Gender and the Gothic
in the Fiction of Edith Wharton

Gender and the Gothic
in the Fiction of
Edith Wharton

Kathy A. Fedorko

The University of Alabama Press

Tuscaloosa and London

The University of Alabama Press
Tuscaloosa, Alabama 35487-0380
All rights reserved
Manufactured in the United States of America

∞

The paper on which this book is printed meets the minimum require-
ments of American National Standard for Information Science-
Permanence of Paper for Printed Library Materials, ANSI
Z39.48-1984.

The illustration on the jacket originally appeared in the *Delineator* in
March 1929. The illustrator was Henry R. Sutter. The photographer
of the illustration is Hans Walther.

Library of Congress Cataloging–in–Publication Data

Fedorko, Kathy A., 1947–
    Gender and the Gothic in the fiction of Edith Wharton / Kathy A.
Fedorko.
        p.   cm.
    Includes bibliographical references and index.
    ISBN 0–8173–0788–5 (alk. paper)
    1. Wharton, Edith, 1862–1937—Criticism and interpretation.
2. Women and literature—United States—History.   3. Gothic revival
(Literature)—United States.   4. Masculinity (Psychology) in
literature.   5. Femininity (Psychology) in literature.   6. Man-woman
relationships in literature.   7. Gender idenity in literature.
8. Sex role in literature.   I. Title.
PS3545.H16Z647   1995
813'.52—dc20   94-38996

British Library Cataloguing-in-Publication Data available

To
Sarah Kathryn Fedorko Macholdt

Contents

Preface

Edith wharton succinctly captures the essence of the Gothic in her description, in *A Motor-Flight Through France*, of the Beauvais cathedral as "an example of what the Gothic spirit, pushed to its logical conclusion, strove for: the utterance of the unutterable." This "Kubla Khan of architecture" seems, Wharton muses, like "some climax of mystic vision, miraculously caught in visible form" (16–17). Wharton's language in this response illuminates the role of the Gothic in her fiction. As a means for exploring areas of experience beyond the realistically expected and accepted, Wharton's Gothic allows her to press the limits of rationality, to utter the unutterable about sexuality, rage, death, fear, and, especially, the nature of women and men.[1]

Gothic art is noted for its agitated, restless, intense straining against limitations, whether sexual, religious, psychological, social, or physical. In expanding the observer's/reader's sense of reality, the Gothic intensifies consciousness of the world both within the mind and beyond the real, "the world of the supernatural, of forces beyond reason, knowledge, and control" (Bayer-Berenbaum 65). A literature of disorienting extremes, the Gothic encourages its readers to enter their fears and know them viscerally. One of the most fundamental fears derives from gender identity and the mutual terror, anxiety, and dread that women and men arouse in one another. The Gothic both critiques and amplifies stereotypical gender roles and the conflict inherent in their idealization (Day 20).[2]

In matters pertaining to the sexes, Wharton talked and wrote sometimes like a misogynist, sometimes like a misandrist, often like an essentialist. Her contradictory views of women and men and feminine and masculine reflect a complicated interweaving of family and social environment, historical time, and individual psychology.[3] They are most apparent in her self-portrayals as woman and artist. Given to undermining her ability as a writer and referring to herself as "rather a housekeeperish person," Wharton was at the same time a highly ambitious, dedicated professional, pleased to be called a "self-made man" (Lubbock, *Portrait* 28, 11). Perhaps as a result of her own gender ambivalence, those who knew her and those who now read and write about her views on gender reflect similar contradictions. According to her contemporaries,

Wharton might be a "very good friend" to her female friends or she might not care much for the society of women, depending on whom one believes (Strachey and Samuels 184). According to recent criticism, her fiction might be pervaded by "a profound misogyny" or distorted by misandry, or she might fear and reject the "feminine-maternal" or yearn for maternal nurturance, depending on which critic one reads.[4] An early book of Wharton criticism written by Grace Kellogg, *The Two Lives of Edith Wharton*, emphasizes the split between the author's personal and creative selves, a theme that is replayed in current discussions of Wharton's attitude toward femaleness and maleness.[5]

Because Wharton was a woman/socialite/writer, "she always suffered the disadvantage of being an outsider," Janet Flanner writes, as a way of explaining Wharton's "repeatedly redomiciling herself" in "various garden cities of the world" (186). Wharton, too, conveys this sense in her reference to herself as "some homeless waif" who, rejected by every country, finally acquires citizenship in "The Land of Letters" (*BG* 119). Wharton was also an "outsider" to the sexes as defined during her lifetime. In *French Ways and Their Meaning*, she denigrates women.[6] But in her letters and diaries and in discussions remembered by others, she can seem as uncomfortable with aloofness, control, and rationality, traits she typically accords men, as she can with vulnerability, passivity, and submission to objectification, traits she typically associates with women. In "the land of letters" she works on a solution to this dilemma.

Gothic fiction, with its "dream landscapes and figures of the subconscious imagination," its sense of being inside a psyche, has always been a useful form for exploring what would otherwise be considered taboo and therefore too dangerous to speak about more directly, that is, realistically (MacAndrew 3).[7] For Wharton the realist, the Gothic served as a kind of psychic theater, a means for creating an interaction between versions of her feminine and masculine selves in a "dialogue with the unconscious" (Wehr 58). She suggests this "personal" function of the Gothic in her comment in *Italian Backgrounds* that "aesthetically, the world is divided into the Gothically and the classically minded, just as intellectually it is divided into those who rise to the general idea and those who pause at the particular instance. The lover of the particular instance will almost always have a taste for the Gothic, which is the personal and anecdotic in art carried to its utmost expression, at the cost of synthetic effect" (183).

Though usually considered a consummate realist, even a "profoundly anti-Romantic realist," Wharton relished the bizarre, ghostly, and ghastly (Wolff 9). "You know I adore horrors & mysteries," she once wrote to Morton Fullerton while also admitting that his friend Hamilton Aidé "never had a more impassioned reader of his 'creepy stories' than I was in my youth" (Lewis and Lewis 147). In *The Writing of Fiction*, Wharton comments that the best stories by Poe, Scott, and Hawthorne are those in "that peculiar category of the eerie which lies outside of the classic tradition" (34). She is most ready to praise "The Turn of the Screw" of all James's work and calls James the "last great master of the eerie in English" (37). And it is Balzac's Gothic tale "La Grande Bretèche" that earns her admiration as "that most perfectly-composed of all short stories" (92).

Wharton adapts distinctive elements from traditional Gothic in her Gothic short stories: concentric narration; a mysterious house; an innocent who confronts the mystery in the house/self; a brutish, arrogant man; a young, passive woman; a would-be rescuer of the woman; threatening weather; a ghost; the suggestion of incest or other sexual malfeasance. My book discusses how Wharton uses and revises these elements in sixteen short stories spanning her career to explore the tension between feminine and masculine ways of knowing and being, and I show how these stories, in turn, are reflected in and revised by the Gothic texts in six of her realistic novels: *The House of Mirth, Ethan Frome, Summer, The Age of Innocence, Hudson River Bracketed,* and *The Gods Arrive.*

Reading the realistic novels in the context of the Gothic stories allows us to see an alternative, "palimpsestic" text in them, that is, a level of meaning "deeper, less accessible (and less socially acceptable)" (Gilbert and Gubar, *Madwoman* 73). Literal imprisonment, ghosts, and tyrants in the short stories are metaphors in the novels, helping us read the Gothic text of gender conflict and, just as significantly, potential resolution to the conflict. I discuss how multiple parallels between female and male protagonists in the "Gothic-marked" novels reveal Wharton's evolutionary rendering of the limitations of both feminine and masculine ways of being and the potential for women and men to become whole selves by integrating elements of both genders.[8]

In short, I read Wharton's Gothic as an enactment of gender tension as well as an experiment in envisioning human beings who are comfortable with both gender selves. My reading is informed by Jung's theory of individuation, that is, the process whereby a person becomes "a separate, indivisible unity or 'whole' " (Jung 9[1]:275). A process rather than a goal, individuation has been explained as an adaptation to internal as well as external reality, to what one is "meant to be—to one's inner truth—which may have little or nothing to do with one's conscious ideas or purposes" (Whitmont 48–49).[9] It involves both claiming the unconscious, previously unacknowledged parts of ourselves and becoming distinct and separate from the unconscious, so as not to be controlled by it (Wehr 50). In Jung's theory, one of the parts of ourselves we confront is the "shadow," the hated and repressed side, "everything that the subject refuses to acknowledge about himself and yet is always thrusting itself upon him directly or indirectly" (Jung 9[1]: 284–85). Knowing and accepting one's anima, the archetypal image of the female in a man's unconscious, or one's animus, the archetypal image of the male in a woman's unconscious, follows the integration of one's shadow (Wehr 63). Achieving wholeness, a Self, thus involves integrating the "feminine" and the "masculine" sides of the personality (Jung 16:261).

I rely most on feminist revisionism of Jung's theory, however, which has encouraged me to use Jung's terminology sparingly. Feminist theorists have convincingly argued for the need of such revision: Jung's ahistorical, "nearly 'contextless'" view of human nature (Wehr 14); his positioning of archetypes as transcendent and therefore unchanging/unchangeable entities of human beings; his confusion of the anima with sexist assumptions about real women; his often condescendingly white, androcentric worldview.[10] Feminist archetypal theory takes the social and cultural context of women's lives into account in its discussion of archetypal patterns. It also integrates woman-centered myth such as that of Medusa and Demeter/Persephone into its discussion of literature written by women, myths and characters to which Wharton alludes throughout her Gothic.[11]

Another theoretical cornerstone to my study is work on the female Gothic, which reads Gothic written by women as a confrontation with the mother. The womb/tomb that terrifies and destroys male characters according to male-centered discussion of the Gothic in a feminist lens becomes the uncanny, dead/undead mother, representing the problematics of womanhood the female character must face.[12] These theories, along with Kristeva's concept of the abject, have helped me formulate my sense of the abyss that Wharton's Gothic characters, both women and men, face.

For key characters in Wharton's Gothic fiction often go through a traumatic "coming-to-awareness" process that revises their sense of who they are, particularly as women and men, and how they relate to their accustomed world.[13] Usually the process is initiated by an uncanny or supernatural encounter in a mysterious house, which often serves as an emblem for a character's vulnerable inner life. The house, in turn, is often beset by symbolic weather—heavy fog, rain, or snow—emphasizing psychic isolation. In coming to awareness, characters are often threatened by the abyss of their inner darkness where they confront fearful qualities that Wharton associates with the feminine/maternal: vulnerability and overwhelmingness, but also receptivity, eroticism, intuitiveness, fierceness, mysteriousness, and rage.[14] Depending on their internal fortitude, characters either try to escape and suppress or to accept and assimilate this encounter into their sense of themselves.

The captive woman under threat and the brutish, sexually threatening man of traditional Gothic appear in Wharton's Gothic, but they are modified and modulated throughout her career as she uses the form to explore and expand the nature of women and men. She soon deconstructs traditional villains and victims, heroes and heroines, by undercutting their gender identification and encouraging the reader to identify with those characters who are most willing to acknowledge the abyss. Those who risk being overwhelmed, who confront and acknowledge the threatening feminine/maternal within, are the ones who deserve our admiration, whether woman or man.

Because I see an evolution in Wharton's portrayal of gender conflict and identity in her Gothic fiction, from gender-bound women and men in the fiction written early in her career to gender mutuality in her late Gothic fiction, my discussion is organized chronologically. Anchored in the particulars of Wharton's life, the four periods—1900–1905, 1906–1916, 1917–1926, and 1927–1937—each include a cluster of Gothic stories and a major novel or two in which the stories are reflected. In my first chapter, "The Gothic Text: Life and Art," I discuss how Wharton perceived the sexual dualism in her own life and the familial conditions in which this dualism developed. Wharton's social class and historical time, Victorian and post-Victorian America, are both reflected and rejected in her extended essay *French Ways and Their Meaning* and in her anger about the repressive Western literary tradition that haunts her own writing. Other factors help account for Wharton's choice of the Gothic as a means for enacting the gender tension that permeated her life as a woman and as a writer: her terror of and attraction to ghost and robber stories, her fascination with incest, her fearful ambivalence about marriage and about women, and her use of houses as signs of self.

Chapter 2, "Fearing the Feminine," discusses how *The House of Mirth* and early Gothic stories—"The House of the Dead Hand," "The Duchess at Prayer," "The Angel at the Grave," and "The Lady's Maid's Bell"—show female characters unable to acknowledge their passivity, unable to make the descent into the dark unknown and lose their maidenly innocence. Because they cannot face the threatening, erotic mother within, the women are unable to accept and act on their own passion. Under the pressure of male domination, they succumb to lives as art objects.

Chapter 3, "Confronting the Limits of Reason," discusses *Ethan Frome*, published in 1911, and the stories written around the same time—"The Eyes," "Afterward," "Kerfol," and "The Triumph of Night." "The Hermit and the Wild Woman," a fable about exaggerated male aestheticism and the female erotic it destroys, allegorizes the female/male conflict of the earlier period but also complicates the gender portrayals. The other Gothic stories dramatize male intellectuals unable or unwilling to acknowledge or cope with the male iniquity and the suppression of the feminine that the supernatural forces they encounter represent. In *Ethan Frome*, where Wharton uses the framing narration she uses in "Kerfol," the male intellectual narrator is enthralled by, while also distancing himself from, the mythic conflict of passive and aggressive female forces he envisions occurring in the Frome household.

Summer (1917) and *The Age of Innocence* (1920), discussed in Chapter 4, "Reclaiming the Feminine," represent a breakthrough in Wharton's use of the Gothic. Gothic elements in both novels, as in *The House of Mirth*, allow the maternal to disrupt the realistic text, countering the language and social constraints of the Father. But Ellen Olenska in *The Age of Innocence*, unlike Lily Bart, faces the Medusa, the terrifying feminine/maternal, and is able to live an independent life with renewed strength, an act of courage the younger Charity Royall in the earlier *Summer* attempts but is less successful at than Ellen. The "Beatrice Palmato" fragment, Wharton's unfinished, unpublished tale of incest written during the time between these two novels, is a dramatic portrayal of the erotic lure meshed with the fatal consequences that incest represents for daughters. In some ways it is Wharton's most Gothic story, illustrating as it does the destructive result when maternal knowledge, awareness, and nurturing are silenced in a daughter's life.

The short stories of this period—"The Young Gentlemen," "Miss Mary Pask," "Dieu d'Amour," and "Bewitched"—portray erotic female power befuddling the men who encounter it and who, in the case of "Bewitched," attempt to destroy it. Present in these stories, as in Wharton's Gothic throughout her career, are severe, cold women, patriarchal gatekeepers at the threshold, who sternly impede the men and women attempting to explore the dark maternal unknown. In this regard *The Age of Innocence* is a breakthrough as well in that Ellen is assisted rather than restrained by two women, mother-surrogates, as it were, in realizing her womanhood.

Hudson River Bracketed and *The Gods Arrive,* published in 1929 and 1932 and discussed in Chapter 5, "Surviving the Abyss and Revising Gender Roles," extend the female power acknowledged in *The Age of Innocence* and *Summer* by transforming the abyss into the mythic, regenerative feminine, source of creativity and renewal. Both a man and a woman learn to respect and understand the dark unknown, the inner parts of themselves and one another, revising the female/male bifurcation that has characterized Wharton's Gothic stories and the Gothic in her novels to this point. The loose romantic epics that result lack the rich texture of her earlier novels, suggesting that the tension between the Gothic and realistic texts is responsible for the charged vitality of Wharton's earlier fiction. "Mr. Jones," published in 1928, and "Pomegranate Seed," published in 1931, each show the triumph of female power over male power. In "All Souls'," written just before her death, Wharton brilliantly and overtly enacts a woman's exploration of her unconscious fears of being overwhelmed by the maternal. That the main character is a woman much like herself attests to the unabated courage with which Wharton descended into the abyss and explored the self she discovered there. That the story's narrator is both nurturing and independent, intellectual and intuitive, yet without an indicated gender, attests to Wharton's career-long evolution of a fe/male self.

Acknowledgments

I AM GRATEFUL to the Woodrow Wilson Foundation for awarding me a Research Grant in Women's Studies in the early stages of my work with Wharton. I am grateful, as well, to the many people whose encouragement of my ideas about Wharton's Gothic kept me writing: Carol Smith and Marianne DeKoven; Claire Kahane; Bob Roth; Lynette Carpenter and Wendy Kolmar; and the members of the Edith Wharton Society, especially Annette Zilversmit, Carol Singley, and Katherine Joslin. Without the help of Barry Qualls at Rutgers University my research would have been much more difficult. The insightful comments and questions of Linda Wagner-Martin and Mary Suzanne Schriber helped me sharpen my ideas. Angela McGlynn's friendship has meant a great deal to me. Ruth Allen, as well as my parents, Nick and Mary Fedorko, took loving care of my daughter Sarah and so allowed me the time and peace of mind to immerse myself in Wharton. I have appreciated the kindness and efficiency of Nicole Mitchell at the University of Alabama Press throughout the process of publication as well as the admirable talent of Marcia Brubeck, my copy editor. Loving thanks go to my husband, Peter Macholdt, who has never wavered in his support of me and my work.

Permissions

The illustration on the jacket is used by permission of the Butterick Company.
Excerpts from the following works by Edith Wharton were reprinted by permission of the estate of the author and the Watkins/Loomis Agency: "Ame Close"; "Pomegranate Seed"; "Mr. Jones" and "Dieu d'Amour" (from *Certain, People*); "Pomegranate Seed" (from *The World Over*); "Preface" and "All Souls' " (from *Ghosts*); *French Ways and Their Meaning*; *In Morocco*; "The Young Gentlemen," "Miss Mary Pask," and "Bewitched" (from *Here and Beyond*); and "A Little Girl's New York."
Excerpts from the Wharton letter to Edward Burlingame dated July 10, 1898, in the Scribner Archives, were published with permission of the Manuscripts Division, Department of Rare Books and Special Collections, Princeton University Libraries.
Excerpts from the Edith Wharton Collection were reprinted by permission of the Yale Collection of American Literature, Beinecke Rare Book and Manuscript Library, Yale University.

Excerpts from *Edith Wharton, A Biography* by R. W. B. Lewis, copyright 1975, were reprinted by permission of HarperCollins Publishers.

Excerpts from *Hudson River Bracketed* were reprinted with the permission of Scribner's, an imprint of Simon & Schuster from *Hudson River Bracketed* by Edith Wharton. Copyright 1929 D. Appleton & Co.; copyright renewed © 1957 William R. Tyler.

Excerpts from *The Age of Innocence* were reprinted with the permission of Scribner's, an imprint of Simon & Schuster from *The Age of Innocence* by Edith Wharton. Copyright 1920 D. Appleton and Co.; copyright renewed 1948 William R. Tyler.

Excerpts from *A Backward Glance* were reprinted with the permission of Scribner's, an imprint of Simon & Schuster from *A Backward Glance* by Edith Wharton. Copyright 1933, 1934 William R. Tyler; copyright renewed © 1961, 1962 William R. Tyler.

Excerpts from *The Gods Arrive* were reprinted with the permission of Scribner's, an imprint of Simon & Schuster from *The Gods Arrive* by Edith Wharton. Copyright 1932 D. Appleton & Co.; copyright renewed © 1960 William R. Tyler.

Excerpts from *The Letters of Edith Wharton* were reprinted with the permission of Scribner's, an imprint of Simon & Schuster from *The Letters of Edith Wharton* edited by R. W. B. Lewis & Nancy Lewis. Copyright © 1988 R. W. B. Lewis, Nancy Lewis and William R. Tyler.

Excerpts from *The Writing of Fiction* were reprinted with the permission of Scribner's, an imprint of Simon & Schuster from *The Writing of Fiction* by Edith Wharton. Copyright 1925 Charles Scribner's Sons; copyright renewed 1953 Frederic R. King.

Excerpts from "The Fullness of Life" and "The House of the Dead Hand" were reprinted with permission of Scribner's, an imprint of Simon & Schuster from *The Collected Short Stories of Edith Wharton* Vol. I edited by Richard W. B. Lewis. Copyright © 1968 William R. Tyler.

Excerpts from "The Letters" were reprinted with permission of Scribner's, an imprint of Simon & Schuster from *The Collected Short Stories of Edith Wharton* Vol. II edited by Richard W. B. Lewis. Copyright © 1968 William R. Tyler.

Abbreviations

AI	*The Age of Innocence*
BG	*A Backward Glance*
CI	*Crucial Instances*
CP	*Certain People*
CSS	*Collected Short Stories*
DM	*The Descent of Man and Other Stories*
EF	*Ethan Frome*
G	*Ghosts*
GA	*The Gods Arrive*
HB	*Here and Beyond*
HM	*The House of Mirth*
HRB	*Hudson River Bracketed*
HW	*The Hermit and the Wild Woman and Other Stories*
"Life"	*"Life and I"*
S	*Summer*
WF	*The Writing of Fiction*
X	*Xingu and Other Stories*

Gender and the Gothic
in the Fiction of Edith Wharton

1 | The Gothic Text
Life and Art

Wharton's conflicting and conflicted views of women and men and feminine and masculine reflect a complicated interweaving of family and social environment, historical time, and individual psychology. These conditions and
the gender tension they foster in turn provide the impetus for Wharton to use
and recast Gothic conventions and narratives in her fiction as a way to dramatize psychic conflict. Indeed, as a dreamlike interaction among parts of the self,
the Gothic in her fiction allows Wharton both to mirror and to revise issues that
inform her life as well as the genre: an ambivalent terror of/attraction to the
supernatural and the threatening; a fascination with incest; a fearful ambivalence about marriage, about breaking out of social restraints, about being "different"; and an attraction to houses as signs of self and to the "abyss" as a state
of being beyond the rational. Wharton's handling of these issues distinctly
evolves throughout her career. In the process, Wharton progressively imagines
a fe/male self, moving from gender-bound women and men in the Gothic-
marked fiction written early in her career to characters in the later fiction who
struggle toward or even attain a degree of gender mutuality.

Family and Society

Wharton's autobiographies—the published version, *A Backward Glance*
(1934) and the unpublished version, "Life and I"[1]—and her autobiographically
colored nonfiction *French Ways and Their Meaning* and *The Writing of Fiction* docu-
ment the personal and professional struggles that drew Wharton to a Gothic
perspective. "Life and I" also vividly dramatizes that perspective, for in it
Wharton remembers her child self as a Gothic heroine—trapped in suffocating
interiors, suppressed by patriarchal restraints embodied by her mother, isolated
by her writing and tortured by her acute sensibilities, but at the same time
pleasurably, even erotically, charged by those sensibilities. As a passionate, secret lover of words and literature, Wharton felt herself to be the isolated, emotionally orphaned heroine, alone in her "other side," a supernatural world
where the flow and energy of words brought ecstatic release while producing
inordinate guilt because she was so "different" ("Life" 23, 36). This intermin-

gling of eroticism and fear, pleasure and pain, is the quintessential Gothic psychology.

"Life and I" demonstrates Wharton's uneasiness with the patriarchal value system that tells women they are worthwhile only if they are attractive, especially to men, and that they risk being excluded if they are intelligent or strong willed or in any other way "unfeminine."[2] "To look pretty" is one of the "deepest-seated instincts of my nature," Wharton writes there. Her clarification of this instinct identifies her as both gazed-at (female) art piece and (male) artist: "I say 'to look pretty' instead of 'to be admired,' because I really believe it has always been an aesthetic desire, rather than a form of vanity. I always saw the visible world as a series of pictures, more or less harmoniously composed, & the wish *to make the picture prettier* was, as nearly as I can define it, the form my feminine instinct of pleasing took" ("Life" 1–2).

Wharton's earliest memory, with which she begins *A Backward Glance*, is of being dressed beautifully while walking with her father and realizing for the first time the value of being a "subject for adornment" (2). Yet at the same time, in "Life and I," she confesses humiliation about being laughed at by her brothers for her red hair and the "supposed abnormal size" of her hands and feet; she was, she felt, "the least good-looking of the family" and therefore intensely conscious of her "physical short comings" (37).

Though pronouncing at a young age that when she grew up she wanted to be "the best dressed woman in New York" like her mother, Wharton felt herself no match and no daughter for the elegant Lucretia Jones (*BG* 20). While she recalls her "tall splendid father" as "always so kind," with strong arms that "held one so safely," and her childhood nurse Doyley as "the warm cocoon" in which she "lived safe and sheltered," she remembers that her mother's abounding interest in flounced dresses and ermine scarves was accompanied by her indolence and capriciousness, that her mother stressed politeness and reserve rather than nurturing (20, 26). This model of old New York womanhood upheld the patriarchy with her "shoulds" and "musts," her withering judgmental demeanor, and her physical reserve, an outcome, perhaps, of her own "internalized oppression" that she encouraged in her daughter (Wehr 18). Sandra Gilbert describes Wharton's situation in her comment that "the more fully the mother represents culture, the more inexorably she tells the daughter that she cannot have a mother because she has been signed with and assigned to the Law of the Father," the law that means "culture is by definition both patriarchal and phallocentric" ("Life's" 358).

Even speaking was a hazardous business for the precocious, acutely sensitive young Edith, because, in Wharton's view, her mother scorned verbal imperfection and risk taking. Over sixty years later the daughter writes, "I still wince under my mother's ironic smile when I said that some visitor had stayed 'quite a while,' and her dry: 'Where did you pick *that* up?' " (*BG* 49). The anger is palpable in the memory that "my parents—or at least my mother—laughed at me for using 'long words,' & for caring for dress (in which heaven knows she set me the example!); & under this perpetual cross-fire of criticism I became a painfully shy self-conscious child" ("Life" 37). And a shy adult. For throughout *A Backward Glance* runs the theme of her "incorrigible shyness" that she blames time and again for missed opportunities of intimacy. The mute girl is mirrored in the passive female Gothic character, holding her tongue, afraid to question, unable to defend herself.[3]

It is worth remembering that "the image of the repressive mother is the daughter's *creation*" and that Wharton's autobiographies should not be assumed to be factual documents (Fryer 359–60 n.4).[4] Although there are hints in *A Backward Glance* about Lucretia's difficult childhood, we have no "backward glance" from Lucretia to counter her daughter's perspective and to help us understand her own childhood pain and losses. Still, however skewed Wharton's memories of her mother, her perception was that she was rejected by a cold mother who criticized and restrained more than she accepted and nurtured. From her Wharton learns the intense self-criticism, the self-hating voice, that women internalize from patriarchal judgment of them as inadequate. Wharton's reiteration in "Life and I" that she "frankly despised" little girls clearly seems to include herself (12). This "self-hater" turns up in her Gothic short stories as the female victim who colludes in her own destruction and as the villainous male who oppresses the passive woman (Wehr 20).[5]

As a child Wharton is beset by "the most excruciating moral tortures" instilled by her internalized mother ("Life" 2). She illustrates this point with an anecdote about telling a little boy in her dance class that their dance teacher's mother looks like an old goat. When she admits to the teacher that she made the remark, she gains a scolding and the tormented sense that her own mother would have thought her "naughty" not to have known how to do the "right" thing ("Life" 7). Noting that she had two "inscrutable beings" to please, God and her mother, and that her mother was the most inscrutable of the two, Wharton confesses that "this vexed problem of truth-telling, & the impossibility of reconciling 'Gods' standard of truthfulness with the conventional obligation to be 'polite' & not hurt anyone's feelings" plunged her into a "darkness of horror" (6–7).

Wharton's intense moral anxiety resembles the impetus for traditional Gothic fantasy of the eighteenth century, springing as it did from uneasiness about "problems of personal moral responsibility and judgement, questions of restrictive convention, and a troubled awareness of irrational impulses which threatened to subvert orthodox notions of social and moral propriety" (Howells 7). Wharton's girlhood, as she perceives it, thus is haunted by a late nineteenth-century version of the "grim realities" of eighteenth-century womanhood that inspired Ann Radcliffe's and Fanny Burney's Gothic, "the restraints on her freedom, all the way to actual imprisonment; the mysterious, unexplained social rituals; the terrible need always to appear, as well as always to be, virtuous; and, over all, the terrible danger of slippage from the respectable to the unrespectable class of womanhood" (Moers 206–207).

Bourgeois men were actors in the eighteenth-century world, and women were passive possessions whose good behavior was often the deciding factor in their material well-being. Female respectability involved passive obedience to male authority, since women were seen as "inescapably Other" (Day 95). Societal emphasis on reason and repression of feeling, the "male" sphere, made that which was repressed, the "female" sphere, all the more threatening and thereby in need of destruction or imprisonment. The rebellious Gothic probed fears, spoke the unspeakable, meddled in the taboo, like rape, sex among the clergy, and, especially, incest. Social institutions like the church and the family, symbolized by the ruined church or castle, were considered claustrophobic and hypocritical because they suppressed and denied part of human experience.

Initially Wharton's "devastating passion" for "making up" stories as a child was a way of finding release from a threatening, confining, judgmental world into a supernatural one ("Life" 11). The sound and sight of words produced "sensuous rapture," regardless of her inability to understand them (10). She writes in "Life and I" that words "sang to me so bewitchingly that they almost lured me from the wholesome noonday air of childhood into some strange supernatural region, where the normal pleasures of my age seemed as insipid as the fruits of the earth to Persephone after she had eaten of the pomegranate seed" (10). Wharton might well be describing immersion in *le sémiotique*, Julia Kristeva's term for a pre-Oedipal, preverbal, sensual state associated with the maternal voice and bodily rhythms. The sensuousness of language thus provides the young Wharton with a haunted maternal bower, a "secret garden."[6]

Even when Wharton learns the meanings of words, it isn't intellectual discourse but rather the language of erotic secrecy and mystery, of supernatural otherworldliness that pervades her descriptions of immersion in books. She feels a "secret ecstasy of communion" with the books in her father's library: Coleridge; Goethe's *Faust* and *Wilhelm Meister; The Duchess of Malfi; The White Devil;* the "Song of Solomon"; Irving's *Tales of the Alhambra,* no small dose of the romantic, the erotic, the Gothic (*BG* 69). These "enraptured sessions" with poetry, philosophy, religion, and drama become part of her "secret retreat" within her where she "wished no one to intrude" (70). "Words and cadences haunted it like song-birds in a magic wood," nurturing the way her mother did not (70). Her father's library becomes analogous to "my strange inner world," conflating the symbolic and spiritual, the paternal and maternal (72). In Wharton's Gothic, startling, disorienting, and often erotic discoveries take place in libraries, as intellectual knowledge is expanded by intuitive, uncanny awareness.[7]

Wharton's dilemma as female child and woman is that intellectual knowledge and activities endow male-identified power at the same time that they estrange her from her female self as it has been defined by her society and her mother. Discovering Sir William Hamilton's *History of Philosophy* in her brother's room gives the young Wharton the hope that "now I should never be that helpless blundering thing, a mere 'little girl,' again!" ("Life" 32–33). But her intense intelligence and engagement with language also increase her sense of abnormality. As she confesses, "it humiliated me to be so 'different' " (36). The social ramifications of difference were clear. According to an 1882 story in the *Newport Daily News* the engagement between Edith Jones and Harry Stevens, when she was nineteen, was broken because of "an alleged preponderance of intellectuality on the part of the intended bride" (Lewis, *Biography* 45).

Her own writing intensified Wharton's gender conflict. This public, and thereby unfeminine, act was met with silent disapproval: "My literary success puzzled and embarrassed my old friends far more than it impressed them, and in my own family it created a kind of constraint which increased with the years. None of my relations ever spoke to me of my books, either to praise or blame— they simply ignored them; and among the immense tribe of my New York cousins, though it included many with whom I was on terms of affectionate intimacy, the subject was avoided as though it were a kind of family disgrace, which might be condoned but could not be forgotten" (*BG* 143–44). In having her own writing avoided as though it were a "family disgrace," Wharton faced the quintessential woman writer's dilemma. Writing is a fearful, "naughty" thing to do, for it involves honesty of feeling, assertiveness, and noticing and talking of things not polite to acknowledge. Like sex, it is fraught with guilt, this uncontrolled, unladylike, other-worldly act. Hélène Cixous, in urging women to "write her self," shows that Wharton's dilemma is still a current one for women: "Where is the ebullient, infinite woman who, immersed as she was in her naiveté, kept in the dark about herself, led into self-disdain by the great arm of parental-conjugal phallocentrism, hasn't been ashamed of her strength? Who, surprised and horrified by the fantastic tumult of her drives (for she was made to believe that a well-adjusted normal woman has a . . . divine composure), hasn't accused herself of being a monster? Who, feeling a funny desire stirring inside her (to sing, to write, to dare to speak, in short, to bring out something new), hasn't thought she was sick?" ("The Laugh" 876).[8]

The denial by silence of Wharton's writing by her extended family and their dread of creativity is not unlike the denial of intense and sometimes supernatural experiences by characters in her Gothic stories. Their attempted suppression of disorienting awareness is undermined when the reader joins Wharton in an act of voyeurism and recognition as the story plays itself out.[9]

Her family relationships and experiences were not Wharton's only impetus for using Gothic conventions and narratives in her fiction as a way to tell the disallowed story of female sexuality and power. Her Victorian/Post-Victorian

Anglo-Saxon society, with its penchant for ignoring what it considered inappropriate human experience, was an impetus as well. In *French Ways and Their Meaning*, Wharton describes maturity in a society as the ability to face primal terrors. "Intellectual honesty, the courage to look at things as they are," she writes, "is the first test of mental maturity. Till a society ceases to be afraid of the truth in the domain of ideas it is in leading-strings, morally and mentally" (58–59).

One of the main aspects of life to which Wharton refers in the phrase "things as they are" is sexuality. The French, she observes, are criticized by Anglo-Saxons for talking and writing freely about sexuality, as if to do so were "inconsistent with . . . purity and morality." Wharton notes approvingly that the French just take sex for granted "as part of the great parti-coloured business of life" (60, ellipsis mine).

Wharton felt that Anglo-Saxon literature had been no better than the society at acknowledging female sexuality in particular. In *The Writing of Fiction* she argues that English novelists create women whose passion is banked by prudery. Scott, for instance, "became conventional and hypocritical when he touched on love and women," substituting "sentimentality for passion" and reducing his heroines to " 'Keepsake' insipidities" (5). Thackeray, Dickens, Brontë, and Eliot were also affected by the "benumbing" restraints of their time (63).

Wharton's own portrayal of passionate women in her novels was hindered not only because, as Elizabeth Ammons argues, she felt the American woman she wrote about "was far from being . . . a whole human being" but also because her society, her background, and the very form of realism resisted such portrayal (3, ellipsis mine). In *A Backward Glance*, Wharton recounts that early in her career she had a reader protest, "have you never known a respectable woman? If you have, in the name of decency write about her!" (126) Those were the days, she remembers, when an editor stipulated that no "unlawful attachment" should appear in her projected novel and when her friend Charles Eliot Norton warned that "no great work of the imagination has ever been based on illicit passion" (126–27). But decades later the situation remained unchanged. The *Saturday Evening Post, Liberty,* and *Collier's* wouldn't publish *Hudson River Bracketed* and *The Gods Arrive* because of the "illicit liaison" in them, and the editor of *Delineator,* which finally did publish them, commented that "the situation, that of a man and woman unmarried and living together, is a little startling for magazine publication" (Lewis, *Biography* 502).

Wharton's anger about the problem of portraying sexuality in literature surfaced most heatedly when she chided younger novelists for not realizing that portraying whole people, complete with passions, had been difficult for their predecessors. In a 1931 letter to Sinclair Lewis she rebukes him for the depreciatory comments he had made about Howells in his Nobel acceptance address;

Wharton points out that Howells had to contend with a country "reeking with sentimentality and shuddering with prudery" (Dupree 265). She returns to the matter in *A Backward Glance,* commenting bitterly that "the poor novelists who were my contemporaries . . . had to fight hard for the right to turn the wooden dolls about which they were expected to make believe into struggling suffering human beings. . . . The amusing thing about this turn of the wheel is that we who fought the good fight are now jeered at as the prigs and prudes who barred the way to complete expression" (127, ellipsis mine).

Contemporary critical discussion of realism has shown that the difficulty of portraying passions in realistic fiction that Wharton pinpointed (and a reason why she relied on a Gothic subtext to show passion constrained) is a problem inherent in the form. The dilemma is the very strength of realistic fiction, Leo Bersani has argued; its recreation of social structures militates against a full portrayal of the forces that would deny their validity. "The technical premises of realistic fiction—the commitment to intelligible, 'full' characters, to historical verisimilitude, to the revealing gesture or episode, to a closed temporal frame— already dooms any adventure in the stimulating improbabilities, of behavior which resists being 'placed' and interpreted in a general psychological or formal structure" (67). Because it keeps characters coherent, "the containment of desire is a triumph for social stability" (73).

Feminist criticism has enlarged the conversation about how this "containment of desire" in deference to "social stability" is a culturally created gender issue, a containment of the "natural" feminine/maternal by the "symbolic" masculine/paternal. Often "submerged meanings" appear in women's writing as surreal or uncanny eruptions in and interruptions of the text (Gilbert and Gubar, *Madwoman* 72). Grace Poole's intrusion into Jane's story in *Jane Eyre* is one of the most discussed examples. A novel such as *Villette,* as well, which seemingly doesn't recognize the Romantic or Gothic, nonetheless can be said to possess a "buried letter of Romanticism" and "the phantom of feminism" conveying "the discourse of the Other, as the novel's unconscious . . . struggles for articulation within the confines of midnineteenth-century realism" (Jacobus, "Buried Letter" 42, 59; ellipsis mine).

Brontë's texts have been called examples of "new" Gothic in that intense feeling and extrarational experience are not only contained in "marvelous circumstance" but interpenetrate the "ordinary world" and thereby enlarge the sense of reality in the novels, especially the reality of women (Heilman 123, 121). Traditional Gothic male villains are deconstructed when "dark magnetic energy" characterizes female protagonists (127). Such a view privileges the realist form with which Wharton was comfortable in her novels but into which, like Brontë, she interwove a Gothic text to accommodate the gender tension central to her life as a writer.

The Abyss

Wharton's sense of being an outsider, the "separated one," as a precocious child and a woman writer, uncomfortable with the male-identified power of writing and the intellect while at the same time lured by the nourishing female-identified "rich world of dreams" and the sound and sight of words, helps explain her use of mystical/supernatural rather than "realistic" language to describe her creative process, the goddess's descent into the soul, as she puts it (Wilt 19; "Life" 12; BG 198). The moment of creation is akin to the mysterious moment just before sleep when "one falls over the edge of consciousness" (BG 198). Similarly, the storytelling process "takes place in some secret region on the sheer edge of consciousness" where characters haunt the brain and names spectrally appear without characters (205). The creative act is "like the mystic's union with the Unknowable" (121) or "that mysterious fourth-dimensional world which is the artist's inmost sanctuary (*WF* 119)."[10]

Wharton's language of creativity—the "unknown depths," the "sheer edge of consciousness," the mysterious and the spectral—is the language of her Gothic as well. Characters anxiously facing the dark abyss of preternatural knowledge or entering a mysterious life removed from society in the Gothic stories and the Gothic-marked novels replicate Wharton's creative process of entering the "unknown depths." Wharton's Gothic thus enacts the writing process as a plunge into awareness beyond the realistic, where the unexpurgated "real" story is told, the "unlabeled, disallowed, disavowed" of which her patriarchal mother and society would not approve (Stein 126).

The omnipresent Gothic abyss traditionally threatens damnation, a fall into "the demonic underworld" that leads to "the rejection of human identity and the embracing of the monstrous" (MacAndrew 49; Day 7). Rather than this chaotic loss of humanity, the abyss as Wharton uses it is a plunge into a realm that threatens loss of the controlled self at the same time that it promises new understanding. And what realm could be more frightening and yet more alluring for this unmothered daughter of the patriarchy than the feminine/maternal darkness, with its overwhelming intimacy and primal power?

Wharton acknowledges the occult power of the maternal when she places the faculty for apprehending ghosts in "the warm darkness of the pre-natal fluid far below our conscious reason" (G vii). Her Gothic portrayals of inner journeys into threatening knowledge take characters into maternal places: houses, cabins, caves. Within the place within the mind of the character, an abyss opens, threatening annihilation at the same time that it promises self-awareness if s/he can acknowledge the experience.[11]

Facing the abyss is crucial to Wharton's Gothic, for the willingness of characters to face the maternal darkness indicates their willingness to understand the inner life, the loss of the known self that has opened before them. Arrogant intellectual men in her Gothic fiction are usually those least willing to acknowledge what they have seen in the abyss and most apt to ignore or deny their experience with the darkness. Wharton seems to be mirroring her sense of the limitations of her own rationality, of the patriarchal symbolic, her sense that, emphasized at the expense of respect for the maternal erotic darkness, such logocentrism becomes tyrannical and repressive.[12] Since the characters, especially in the stories, are themselves too timid to fully assimilate what they have experienced, Wharton depends on the reader to decipher their lost knowledge. Thus the woman's story is heard despite the attempts of the male narrator or other (usually male) character to deny or suppress it.

Contemporary feminist criticism of the Gothic argues that what draws a woman in particular to the "forbidden center" of the Gothic mystery is not threatened incest within the Oedipal plot, a reading that privileges the male reader, but rather "the spectral presence of a dead-undead mother, archaic and all-encompassing, a ghost signifying the problematics of femininity which the heroine must confront" (Kahane, "Gothic Mirror" 336).[13] The "ubiquitous Gothic precipice on the edge of the maternal blackness" thus draws female characters to a confrontation with the mysteries of identity (340).

Sexual maturity, the secret knowledge and power of the mother, is both feared and desired. "Bad" women the heroine confronts in the Gothic text are the "monstrous" other parts of herself, and the parts of the mother, that she cannot accept—her passions, her ambitions, her energy (Stein 123ff.). The Gothic gives "*visual* form to the fear of self," the dark, knowing mother/self who might appear in the fiction as a mad woman or a freak or a sexual monster and therefore beyond the pale of respectable society (Moers 163). Wharton gives such "visual form to the fear of self" when Lily Bart has her disturbing vision of herself in the mirror early in *The House of Mirth* and in the mirror of her thoughts after Trenor's attempted rape. Wharton's own fear of her sexual self is reflected in the exaggerated mirroring of Lily's vaguely erotic activities by the omnivorously sexual Bertha Dorset.

Wharton's use of the abyss in her Gothic fiction as a character's disorienting confrontation with primal human emotion or experience recalls Jung's theory of individuation, "the process by which a person becomes a psychological 'in-dividual,' that is, a separate, indivisible unity or 'whole,'" by assimilating knowledge from the unconscious as part of consciousness (9[1]:275). This process has been called an adaptation to inner reality as well as outer, to what one is "meant to be"; one recognizes the next step in what one is meant to be by looking for what attracts and frightens at the same time (Whitmont 48–49, 62). The "rebirth journey," as individuation has been called, brings to consciousness "the lost values of the psyche, which lie so largely in the realm of Eros, and by this means the human being becomes more complete" (Harding 245). The goal of the journey is an assimilation of gender selves, inner and outer worlds, consciousness with unconsciousness.[14]

Jung conforms with most androcentric Western theory in his association of consciousness with the masculine and unconsciousness with the feminine. "Psychologically the self is a union of conscious (masculine) and unconscious (feminine). It stands for the psychic totality" (9[2]:268). These realms accrue, however, the sexist associations of reasonable, reasoning masculine consciousness as opposed to feared, fearful feminine unconsciousness. In Jung's theory the male hero's plunge into the abyss of the unconscious involves confronting his "shadow," the hated, repressed side of the personality and thereafter the "anima," the archetypal image of the female in a man's unconsciousness, an awesome, organic power associated with the Terrible Mother or with a dual mother, part destructive, part creative (Wehr 59–67, 112–13). The ultimate encounter is thus with an Other that must be overcome to be assimilated.

Feminist archetypal critics have revised Jungian theory to make it more compatible with women's experiences as women themselves have written about them. The shadow a woman confronts often carries with it the gynophobia of the social world that fuses with the animus (the archetypal image of the male in a woman's unconscious) into "a masculine character who loathes the woman as much as she loathes herself" (Pratt, "Spinning" 104). Annis Pratt cautions that for women the rebirth journey entails psychological risk that is as likely to lead to madness as to renewal (*Archetypal* 142). But women may also overcome this self-destructiveness and assimilate a mother/self that engenders a sense of female power and erotic independence by accepting rather than fearing the life forces of sexuality, birth, and death. Thus "the woman's encounter with a feminine figure at the depths of her psyche . . . is more a fusion than an agon; the woman encounters a being similar to herself which empowers even as it exiles her from the social community," since she then becomes a woman unreconciled to a patriarchal world (Pratt, "Spinning" 106, ellipsis mine). In imagining this feminine archetype encountered in the inner world, women writers often draw on female-identified mythology: Demeter/Persephone, Celtic Grail legends, Ishtar/Tammuz rebirth legends, and witches and other wise women (Pratt, *Archetypal* 170). This is Wharton's practice in her Gothic-marked fiction.

While male reading of the Gothic places the "maternal blackness" beneath the ruined castle, "the crumbling shell of paternal authority," as imprisoning womb/tomb, feminist reading is more apt to identify the castle or other enclosure as the mother, "mother as nurturer, as sexual being, as body, as harboring a secret, as an indifferent hardness" (Fiedler 112; Holland and Sherman 289). The mother, especially for the woman reader, threatens nothingness, overwhelmingness, nonseparation (Holland and Sherman 283). The female Gothic character's entrapment in or exploration of a Gothic house is thus an extension of her relationship to the maternal body she shares (Kahane, "Gothic Mirror" 338).[15]

Kristeva's theory of the abject provides another way to read the abyss in Wharton's Gothic. Though Kristeva emphasizes the abject as a reiteration of *separation* from the maternal, her discussion of the self-awareness gained in the process of struggling against and being pulled into the abject sheds light on the response of Wharton's Gothic characters. Lying just on the edge of meaninglessness and nonexistence, the abject represents "our earliest attempts to release the hold of *maternal* entity even before ex-isting outside of her, thanks to the autonomy of language" (13). "The phantasmatic mother," constitutes, in the history of each person, "the abyss that must be established as an autonomous (and not encroaching) *place,* and *distinct* object, meaning a *signifiable* one," so that the person might "learn to speak" (100). In spite of this "placing," one does not "cease separating" from the abject; it retains the power to recreate the act of attempting to break away from the maternal entity punctuated by the pull back from it (13).

Reexperiencing the act of separation from the mother forces the limits of one's psychic world and the limits of self-knowledge. "The abject shatters the wall of repression and its judgments. It takes the ego back to its source on the abominable limits from which, in order to be, the ego has broken away. . . . Abjection is a resurrection that has gone through death (of the ego). It is an alchemy that transforms death drive into a start of life, of new significance" (15, ellipsis mine).

Such a definition of the abject as a rebirth into new understanding through the pull of the maternal abyss helps explain why Wharton's characters are both terrified of and attracted to extrarational experiences. Wharton's Gothic emphasizes the maternal abyss as "repellent and repelled" to those most frightened by it, yet Wharton also emphasizes that it is also a state of being that one must assimilate within oneself rather than reject or pull away from (6). In dramatizing primal experiences in her Gothic fiction—of ghosts, madness, and sexual threat—Wharton is courting disorder. She is pressing the limits of rationality and having her characters risk temporary egolessness for the sake of greater awareness, particularly of the feminine. She is speaking about those things considered unspeakable by her family and society—the erotic, the antisocial, the grotesque, the energetic, the fearful—those emotions and conditions that, like the regression to the maternal, threaten to overwhelm one.[16]

Wharton dramatizes the power of the uncontrollable and overwhelming in her autobiographical account of recuperating, when she was nine years old, from a near-fatal bout of typhoid and of being given a book to read: "To an unimaginative child the tale would no doubt have been harmless; but it was a 'robber-story,' & with my intense Celtic sense of the super-natural, tales of robbers

& ghosts were perilous reading. This one brought on a serious relapse, & again my life was in danger" ("Life" 17).

Thereafter, until she was a "young lady," she lived in "chronic fear" of an unexplained terror, "like some dark undefinable menace, forever dogging my steps" (17). Most terrifying was returning from daily walks outside with nurse, governess, or father and, while waiting for the door to her home to be opened, feeling the menace behind her, on top of her, and being "seized by a choking agony of terror" until she could escape inside (18). The memory suggests an overwhelming need to reconnect with the sheltering maternal body/house across the threshold. But the intensity of the "undefinable menace" that sends her to the mother also suggests an anxious fear of separation intensified by never having felt solidly connected in the first place. In Wharton's Gothic fiction, terror of the outside unknown is transmuted into terror of the internal unknown, within the house/mother rather than outside of it. Facing that terror is a courageous means of claiming and transforming it.

Wharton states, in "Life and I," that until the age of twenty-seven or twenty-eight, she "could not sleep in the room with a book containing a ghost-story" (19). Using the progressive tense of recent occurrence, she admits, "I have frequently had to burn books of this kind, because it frightened me to know that they were down-stairs in the library!" (19). Such a sensational reaction to the threat posed by the supernatural—such books almost killed me and I subsequently burned them—reveals how much Wharton feared the uncontrollable and how much power she granted fiction as a means of recreating the terror of uncontrollable forces. Julia Briggs's idea that "by recounting nightmares, giving them speakable shapes and patterns" in "stories of the terrific unknown," we hope to "control them and come to terms with them" might well account for both Wharton's autobiographical "confession" and her Gothic fiction that draws one into the "terrific unknown" (11).

In recasting the "abyss" as a restorative, regenerative place for those courageous enough to face it, Wharton reconceives its destructive power. Her several nervous breakdowns and her bouts of "occult and unget-at-able nausea" and overwhelming fatigue during the period when she was most conflicted about her identity as writer/wife/socialite/intellectual/homemaker made her familiar with the risks of the journey into the self (Wolff 52). Wharton's experience with the Weir Mitchell Rest Cure for her nervous collapse was more salutary than the experiences of Charlotte Perkins Gilman or Virginia Woolf, since she was encouraged to write during her time of separation from the outside world (Lewis, *Biography* 84). Nonetheless her imposed infantalization, during which she was barred from visitors yet felt "ghostly presences . . . peering in on her morning and night," reappears as a dominant theme in many of her Gothic stories (84). Walter Berry's comment in his letter of November 9, 1898, that he is "delighted to hear" that Wharton had "loosened the first stone in your cell toward an escape" suggests that Wharton saw herself as a prisoner during her "cure" (Beinecke).

Her visit with her dear friend Henry James during his period of despair in 1910 is another encounter with the abyss. She observes that his eyes are those of a man who "has looked on the Medusa," and as she sits beside him, she looks "into the black depths over which he is hanging—the superimposed 'abysses' of all his fiction" (Lewis and Lewis, *Letters* 202). Most notable for Wharton is that James is no longer in control of his emotions: "I, who have always seen him so serene, so completely the master of his wonderful emotional instrument . . . , I could hardly believe it was the same James who cried out to me his fear, his despair, his craving for the 'cessation of consciousness,' & all his unspeakable loneliness & need of comfort, & inability to be comforted!" (202, ellipsis mine).

Wharton later comments how "haunted" she has been by James's condition (203). The tension between complete mastery over one's emotions and being incapacitated by them is part of the gender-identified duality that Wharton dramatizes in her Gothic fiction. Ellen Olenska in *The Age of Innocence* is perhaps her most successful example of a character who exemplifies balance between the extremes, though it comes at the cost of "leaving home" for good. Because she has faced the Medusa and the darkness of the abyss, Ellen possesses a maturity of mind and spirit that Newland Archer admires, even marvels at. He himself skirts the edge and the Medusa's gaze, thereby sacrificing the "flower of life" (*AI* 350).

Confronting the Medusa, without the deflecting mirror in which Perseus sought refuge, is one of Wharton's favorite ways of describing the act of facing powerful femaleness directly, unflinchingly. Yet the drama and tension of traditional female Gothic is in good part dependent on the *concealment* of female knowledge, the mysteries of birth, death, and sexuality, within the threatening maternal space of dungeon, castle, or haunted room. One female reader of the form, Leona Sherman, describes recreating in the Gothic a figurative confrontational dance with her mother about the essence of femaleness: "I know she knows but she won't tell me. I know I know, but I doubt because she won't tell me. She says one thing, but I see another on her face. I feel we can't really talk about what we know, because she would be calling her whole past life into question and endangering her present. She thinks the concealment necessary for my survival, and finally, she loves me and wants to protect me above all. The mysteries are the issues of sex and birth and death and, too, the necessity of concealing them" (Holland and Sherman 287).

Wharton describes in "Life and I" just such an evasive encounter with her mother about sexuality. I quote this much quoted passage in its entirety because Wharton's dramatic, even melodramatic, rendering of her request for information about the secret of sexuality so uncannily mirrors Sherman's description of a woman reading/recreating a Gothic story:

> . . . a few days before my marriage, I was seized with such a dread of the whole dark mystery, that I summoned up courage to appeal to my mother, & begged her, with a heart beating to suffocation, to tell me "what being married was like." Her handsome face at once took on the look of icy disapproval which I most dreaded. "I never heard such a ridiculous question!" she said impatiently; & I felt at once how vulgar she thought me.
>
> But in the extremity of my need I persisted. "I'm afraid, Mamma—I want to know what will happen to me!"
>
> The coldness of her expression deepened to disgust. She was silent for a dreadful moment; then she said with an effort: "You've seen enough pictures & statues in your life. Haven't you noticed that men are—made differently from women?"
>
> "Yes," I faltered blankly.
>
> "Well, then—?"
>
> I was silent, from sheer inability to follow, & she brought out sharply: "Then for heaven's sake don't ask me any more silly questions. You can't be as stupid as you pretend!"
>
> The dreadful moment was over, & the only result was that I had been convicted of stupidity for not knowing what I had been expressly forbidden to ask about, or even think of! ["Life" 34–35]

Wharton recreates herself here as the traditional Gothic heroine probing the dread-producing mother/castle for answers about "the whole dark mystery" of sexuality, but she leaves both uninformed and humiliated because she is so uninformed.

Perhaps because Wharton didn't believe, as Sherman posits, that the mother/Gothic denies the knowledge to the questing daughter because she "loves me and wants to protect me above all," in her own Gothic fiction Wharton turns the "Gothic denial" of "the whole dark mystery" of sexuality, birth, and death figured by the woman/mother on its head (Holland and Sherman 292, 287). By denying access to the mother and thereby to femaleness, both women and men wield patriarchal power, power defied by characters such as Charity Royall in *Summer* and Lady Jane Lynke in "Mr. Jones." More often, a character shrinks from rather than claims this powerful knowledge, and the reader is left with an awareness of the sacrifice that the character has made because of her or his timidity.

Women and Men

Wharton seems, at first glance, to be arguing for sexual equality on the social as well as the fictional front in her indictment, in *French Ways and Their Meaning*, that America's hypocritical Puritan heritage concerning "the danger of frank and free social relations between men and women" has been the main retardant to "real civilization" there (112–13). "The two sexes complete each other," Wharton insists (103). Yet *French Ways* reveals the same kind of gender tension that her autobiographies do as well as a denigration of women. Her stress on equal relations between women and men as keys to a mature culture is contradicted by her relegation of women, in the same book, to subservient roles of muse, patient listener, faithful attendant, and helpmate (113; see esp. pp. 112, 26, 121). Although herself a devotee of "good talk," one whose delight in it her friend Gaillard Lapsley once described as that of "an emancipated feminist conscientiously practicing free love" (Lubbock, "Memoirs"), Wharton writes in *French Ways* that a woman has "no place" in a conversation, "unless her ideas, and her way of expressing them, put her on an equality with the men; and this seldom happens. Women (if they only knew it!) are generally far more intelligent listeners than talkers" (25). After all, she adds, "intelligent women will never talk together when they can talk to men, or even listen to them" (26).

Wharton's accolades in *French Ways* go to the "man's woman," one "whose mind is attuned to men's minds" and so doesn't possess the fussiness and spitefulness of the woman who spends time with other women (119). This denigration of women is echoed in a 1923 letter to Minnie Jones in which Wharton writes that she is "not much interested in traveling scholarships for women" and that "they'd much better stay at home and mind the baby" (Beinecke). "Emancipated" young women are a " 'monstrous regiment' . . . taught by their elders to despise the kitchen and the linen room," to their own demise (*BG* 60). It isn't difficult to see why an acquaintance of Wharton's would assume that "being a very normal person she preferred men to women, and often terrified the latter with a cold stare" (Lubbock, *Portrait* 28).

The impression was reinforced by Wharton's cultivation of a coterie of admiring male friends with whom she surrounded herself and for whom she often played the part of Great Mother. Adrienne Rich's discussion of the "motherless" woman seems particularly applicable to Wharton in this regard. Such a woman may deny her own vulnerability, deny she has felt any loss or absence of mothering by "mothering" others. In this way she gives to others what she has lacked. "But this will always mean that she needs the neediness of others in order to go on feeling her own strength. She may feel uneasy with equals—particularly women" (246).

At the same time, Wharton's misogynist talk and that of her acquaintances about her is belied by her strong and enduring friendships with many women, among them Sara Norton, "so beloved and frequent a visitor" to the Mount; sister-in-law Minnie Jones, of whom Wharton writes, "To me she became closer than a sister of my own blood"; Minnie Bourget, with whom, from their first meeting Wharton felt "a deep-down understanding established itself between us"; her niece and frequent correspondent the landscape architect Beatrice Farrand; Elisina Tyler, a companion in her war projects who was with her when she died; Rosa de Fitz-James, with whom she traveled; and of course her personal maid Elise and Gross, her housekeeper for forty-five years, "two faithful women (who) kept the heartfire burning" (*BG* 155, 104; Lewis, *Biography* 514). Fifteen years after *French Ways*, in *A Backward Glance*, Wharton admits her intense admiration and affection for the "intellectually ardent" Vernon Lee, "the first highly cultivated and brilliant woman I had ever known" (Lewis, *Biography* 321; *BG* 132). She also acknowledges that Lee, along with Matilde Serao, a Neapolitan journalist and novelist, and Madame de Noailles, a French poet, has the gift for great talk that she has heretofore only found in men.[17] Mary Berenson provides an illuminating glimpse into Wharton as a woman friend in her observation that Wharton "said she wasted her youth trying to be beautiful, but now that she has given up all hope she feels freer. She *is* heavy-handed, but when you like her it becomes rather endearing. I think she is a very good friend to her friends" (Strachey and Samuels 184).

Nonetheless, in her professional persona, Wharton usually disparages the intellect and strength of women. One reading of this disparagement is that she sensed the danger inherent in a woman's immersing herself in male-identified qualities, especially to the exclusion of the kind of nurturing relationships she could share with female friends. The dominance, severity, and self-engrossment that Wharton felt had distorted her own life and denied her needed nurturance were, after all, her mother's qualities. Another reading is that Wharton saw her professional self as male and special compared to that of all other women, a self Kathryn Allen Rabuzzi denotes a "pseudo-man" unable to risk acknowledging the vulnerability and weakness inherent in "typical" women (136).[18] Still another reading, and the one on which I build my discussion of Wharton's Gothic, is that this disparagement reflects her profound discomfort with these male-identified qualities in herself. So out of keeping with the expected norm of femininity are her ambition, drive, passion, and intellect that they must be continually disowned, distanced, and kept in their place by patriarchal severity and scorn directed at other women. Mary Daly calls such a response "feminine antifeminism," possessed by women whose internalized "patriarchal presence" leads them to express "disapproval and hostility" toward women who threaten the gender status quo (52). All of these readings speak of a dissonant relationship with both genders as Wharton defined them and a persistent fear of the aware self that would acknowledge and accept the multivalent nature of femininity that she herself possessed.

Marriage

In traditional Gothic, the heroine escapes self-knowledge and personal authenticity through marriage; "profound uncertainty gives way to confidence and reason: married love conquers fear" (Nichols 188). This "happy ending" allows the heroine and the reader to have it both ways; romantic love acts as a defense against male sexuality, which the woman both fears and desires, and so it provides a solution certified by society (Holland and Sherman 286). Although in *French Ways* Wharton extols marriage as a woman's badge of maturity, in her Gothic stories marriage is what causes fear and distress. The Gothic version is closer to Wharton's own marital experience. Edith Jones's passionless marriage to Teddy Wharton, the handsome, compliant, and even supportive gentleman who so epitomized the restrained, unintellectual society that bred him, was physically draining for her and eventually mentally and emotionally imprisoning as well. Even as Wharton actively traveled, entertained, and bought and renovated houses, she perceived herself during her marriage as "a dim woman cloistered in ill-health" (Donnée Book). Attacks of asthma struck whenever she was forced to share a bedroom with Teddy (Wolff 51). Wharton uses the Gothic to speak, not about "melancholy, anxiety-ridden sentimental love" that ends in marriage, but rather about patriarchal restraints on the female person and spirit within the domestic setting (Howells 5). At the end of her Gothic stories the heroine is often dead or imprisoned rather than able and willing to resume the "quiescent, socially acceptable role" of the expectable Gothic ending (Kahane, "Gothic Mirror" 342). In Wharton's Gothic, marriage is therefore not a defense against the male, sexual forces that menace and attract a woman in traditional Gothic but rather is apt to be the very source of the threat against a woman because it controls her sexuality and sometimes even kills her (Holland and Sherman 286).

Wharton's Gothic consistently magnifies the constraining, even destructive effects of marriage on women, even though elsewhere in her writing she is as contradictory about marriage as she is about what a woman should be. Several references to marriage suggest Wharton's belief in the institution: her much cited remark about "the poverty, the miserable poverty, of any love that lies outside of marriage" during her affair with Morton Fullerton; her argument in *French Ways* that marriage completes a woman; and her comments in *The Gods Arrive,* via the intellectual, unmarried George Frenside, about the need for the framework of marriage—"Marriage may be too tight a fit—may dislocate and deform. But it shapes life too; prevents growing lopsided, or drifting" (Lewis, *Biography* 317–18; *GA* 311). Wharton's unpublished notebooks reveal a darker, more sardonic view of marriage, such as the 1913 dialogue insert:

> "Did you know that John and Susan committed suicide together on Tuesday?"
> "What? No—How?"
> "They got married." [Donnée Book]

The questionable ideal of marriage as the union of two "equal" souls in the early story "The Fullness of Life" is consistently refuted in the Gothic stories and the novels with a Gothic subtext, where marriage is more apt to be suffocating captivity. Eventually, in her last two completed novels, Wharton resolves the still-prominent question of whether such a union of equal souls is possible by showing that the true union must be *within* the woman and man, between the feminine and masculine parts of the self. A marriage of selves can occur when a person confronts and accepts the feminine/maternal within, an act that Wharton perceives as a *human* (rather than an exclusively female) act of courage.

Incest

Wharton's allusions to incest and, in the "Beatrice Palmato" fragment, dramatization of it is in keeping with her use of the Gothic to probe the "unacknowledged, disavowed, disallowed" story about female sexuality (Stein 126). Her career-long attraction to incest has been discussed as an outgrowth of her own incest experiences.[19] But reading Wharton's Gothic as an exploration of gender, as I do, opens up other possible readings of the incest motif. Jung posits that whenever the drive for wholeness appears, that is, the union of feminine and masculine, "it begins by disguising itself under the symbolism of incest" (16:263). To a degree this tendency helps explain Wharton's interest in sexual union as a fusion of conflicting yet related forces. Since, however, incest is destructive to women in Wharton's Gothic fiction, her use of it seems instead to be a dramatization of the longing of a woman to lose her sense of powerlessness by merging with the masculine power that controls her. The warning that too often a woman "cannot distinguish between her unmothered need for the mother and her need for a male partnership," which she assumes will fill her with "patriarchal authority," helps explain the dilemma of unmothered characters such as Sybilla Lombard in "The House of the Dead Hand" and Beatrice Palmato in the fragment bearing her name (Perera 162). The desire of both women for self-definition results instead in absorption by those patriarchal figures who possess self-defined power and control.

Houses

Wharton's Gothic reveals that female self-definition is most successfully achieved, not through a man, but through the reclaiming of a house, which serves as her most powerful sign of body/self. This is in keeping with Gothic tradition. As Elizabeth MacAndrew notes, "The omnipresent old house or castle is one of the most stable characteristics of the Gothic," and as those who have written about female Gothic have subsequently argued, the house/castle embodies the feminine/maternal (48). In *A Backward Glance* Wharton recalls being frightened, as a small child, by the "intolerable ugliness" of her aunt's Hudson River Gothic estate called Rhinecliff (28). "From the first," she writes, "I was obscurely conscious of a queer resemblance between the granitic exterior of Aunt Elizabeth and her grimly comfortable home, between her battlemented caps and the turrets of Rhinecliff" (28). Within this female house/body, Wharton has a terrifying nightmare of a Wolf under her bed, one of the first of her "other similar terrifying experiences" of being haunted by "tribal animals" (28). The adult Wharton hints at but skirts the observation that destructively uncontrollable power haunts the female body.[20]

In one of her earliest stories, "The Fullness of Life," which Wharton in a 1898 letter to Edward Burlingame, her Scribner editor, self-consciously called "one long shriek," the narrator, a dead woman and so the ultimate passive character, compares a woman's nature to a "great house full of rooms" (Scribner Collection; Lewis, *CSS* 1:14). In most of the rooms, friends and family come and go, "but beyond . . . are other rooms, the handles of whose doors perhaps are never turned; no one knows the way to them, no one knows whither they lead; and in the innermost room, the holy of holies, the soul sits alone and waits for a footstep that never comes" (Lewis, *CSS* 1:14, ellipsis mine).

The narrator's unresponsive husband never ventures into her inner self, "full of treasures and wonders" (14). The woman confers with the "Spirit of Life," about being granted a "soul-mate" for eternity, but she rejects the boring ideal for the unhappy but comfortable tension with her husband. When the Spirit points out that the choice is forever, she counters, "Choosing! . . . Do you still keep up here that old fiction about choosing? I should have thought that *you* knew better than that. How can I help myself?" (20, ellipsis mine) "How can I help myself?" is the central question, suggesting as it does that helping herself is both a possibility and an impossibility.

By 1917 this passive early character's creator has realized that a woman can nurture her own fulfillment rather than having to depend on a man for it. In a letter written to her close friend Mary Berenson urging her to help heal herself after a nervous collapse, Wharton again calls on the house/self image: "I believe I know the only cure, which is to make one's centre of life inside of one's self, not selfishly or excludingly, but with a kind of unassailable serenity—to decorate one's inner house so richly that one is content there, glad to welcome any one who wants to come and stay, but happy all the same in the hours when one is inevitably alone" (Lewis, *Biography* 413). Wharton's notebook entries about the blessedness of being alone at her home in Hyères illustrate how happily she had learned to live in her own inner house.

In "A Little Girl's New York," an essay written near the end of her life, Wharton reads women's sexually suppressed bodies in their overly decorated houses. In the 1890s the uniform brownstones marched up Fifth Avenue like "disciplined schoolgirls." Her description "penetrate[s] from the vestibule . . . into the carefully guarded interior" of one of the brownstones, which could easily have been her mother's on West Twenty-third Street:

> Beyond the vestibule (in the average house) was a narrow drawing-room. Its tall windows were hung with three layers of curtains: sash-curtains through

which no eye from the street could possibly penetrate, and next to these drap-eries of lace or embroidered tulle, richly beruffled, and looped back under the velvet or damask hangings which were drawn in the evening. This window garniture always seemed to me to symbolize the superimposed layers of under-garments worn by the ladies of the period—and even, alas, by the little girls. They were in fact almost purely a symbol, for in many windows even the inner "sash-curtains" were looped back far enough to give the secluded dwellers a narrow glimpse of the street; but no self-respecting mistress of a house (a brownstone house) could dispense with this triple display of win-dow-lingerie, and among the many things I did which pained and scandalized my Bostonian mother-in-law, she was not least shocked by the banishment from our house in the country of all the thicknesses of muslin which should have intervened between ourselves and the robins on the lawn. [358]

Wharton becomes the male-identified "penetrator" of this house and cus-tom by becoming writer and house designer. Her first published book, *The Deco-ration of Houses*, written with Ogdon Codman and the source of her first royalty check, is a declaration of independence in several respects. In it Wharton stresses that the house is an "organism" and that decoration is not a "superficial application of ornament" but a branch of architecture that is itself an expression of the "tastes and habits" of the people living in the house (xxx, 17). Art and life are organically conjoined in successful house creating, she argues, and both are guided by symmetry, proportion, and simplicity.

These classical principles guided her creation of her "first real home," the Mount, a palatial house on a hill overlooking Lake Laurel outside Lenox, Mas-sachusetts, whose building she designed and supervised herself and for which she paid in part from the earnings of *The House of Mirth* (*BG* 125). These princi-ples also guided her renovation of her two French homes, Pavillon Colombe in St. Brice-sous-Forêt, outside Paris, France, and Ste. Claire du Vieux Chateau, in Hyères on the Mediterranean, self-created havens established after her divorce from Teddy. Part of the appeal of both places was their woman-centered histo-ries, one sensual, one spiritual. Wharton was delighted that Pavillon Colombe had been named after two actress sisters of erotic fame "installed there" by their lovers around the mid-1700s. Ste. Claire, by contrast, was a former convent, built within the crenelated walls of an old château and overlooking Hyères and the sea, a place Wharton once called "the garden of my soul" (Notebook 1924–34). Another part of the appeal of both houses was their need for extensive renova-tion; out of the ruins Wharton created classically ordered, impeccably orches-trated households.[21]

In her Gothic, Wharton seems to be deliberately testing and countering the classical control she imposed on her own houses. In the short stories and Gothic-marked novels, dilapidated, disordered, or eerie houses embody, for those who become aware of it, an alternative reality, a way of knowing that is visceral rather than rational, frightening more than soothing, disruptive of the status quo rather than supportive of it. Like castles in traditional Gothic, Wharton's Gothic houses hold secrets about ungovernable passions: greed, lust, rage, fear, jealousy. Locked up or otherwise kept inaccessible by patriarchal heavies, these houses embody the suppression of women's (and sometimes men's) stories and lives, to the detriment of women and men alike.

Thus the question of who controls the house and its environment is a crucial source of gender conflict in the Gothic fiction. Female protagonists in the early Gothic stories—"The House of the Dead Hand," "The Lady's Maid's Bell," "The Duchess at Prayer"—are held captive in houses as much by their own passivity as by patriarchal power, which in turn is partly a projection of their own feared assertive self. In *The House of Mirth, Summer,* and *The Age of Innocence,* a woman's search for a home is a search for a way of being in society that is defined by oneself rather than by society or by a man.[22] Judith Wilt's comment about place and the Gothic is appropriate to Wharton's view: "Power, the Gothic says, resides in place, and . . . overwhelmingly, the kind of power that resides in place, in placement, seems to be male, and the power that challenges it, evades it, or that seeks place from a position of placelessness, is female" (276–77, ellipsis mine).

Wharton revises this dynamic in her Gothic stories and novels written in the 1920s and 1930s—"Miss Mary Pask," "Dieu d'Amour," "Bewitched," *Hudson River Bracketed,* and *The Gods Arrive*—by making houses more female-identified, or by having caves and cabins serve as female spaces. The timid, usually male, characters who enter these mysterious, dark, sensuous places, "the maternal body with its related secrets of birth and sexuality" as well as death, feel threatened by annihilation, and they flee in terror (Holland and Sherman 286). Male characters like Orrin Bosworth in "Bewitched" and Vance Weston in *Hudson River Bracketed* and *The Gods Arrive,* who are unafraid of female-identified places, are also able to hear and assimilate women's stories and respect female experience. Female characters who reclaim houses, such as Jane Lynke in "Mr. Jones" and Halo Spear in *The Gods Arrive,* reclaim their female history and control over their lives. Sara Clayburn's anxious nighttime search for her servants through her cold, silent house in "All Souls'," written shortly before Wharton's death, vividly dramatizes a woman's terrified realization that her feminine self is alien and empty.[23] That Wharton never indicates the gender of the scholarly narrator who tells Sara's story, comforts her after her ordeal, and frames her surreal experience with references to women's supernatural powers is fitting as a coda to Wharton's career-long conversation about women and men and feminine and masculine in her Gothic fiction.

2 | Fearing the Feminine

I~N THE GOTHIC~ stories written early in her career, between 1900 and 1904—"The House of the Dead Hand," "The Duchess at Prayer," "The Angel at the Grave," and "The Lady's Maid's Bell"—Wharton enters the world of women who, unable to accept or act on their sexuality and autonomy, accede control to their self-hating masculine selves, portrayed by the villainous, controlling men who at worst tyrannize them and at best restrict their lives. Wharton is testing her creating self, examining the dangers of allowing art and intellectualism to control and restrain femininity.[1] These early Gothic stories mirror the psychic struggle between female sexuality and autonomy and male attempts to suppress it, a struggle not unlike Wharton's own in accommodating her femininity to the artist she was becoming. The Gothic form, with its dreamlike tension between female/male counterforces in enclosed spaces, is an allowable way for Wharton to express the painful fear of femininity that permeated her life and fiction while also allowing her to enter emotional and psychic depths. The early Gothic stories express, too, Wharton's fear of her art and her intellect as dominating, destructive forces subsuming and destroying her sexuality and liberty. This "ambivalence toward imaginative power" has been called "central to American Gothic tradition" (Johnson 527).

Lily Bart's passivity and fear of self-awareness in *The House of Mirth*, published in 1905, reflects the female (self)victimization found in these early Gothic stories. Lily's objectification of herself and her willingness to be objectified by others, countered by her anxiety about her role as art object, however, places the male/female conflict of the stories *within* Lily. Another distinction in Wharton's handling of the Gothic in the realistic novel compared to the short stories is the parallel she draws between Lily and Selden. In *The House of Mirth*, as in all of the Gothic-marked novels I discuss, Wharton uses similarities between the protagonists to stress the commonalities of female and male ways of being and, thereby, the possibility of a fe/male self not usually found in the Gothic stories. At the same time Wharton realistically describes the social forces defining the parameters of gender.

"The House of the Dead Hand," one of the earliest stories of this early period, is the rawest, most blatant example of conflict between woman as art object and man as intellectual in the Gothic fiction. It shares many Gothic elements with "The Duchess at Prayer," "The Angel at the Grave," and "The Lady's Maid's Bell": a dreary house; a young woman living a constrained life within it; an overbearing, usually brutish man threatening the woman's well-being; and an ineffectual "savior" of the woman. Though the treachery and power of the father in "The House of the Dead Hand" and the husband in "The Duchess at Prayer" are indisputable, the women controlled by them also exhibit a submissive, unaware collusion in their restraint. By contrast, the heroines of "The Angel at the Grave" and "The Lady's Maid's Bell" stare into the darkness of their own fears, indicating nascent self-awareness that heroines in stories and novels later in Wharton's career develop and act on. Significant too, in "The Lady's Maid's Bell," is the unnourished but nonetheless potentially supportive relationship among women, a dynamic that Wharton explores more substantially in *The House of Mirth* and *The Age of Innocence*.

Sybilla Lombard, the passive young heroine of "The House of the Dead Hand," has been coerced by her overbearing father to use an inheritance from her grandmother to buy a Leonardo painting which the father keeps locked up. Her mother, who is vacuously unaware of her husband's cruel condescension to her, clearly isn't capable of nurturing or protecting her daughter. That Sybilla's very life and will are held captive by her rapacious Renaissance scholar father becomes clear when the funereal house they inhabit in Siena is visited by an outsider named Wyant. Asked by a friend to see and try to copy the Leonardo, Wyant views not only the painting but the drama of a woman paralyzed into inactivity by her submission to male power. Wyant is a common character in Wharton's Gothic short stories, an outsider, usually male, who blunders into domestic emotional complexity and evades his moral responsibility to act on what he learns about male abuse of power and female victimization. He represents the reticent social observer, intelligent enough to recognize the turgid emotional struggle he is observing and too timid to acknowledge his observations fully.

It doesn't take long for the reader to realize that the "dead drooping hand" of sallow marble over the Lombard doorway, which gives the house its name, represents Sybilla's spirit and, through her, the feminine spirit, "convulsed and helpless, as though it had been thrust forth in denunciation of some evil mystery within the house, and had sunk struggling into death" (Lewis, *CSS* 1:509).[2] When Wyant enters the sunless, morguelike villa, he immediately notices Sybilla's sullen drooping mouth and her inanimateness, especially in contrast to her father's "fierce vitality" (510).

The same contrast between lethargy and animation exists between the vivid religious and sensual elements of the Leonardo painting and the mechanical detachment with which Sybilla goes through the motions of describing them to Wyant. The central figure of the artwork—part Virgin, part Circe—has one hand "drooped on the arm of her chair" and is surrounded by symbols of sensuality (513). Yet it seems to have sucked out Sybilla's own spirituality and sensuality. The female sexual iconography of the scene through which one travels to reach the painting accentuates the sense that the artwork embodies Sybilla's sexuality. First the girl draws aside a tapestry hanging and fits her key into a concealed door that takes the viewers of the painting down a narrow stone passage to another door and another lock into which the girl fits another key. Once in a small dark room, the father has Wyant place his left foot on the pomegranate bud in the carpet while Sybilla pulls the hidden cord behind the velvet curtain. She mechanically chants St. Bernard's invocation to the Virgin from Dante's *Paradise* as her father directs, and "the folds of velvet slowly parted" to reveal the painting (512). Having Wyant place his foot on the clitoral emblem of fertility so that he can see the image of sensuality behind the labial folds of the curtain accentuates Lombard's sadistic control over his daughter's sexuality.[3]

For in sacrificing her matrilineal heritage to buy this painting, Sybilla has sacrificed all possibility of living a life of her own. Despite her father's portrayal of her as a "votary of the arts," she has clearly bought the painting only to satisfy his obsessive immersion in the Italian Renaissance (511). His passionate cry to her, "swear to me that the picture shall never be reproduced," echoes his implied insistence that Sybilla herself not reproduce, that she have no sexuality (516).[4]

Indeed, Sybilla's feeble attempt to save her life by arranging an assignation with a suitor, a scheme in which Wyant becomes enmeshed, fails as much because of her timidity as because of his. Even after her father dies, Sybilla is controlled by his power over her and so is unable to sell the picture she hates to buy her freedom. "I found it was impossible," she tells Wyant when he returns several years later. "I tried again and again; but he was always in the room with me" (529). She blames Wyant for not helping her when she had a chance to escape, but her desire to be other than subsumed by art is suspect. It is her own fear of her sexuality as much as her father's control over it that keeps it hidden and objectified in art rather than lived. Sybilla is one of Wharton's most pathetic examples of a woman unable and unwilling to save herself from her external and internal male domination. As in Mary Wollstonecraft's *Maria*, "The House of the Dead Hand" tells the ironic story that a woman becomes a typical Gothic heroine by self-destructively "giving up power, by refusing to act in her own behalf" (McMillan 56).

"The Duchess at Prayer" and "The Angel at the Grave," published in the 1901 collection *Crucial Instances,* are better written than "The House of the Dead Hand"; the situations are more complex, the language is more subtle, the female characters are more aware of their restrained condition and more spirited in their response to it than Sybilla. "The Duchess at Prayer" shares many characteristics with Balzac's Gothic story "La Grande Bretèche," which Wharton greatly admired. It has the same Italian setting, the beautiful and spirited young wife of a sullen husband, the live burial of the woman's lover, the tomblike house in which the drama occurs, the several and thus unreliable narrators. What is Wharton's own, however, is her emphasis in both "The Duchess at Prayer" and "The Angel at the Grave" on imperious male culture and the spontaneous female energy suppressed by it.

The multiple narrators in "The Duchess at Prayer" give the eerie sense that one is entering a state of mind. The narrator who guides the reader into the villa that has been vacant for two hundred years is himself guided by an old man who tells the story of the Duchess told to him by his old grandmother, once a sewing girl to the Duchess. The old man's querulous refrain, "What do I know?" when cross-examined by the narrator is appropriate, for ambiguity is at the heart of the story.[5] The narration encourages the reader to feel herself inside what Elizabeth MacAndrew calls "the inner landscape of the mind itself," where "rather than discerning transcendent truths beyond it," one sees "the fearful outlines of the subconscious—flitting shadows and cornered trolls— which can only be exposed to full daylight at great risk" (217).

The "fearful outlines of the subconscious" in "The Duchess at Prayer," as in "The House of the Dead Hand," involve a heroine who has her youth and sexuality constrained by a man who replaces her with a piece of art. The Duchess is "all for music, play-acting, and young company," but unfortunately she is married to a dour Duke, whose portrait reveals a "quibbling mouth that would have snapped at verbal errors like a lizard catching flies" and who, when he is at home, spends his time "forever closeted in his library, talking with learned men" (CI 10, 4).[6]

One of the Duke's companions is a resident chaplain, usually "buried in his library like a mouse in a cheese," whose request to the Duchess for a large sum of money to buy books is laughed away by her with the dismissive retort, "Holy Mother of God, must I have more books about me? I was nearly smothered with them in the first year of my marriage" (15). The chaplain's embarrassment at the rebuff exacerbates the struggle in the story between sensuality and intellect that already exists between the wife and the husband.

The tension is reminiscent of that in Robert Browning's "My Last Duchess," to which Wharton may well be alluding in writing her story. Just as Browning's Duchess had what her possessive husband called "A heart . . . too soon made glad, / Too easily impressed; she liked what'er / She looked on, and her looks went everywhere," so Wharton's Duchess "was always laughing" (204, ellipsis mine). That her laughter makes her husband wince "as if you'd drawn a diamond across a window-pane" is eerie warning to the reader that Wharton's Duchess will fare no better than Browning's (CI 11).

In between her husband's twice yearly visits to the villa, the lively young wife in Wharton's story does her best to entertain herself—planning gardens and bringing in fortune tellers, astrologers, and trained animals. But she is most buoyed by visits from her husband's handsome and fun-loving young cousin Ascanio. The two are attracted to one another like bees to lavender, the old guide tells the narrator. The jealous husband becomes aware not only of the attraction but of his young wife's beauty on one of his visits, and he offers the cousin a ride away from the villa as he leaves. The chastity the Duke expects to enforce by keeping the Duchess isolated in the dreary villa is threatened by her natural desire for stimulation and companionship.[7]

With the help of the chaplain's scrutiny and more frequent visits home than usual, the Duke apparently figures out that his wife's daily visits to the villa's chapel and the crypt beneath it are as likely due to assignations with his cousin Ascanio, hiding in the crypt, as to religious devotion. To control the sexually alive young wife whom he leaves alone most of the year, the Duke has a life-sized marble statue made of her kneeling in prayer, which he brings to the villa unexpectedly one day, "shrouded" in white as if "wrapped in death-clothes" (20, 22). The death imagery is apt, since the Duke intends to place the sculpture over the entrance to the crypt where the Duchess has knelt, sealing Ascanio within it.[8] It is also apt because he kills his wife, covertly by tauntingly toasting the "long life" of Ascanio and overtly with poison in the goblet of wine she drinks for the toast. That the Duke brings home a new Duchess the next year is another allusion to Browning's poem about the killing of a lively, independent woman's spirit, her reduction to a piece of art, and her replacement by another Duchess who will probably be more compliant.

The Gothic touch by which the sculpture's face changes after the Duchess's death to reflect the agony she experienced during her last hours alive reflects the intense anxiety the story expresses about the power of male gynophobia to transmogrify spontaneous life into static art. The sadistic male intellectual in "The House of the Dead Hand" and "The Duchess at Prayer" is modulated in subsequent Gothic stories and in the Gothic-marked novels, but Wharton continues to enact the sacrifice of female autonomy and energy to the male control of art and intellectualism.

"The Angel at the Grave" is the least overtly Gothic of the early stories. But Paulina Anson's attempt to assume the intellectual isolation of her grandfather in her sober ancestral dwelling known as "the House," to the detriment of her own life spirit, definitely links this story to Wharton's other Gothic stories. At the same time it is distinguished by its deliberate intermingling of the masculine and feminine spheres, which the other stories have portrayed more distinctly as separate male and female characters. In her name and her actions, Paulina embodies both genders.

The only granddaughter of Orestes Anson, Paulina is also the only one in the family who has tried to read the famous philosopher's works on free will and intuition, so she becomes the keeper of the Anson shrine, "the House," where he lived before his death. Even Paulina, however, gets primarily "verbal pleasure" from her grandfather's "sonorous periods, his mystic vocabulary, his bold flights into the rarefied air of the abstract" (*CI* 41). Eventually she gets "crumbs of meaning" from the rhetoric, but overall her appreciation of the man who has become legend enough to have pilgrims visit his home with regularity entails a Romantic admiration bred of sensation rather than intellect. Indeed, we learn that Paulina "was the type of woman who transmutes thought into sensation and nurses a theory in her bosom like a child" (42). She "feminizes" the intellectual, living it as sensual experience rather than using it as an outward means of control.

Nonetheless, when a suitor with flagrant disregard for her grandfather's reputation tries to court Paulina, her rejection of him, the narrator suggests, comes not only from the spirit of her grandfather emanating disapproval from the very house itself (just as Lombard's control emanates from the House of the Dead Hand after his death) but also from Paulina's own fear of an independent, sexual life, which is like Sybilla's. Paulina, however, "hung a moment over the black gulf of temptation" peering, as Persephone might have, "half-consentingly down the abyss that opened at her feet" (43). In borrowing a man's intellectual life as her own, she has grown afraid of her femininity and so shrinks from the "black gulf" of self-awareness that full acceptance of it would bring. Wharton suggests here a revision of the Greek version of Persephone's abduction into the underworld, similar to the earlier Sumerian story of Inanna's "life-enhancing descent into the abyss" (Perera 142).

Only after putting in years of work on a biography of her grandfather that is rejected by his former publisher does Paulina understand the sacrifice she has made of her own life to his. The realization that he was really a minor figure compared to the New England eminences Emerson and Hawthorne, with whom he had corresponded, comes to Paulina like a ghost. With it comes the even more Gothic realization that "she had been walled alive into a tomb hung with the effigies of dead ideas" (*CI* 51). Suddenly she realizes her desperate longing "to escape into the outer air, where people toiled and loved, and living sympathies went hand in hand" (51). More subtly but no less destructively than Sybilla in "The House of the Dead Hand" and the Duchess in "The Duchess at Prayer," Paulina has become an artifact, a willing victim of intellectual domination. In immersing herself in a male life to the exclusion of her own, she ironically loses the free will and intuition her grandfather had written about.

The twist in this story comes with the help of George Corby, an unexpected visitor who arrives at the house when Paulina has aged enough to use a cane. He informs her that her grandfather had done other work far more original than his philosophy but that it had been silenced by the rejection of his peers. That the original discoveries were about the *amphioxus,* a fishlike sea animal, adds complexity to the Orestes allusion of her grandfather's name. For the man named after a matricide has a secret side to him, one centered in the sea, a feminine element, and in an animal resembling a fish, a symbol of the fertility goddess (Neumann 276, Gimbutas 238). Paulina's explanation to Corby for why she had not burned the manuscript, as her grandfather had intended, suggests what often happens to women's voices and women's stories: "to burn it was like shutting the door against his voice—against something he had once wished to say, and that nobody had listened to" (*CI* 59).

Young Corby's enthusiasm for Anson's unappreciated work encourages Paulina to express her grief at having sacrificed her life for her grandfather's philosophical ideas. "It ruined my life! . . . I gave up everything . . . to keep *him* alive" (60, ellipsis mine). At the same time, Corby's reassurance that Paulina's love had kept alive other hidden ideas that might have otherwise gone undiscovered rekindles both her intellectual excitement and her feelings of youthful sexuality.

Like Sybilla in "The House of the Dead Hand," Paulina has feared and thus constrained her sexuality and autonomy. Unlike Sybilla, Paulina is an intellectual, a writer and lover of ideas, who eventually finds a way of acknowledging, however briefly, both her feminine and masculine self, as Wharton has defined them.

Wharton's first ghost story, "The Lady's Maid's Bell," was written in 1901, within six months of her mother's death. R. W. B. Lewis's tantalizingly unexplained comment that, "with the source of the childhood terrors removed, the mature writer could now deploy her memory of them to expert literary purpose," meshes with my own sense that "The Lady's Maid's Bell" is also Wharton's first Gothic story to acknowledge not only the terror but also the attractive pull of the feminine/maternal darkness signified by a female ghost ("Powers" 646).

Our first hint of the story's center in the female experience is that it is named after a bell, a yonic symbol that links the three female characters by allowing them to communicate with one another.[9] Hartley, the most recent maid to frail Mrs. Brympton of Brympton Place and called by her last name, learns quickly that Mrs. Brympton doesn't ring the lady's maid's bell. Yet the bell *does* ring in the middle of the night, calling Hartley to aid her mistress, weakened by the sexual advances of her bully husband. The clitoral image of "the little hammer still quivering" in the bell after it has rung and the concurrent presence of the ghost of Emma Saxon, Mrs. Brympton's maid for twenty years, going down to her mistress's room ahead of Hartley, connect all three women in a drama of female sexuality (*DM* 260).

"The Lady's Maid's Bell," like "The Duchess at Prayer," includes an overbearing, brutish husband, whom Hartley describes as "a big fair bull-necked man, with a red face and little bad-tempered blue eyes: the kind of man a young simpleton might have thought handsome, and would have been like to pay dear for thinking it" (252). True to his egocentric character and like the Duke in the earlier story, Mr. Brympton leaves his wife at home for long periods of time while he no doubt lives a full life of pleasure. When he infrequently returns for short periods, he jangles the household staff, drinks heavily, and leaves his wife "white, and chill to the touch" after visiting her in her room (253). His "once-over" of Hartley when he is first introduced to her tells her that "I was not the kind of morsel he was after. The typhoid had served me well enough in one way: it kept that kind of gentleman at arm's length" (252). Both Hartley and her mistress are potential victims of Mr. Brympton's sexual aggression. Significantly, however, unlike the earlier villains Mr. Lombard, the Duke, and even Orestes Anson, Mr. Brympton isn't an intellectual and doesn't use his power to freeze his wife's vitality into a piece of art. His power over her is more limited to the physical, suggesting a power more easily overcome if a woman were strong enough.

His wife, Mrs. Brympton, is herself both like and unlike the typical female Gothic characters whom Wharton has introduced to this point. Like Sybilla and the Duchess in their somber dwellings, Mrs. Brympton is virtually an inmate of the gloomy country estate in which she lives on the banks of the Hudson. But her physical frailty—she is "nervous, vapourish" in her aunt's words—victimizes her as much as the "coarse, loud, and pleasure-loving" man she married (244, 255). Hartley's musing that "it might be the heart that ailed her" suggests not only physical ailment but a failure of vitality (256). The latter view is supported by Hartley's observation that Mrs. Brympton was "quiet, retiring, and perhaps a trifle cold," no doubt "a little offish" to "a gentleman as free as Mr. Brympton" (255).[10] Such detail about the marital relationship of these characters adds subtlety to otherwise typical Gothic figures. "The Lady's Maid's Bell" extends the suggestion of "The Duchess at Prayer" that marital incompatibility and the domestic tension that results from it are just as powerful a source of fear and trauma as a chaste single woman being pursued by a villain in traditional Gothic.

The third component of Wharton's Gothic plot in "The Lady's Maid's Bell" is the ineffectual lover of the heroine, in this case friendly Mr. Ranford, with whom Mrs. Brympton shares books.[11] Though he attempts an assignation, like the one planned by Count Ottaviano to carry away Sybilla in "The House of the Dead Hand," the act is foiled by the deliberate return of Mr. Brympton late in the night. Wharton consistently revises the typical Gothic hero, the savior who usually rushes to the defense of the tormented heroine, under attack by the villain. Ranford suggests the role of "male foil" in modern Gothic in that he is a gentle and passive romantic companion for the heroine who is "usually overwhelmed by events" (Radway 150). Ranford's limp at Mrs. Brympton's funeral confirms him as a "castrated" hero (Stengel 8). That Wharton's men consistently fail to come through for the heroines, however much companionable diversion they provide, is Wharton's caustic comment on the myth of the hero who will save the woman from her own victimization. Mrs. Brympton's death makes clear that another lover is not what the woman needs to save herself. This same theme of the ineffectual hero/savior plays prominently in Wharton's Gothic-marked novels: *The House of Mirth, Ethan Frome, The Age of Innocence, Summer, The Gods Arrive* and *Hudson River Bracketed*.

The ghost of Emma Saxon, the former maid to Mrs. Brympton, provides the text of "The Lady's Maid's Bell" with the "expansion of consciousness" basic to traditional Gothic and key to Wharton's revision of the form (Bayer-Berenbaum 21). Emma's appearance speaks for not only Mrs. Brympton's sexuality but also for her isolation and silence. As the former maid of twenty years, she plays a mother role to Hartley, the young replacement, as well as to the frail Mrs. Brympton, who is both child and mother to the younger Hartley. Emma represents the dark knowledge of the maternal erotic that Hartley consistently pushes from her mind. She is Hartley's aware self, her dark double, the first name to her last. From the start, when Hartley spontaneously blurts out to Mrs. Brympton that she won't feel lonely in the country house if she is with her mistress, she feels herself taken over by a spirit that she comes to know as Emma's. As she gets drawn into her mistress's sexual drama, her mistress mistakes her for Emma, and she is pulled to look into the abyss of awareness that Emma represents.

As the inhabitant of the locked room across the hall from Hartley's, the thought of which Hartley admits begins to weigh on her, Emma becomes for the reader the keeper of the secret of the house, the secret of the Brympton marriage that Hartley both wants and does not want to know. Her ghostliness also speaks of women's silence and isolation in the story. Just as Hartley constantly vows to hold her tongue and not ask any questions about the mysterious happenings in the house, so she thinks of Mrs. Brympton as one of the class of ladies who "have to endure and hold their tongues" when faced with their husbands' drunken advances (*DM* 254). Such reticence prevents all the women from helping one another. As Mrs. Brympton's strength and spirits continue to wane, Hartley's affection for her grows, but the young woman admits, "after all there was little I could do to help her" (269). Her sense of powerlessness is accentuated when she sees Emma in a doorway, her face "just one dumb prayer to me" (270). "How in the world was I to help her?" she asks of the ghost, her response echoing what she says of her mistress and linking them all in a common bond of helpless silence (270).

As Emma leads Hartley to Ranford's house and then disappears, Hartley feels desolate that the ghost "had left me all alone to carry the weight of the secret I couldn't guess" and certain that "*she* knew what it was; she would tell me if she could" (273, 272). Then Hartley faints. Her frustration that the ghost knows but won't reveal "the secret" recalls Wharton's discussion about sex with her mother. The mystery is too overwhelming to be probed by a cautious woman afraid to ask questions.

That it is the weighty secret of female sexuality Emma leaves with Hartley becomes clear to the reader when Emma appears to her twice more, at the head of the stairs, "peering dreadfully down into the darkness" into which she disappears and then "on the threshold" of Mrs. Brympton's dressing room with the darkness behind her (275, 277). Fraught with connotations of sexuality, the threshold on which Emma stands leads into the darkness of the underworld, the unconscious, the feminine (Rabuzzi 88–89).

Emma has a story to tell, about an affair between Mrs. Brympton and Mr. Ranford, about the Brympton marriage, about her relationship with Mrs. Brympton, or perhaps about her own death. That she does not tell her story, and in fact asks helplessly, leaves an emptiness where a resource should be. In her disembodiment and muteness she is a sign of the untold female story.

Alice Hartley is no help either in clarifying the mystery. Although sensitive to the menace in her situation, she is not courageous enough to ask questions and probe for the secret of the house. Through her, Wharton portrays female ambivalence: to see the horror of one's situation and not speak, to be afraid of one's aware self, of the darkness that yields knowledge. The pale, bodiless Emma, whose eyes have "an asking look" and who silently stares, is an exaggerated version of the pale, thin Hartley, unwilling to ask questions, and her pale, thin mistress, who suffers silently. Given that blood is, as Susan Gubar has written, a central symbol furnished by the female body, these women seem bled of their femaleness, made sick by their silence ("Blank Page" 83). The unspeakable domestic horror they are experiencing without sharing has made ghosts of them all. Their ghostliness is a visual representation of their story, only wisps of which are known.

"The Lady's Maid's Bell" extends Wharton's use of the Gothic into an exploration of women's sexuality that she continues to explore as part of the Gothic subtext in *The House of Mirth, The Age of Innocence, Ethan Frome,* and *Summer* as well as in "Bewitched," "Pomegranate Seed," and "All Souls'." Gothic fear, "The Lady's Maid's Bell" tells us, derives as much from confrontation with one's own femaleness, with the secrets of the erotic, as it does from male oppression. Unlike traditional Gothic heroines, who only flirt with this awareness and then lose themselves in domestic denial, Wharton's heroines are a precursor of those created by modern female Gothic writers, such as Margaret Atwood, Shirley Jackson, and Flannery O'Connor, for whose characters the female body is often the primary terror.

The fate of Sybilla in "The House of the Dead Hand" and the Duchess in "The Duchess at Prayer," to have their lives figured by a painting and a piece of statuary, is both mirrored and revised by Lily's story in *The House of Mirth.*

Bred by her mother to be a beautiful object, worthy of purchase in the social system of exchange, scheming to sell herself to the highest bidder, Lily tries to live her life based on this patriarchal means of being female that the Gothic stories of this period dramatize. With the stories as context, the horror of Lily's life role is accentuated. Her fear of her sexuality and autonomy, which evolves from this objectification and a lack of maternal nurturing much like Sybilla's, gravely affects her experiences in the house of mirth that is her society. Whether encountering the villain, the femme fatale, the mean aunt, or her own reflection in a mirror, she experiences fear and dread because of her tenuous sense of self.[12] Like the orphaned heroine in traditional Gothic, Lily wanders from house to house and finds most of the houses oppressive and threatening. Unlike the traditional heroine, Lily has no happily-ever-after marriage at the end of her wanderings.

Reading Lily's story in the context of the Gothic short stories also reveals how profoundly courageous she is in spite of her fears and in spite of having, like most Gothic heroines, almost no support from others. Instinctively she resists being owned by a man, unlike Sybilla and the Duchess. And while Paulina, in "The Angel at the Grave," hangs "a moment" over the black abyss that is the autonomous life of a mature, sexually aware woman, and Hartley, in "The Lady's Maid's Bell," stares briefly at the ghost Emma, who peers into the darkness of female self-knowledge, Lily endures a "dark night of the soul" during her last hours alive. She hangs near "the dizzy brink of the unreal," intensely aware of her sense of isolation, of her uselessness, of her "inner destitution" (*HM* 520, 515). Though Lily eventually drowns the self-awareness in chloral, her courageous confrontation with the dark abyss of her inner self contrasts with the fleeting glances into the darkness of the heroines in the earlier Gothic stories.

Lily has been raised by a mother who, like the husband in "The Duchess at Prayer" and the father in "The House of the Dead Hand," transforms her daughter into an artistic commodity. In contemplating Lily's beauty, Mrs. Bart "studied it with a kind of passion, as though it were some weapon she had slowly fashioned for her vengeance. It was the last asset in their fortunes, the nucleus around which their life was to be rebuilt. She watched it jealously, as though it were her own property and Lily its mere custodian" (53). It is what Lily learns best about herself, that her beauty is all of her, that it is an asset to be used for financial gain, and that it is hers only until it is owned by a husband. Encouraged by her mother and then by Lawrence Selden in her patriarchal values, Lily becomes, in a sense, her own villain, trying to make herself into an art object.

Like most traditional Gothic heroines, the orphaned Lily is proud of her ability to survive on her own but at the same time fearful about her precarious social situation (Radway 146). Intuitively she fears the consequences of becoming the prized possession of a man who will lavish money on her maintenance. She senses that selling her sexuality and individuality for financial security in a proper and probably stultifying social marriage will mean being a captive in a house and a tradition. Marrying Percy Gryce, for instance, means becoming part of the furnishings of the coffinlike Gryce family home, "an appalling house, all brown stone without and black walnut within, with the Gryce library in a fire-proof annex that looked like a mausoleum" (*HM* 33). Aptly, given the claustrophobia Lily feels at the thought of future years with Percy, the Gryce family money has come from "a patent device for excluding fresh air from hotels" (34). Putting up with Percy's dullness "on the bare chance that he might ultimately decide to do her the honour of boring her for life" is a "hateful fate" to Lily, but one for which she feels she has no alternative (39).

Lily can conceive of no alternative to marrying Gryce because she has nothing to replace the object-self her mother has instilled in her. Receiving no nurturing from her mother, or none that carries the psychic weight of the manipulative molding the narrator has us believe she most remembers, Lily lacks the "solid ego-Self connection" that strong nurturing can provide (Perera 140). An unmothered woman, she distrusts women and femaleness, whether her own or that of other women. "What a miserable thing it is to be a woman," she laments to Selden, not only because she can't have a place of her own the way he can, but because her life is so precarious and lonely (*HM* 9). Lily's hyperbolic comment about "the other women—my best friends," that "they use me or abuse me; but they don't care a straw what happens to me," marks her as the motherless woman whom Adrienne Rich discusses in *Of Woman Born*, who is uneasy around and suspicious of other women (13). Lily feels the "self-loathing and a deep sense of personal ugliness and failure" characteristic of "daughters of the patriarchy" when she can't be the perfect art piece into which her mother has tried to make her (Perera 40–41).

Lily's fear of her physical self seeps out early in the novel when, worried about her bills, she sees her "hollow and pale" face in the mirror and is frightened by two tiny lines near her mouth (*HM* 43). As she peers at herself between the candle flames, "the white oval of her face swam out waveringly from a background of shadows, the uncertain light blurring it like a haze; but the two lines about the mouth remained" (43). This ghostly image—wan, wavering, and insubstantial—reflects the tenuousness of Lily's beautiful self, her anxiety that without her physical beauty she is drained of her substance. Mirrors, on the wall and in her mind, have the power to throw Lily into a state of fear as powerful as that experienced by Gothic heroines in haunted houses, because both involve a confrontation with eroticism and vulnerability, the unacknowledged feminine self.[13] This scene is reminiscent of the one in Emily Brontë's *Wuthering Heights* in which Catherine, looking into the mirror, thinks she is seeing a ghost when she is actually seeing her own reflection. While Catherine has been called "the first Gothic heroine to acknowledge the dark side of her soul," at this point Lily experiences only the fear without the recognition (Conger 102).

Lily might have had a nurturing surrogate mother in her aunt, Mrs. Peniston, as Ellen Olenska has in her aunt, Medora Manson, later in *The Age of Innocence.* Instead, Mrs. Peniston, who has reluctantly taken Lily in when no one else in the family would have her, is a "demonic madonna," as judgmental of Lily as Wharton would have us believe her own mother was of her, a cruel surrogate mother who only exacerbates Lily's self-loathing (Wolstenholme 114). When Lily returns to her aunt's house after hearing that Percy Gryce is to marry someone else, the repetitive scenario of another lost marriage opportunity and the "bright indifference" she must again feign make her feel a deep "self-disgust" (*HM* 158). This "moral repulsion" intensifies "the haunting sense of physical ugliness" engendered by her room in her aunt's house, a conflation of room/self common to female Gothic (158, 177). Lacking male affirmation of her worth as a beautiful collectible, she projects her self-loathing onto the room she occupies.

Lily's depression about her failure to be bought in marriage accentuates her perception that Mrs. Peniston's house, in its "state of unnatural immaculateness and order," is "as dreary as a tomb" and her room in it "as dreary as a prison" (160, 176). The language cues us into the Gothic text of Lily as lonely, penniless heroine, feeling "buried alive in the stifling limits of Mrs. Peniston's existence" in a house that personifies its restraining, repressive owner (160). Eve Kosofsky Sedgwick's reminder of "the psychoanalytic application of 'live burial' to the repression of the libido" is appropriate to Lily's plight in her aunt's care (5).

Mrs. Peniston provides Lily no healthy way of being female. She keeps Lily from growing up and developing some self-respect by doling out small allowances contingent on good behavior and by restraining her assertion of her "eager individuality" (*HM* 162). Barbara Bowman's description of the aunt figure in modern Gothic novels as "oppressive upholders of tradition—conventional and unadventurous" who "disapprove of the heroine's high spirits and ambitions" aptly fits Mrs. Peniston (72).[14] Mrs. Peniston's bronze box with the miniature of Beatrice Cenci in the lid, whose "pink-eyed smirk" is associated in Lily's mind with her aunt's disapproval of her, reminds the reader of what comes to those who resist entrapment and victimization (*HM* 274). By recalling the young Roman noblewoman's horrible life—brutalization and imprisonment by her father, various attempts to escape, then torture and execution because of his assassination—the image brings Lily's less dramatic but nonetheless traumatic situation into relief.

Appropriately Lily faces Mrs. Peniston in the room with the Beatrice Cenci bronze box the day after Gus Trenor's attempted rape. The encounter with Gus recalls the threatening sexuality in "The Lady's Maid's Bell" and the incestuous threat of traditional Gothic narratives. Like the red-faced, bull-necked Mr. Brympton in "The Lady's Maid's Bell," Trenor is "red and massive," with a "heavy carnivorous head" and a "broad expanse of cheek and neck" (128, 87). He is also, as Mrs. Peniston puts it, "a fat, stupid man almost old enough to be her father," one who gives Lily her "allowance" in the form of supposed returns on her investment (200).

The empty, dark town house with its shrouded drawing room to which Trenor lures Lily is reminiscent of Mrs. Brympton's isolation in dark Brympton Place. Trenor's comment, "Does n't this room look as if it was waiting for the body to be brought down?" suggests not only a traditional Gothic plot device, dead body in dark threatening house but also the alternative Gothic text Wharton is evolving, of Lily "brought down," overpowered by male aggression and her own internalized patriarchal self-hatred (227).

The encounter with Gus forces Lily to acknowledge the sexual dark self she has denied. Once escaping into the cab, she reveals that she "seemed a stranger to herself, or rather there were two selves in her, the one she had always known, and a new abhorrent being to which it found itself chained" (238). Later, at Gerty's, she refers to the incident with other images of self-loathing: "Can you imagine looking into your glass some morning and seeing a disfigurement—some hideous change that has come to you while you slept? Well, I seem to myself like that—I can't bear to see myself in my own thoughts—I hate ugliness, you know—I've always turned from it" (265). Lily is encountering her "shadow self," Jung's phrase for the usually despised, repressed side of one's personality, into which we project denied sexual desire, anger, and other "inappropriate" feelings (Wehr 59–61).

Rather than expressing anger or fear about Gus, Lily feels hatred and loathing about *herself* after this incident. Her confession to Gerty that she is "bad—a bad girl—all my thoughts are bad—I have always had bad people about me," reflects her awareness that she has teased Gus Trenor into his rage for "payment" by playing along with his investment game (*HM* 266). Her complicity has, up to this point, been one of those "doors she did not open" in her consciousness (131). Just as Hartley fears the locked door in "The Lady's Maid's Bell" because of the ghost and, by extension, the knowledge it withholds, Lily fears the knowledge she has kept from herself about herself, particularly about her sexuality and the use to which she has put it.

But Lily also takes more than her fair share of the responsibility for what has happened. Unable to accept herself as a woman capable of mistakes but still worthy of respect and self-love, she unforgivingly sees only the ugly and monstrous in herself and rejects it. As she comments to Gerty, she can't bear to see herself in the mirror of her thoughts, because she sees herself as hideously disfigured. This compulsion "to give *visual* form to the fear of self, to hold anxiety up to the Gothic mirror of the imagination," which Ellen Moers sees as a particularly female expression of despair, reflects Lily's conflation of physical disfigurement and emotional shame when the beautiful object she thought herself to be turns out to be a human woman (163). Her disjunction from her physical female self has led to "feelings of self-disgust and self-fear rather than fear and disgust of something outside her" when that sexual self is threatened (Fleenor 11). At the same time Lily's ability to acknowledge this abhorrent stranger in herself is a tribute to her emotional courage that might rejuvenate her were she able to act on it.[15]

Gerty Farish might have helped Lily understand and accept her sexuality after the encounter with Gus were Gerty more comfortable with herself. Lily thinks of her as a comforting mother, provider of "darkness made by enfolding arms, the silence which is not solitude, but compassion holding its breath" (*HM* 240). Gerty *is* compassionate, ministering to Lily, urging her to share her warm bed, pillowing her head in the hollow of her arm "as a mother makes a nest for a tossing child" (270). But the insecurity, anger, and envy Lily fans in Gerty only accentuate Gerty's limited sense of herself. Gerty's narrow bed, on which she "lay with arms drawn down her side, in the motionless narrowness of an effigy," is matched by the narrowness of her stairs and her cramped apartment (270). Perceptively Lily complains, "how beautifully one does have to behave in a small flat!" when her vehement gestures almost knock over Gerty's tea table (427). Like her home, Gerty's understanding and experience of a woman's full being is narrow. So though Gerty tries to help Lily, as Nettie Struther later tries to, neither can really understand her predicament.

The moment Lily sees in her mental mirror a "new abhorrent being" chained to her known self after the encounter with Gus, she also imagines herself pursued in darkness by the relentless Furies of the *Eumenides* (238–39). These symbols of rage, who torment Orestes because of the matricide he has committed, pursue Lily because she has began playing a role that, together with the system she plays it in, have killed the nurturant feminine/maternal spirit in her.[16] She has tried to deny the feminine power that now angrily haunts her, demanding acknowledgment. There is an uncanny similarity between Lily's cry, "Oh Gerty, the furies . . . you know the noise of their wings—alone, at night, in the dark?" (264–65) and that of the guilt-stricken nun Signora Laurentini in Ann Radcliffe's *The Mysteries of Udolpho:* "O! could I strike from my memory all former scenes—the figures, that rise up, like furies, to torment me!—I see them, when I sleep, and when I am awake, they are still before my eyes! I see them now—now!" (575). "Sister! beware of the first indulgence of the passions," she later warns the virginal Emily St. Aubert, for "their force is uncontroulable [sic] . . . and the spectres of conscience will not fly!" (646, ellipsis mine).

Lily's relative innocence compared with the sexual indiscretions of the Gothic nun suggest not only how little she has to be ashamed of but also how tormented she and Signora Laurentini have been made by patriarchal repression and rebuke of female passion. Lily sees herself as she believes her patriarchal society sees her, shameful, but the sexual shame is mingled with shame that she desires more in her life than she has. As she cries out to Gerty: "I am bad through and through—I want admiration, I want excitement, I want money—yes, *money!* That's my shame, Gerty—and it's known, it's said of me" (*HM* 268). In Lily's mind, to be other than the unambitious, passive woman deemed correct by her society is to be monstrous.

Lily's female foil and dark double, Bertha Dorset, plays just the role Lily fears being labeled with.[17] Emphasizing Lily's innocence through her own ambitious sexuality, Bertha is the assertive, manipulative "bad" woman, the femme fatale of traditional Gothic, who stays married for the money but has one affair after another. Bertha is a metaphorical ghost, as menacing, intriguing, and bewildering to Lily as Emma is to Alice Hartley in "The Lady's Maid's Bell." The narrator in *The House of Mirth* tells us that, next to Lily, Bertha's small pale face "seemed the mere setting of a pair of dark exaggerated eyes, of which the visionary gaze contrasted curiously with her self-assertive tone and gestures; so that, as one of her friends observed, she was like a disembodied spirit who took up a great deal of room" (36). Both Bertha and Emma represent sexual knowledge that Lily and Alice fear facing, but Bertha is also the ghostly representation of all that is wrong with a social system in which women can make money only by marrying it and can be sexual only on the sly. She is a distortion of the "impersonal feminine potency," the "erotic and active-assertive" side of the feminine self, in that she uses her sexuality as a weapon, particularly against other women, in the male system of exchange (Perera 163, 165).[18]

Bertha is all that Lily could be, Lily's dark possibility, but that which Lily keeps preventing herself from becoming by scaring off one wealthy potential husband after another. Bertha is "dangerous," in Judy Trenor's words, nasty while Lily is not (*HM* 69). Bertha has a "reckless disregard of appearances" while Lily struggles to maintain them (335). Lily stands in for Bertha as George's companion while Bertha pursues her sexual adventures, and Lily is the one, rumor has it, whom George would marry if he were to divorce his wife. Bertha is the temptress who lures all the men Lily tries to charm with her grace and beauty: George, Percy, Gus, and Selden. Bertha writes passionate love letters to Selden, while Lily's love for him goes unvoiced. Nonetheless, the charwoman's mistaken notion that Lily rather than Bertha is the writer of the letters places them in her hands, enhancing the suggestion that the women are one and the same.

The letters represent both female sexuality and the verbalization of it that the novel's society prefers not to acknowledge, "the volcanic nether side of the surface over which conjecture and innuendo glide so lightly till the first fissure turns their whisper to a shriek" (167). The intensity of this language accentuates how dangerous to the status quo the passion is that the letters express. For Lily, possessing Bertha's letters, her expression of female passion, is an experience of great anxiety, a confrontation with dark sexual knowledge but also with the alternative between self-saving action and a larger moral good. The "horror" of Rosedale's idea of using them for blackmail holds her momentarily "spellbound" (416). When she refuses, the letters become the catalyst for Lily's moral decision to give up her last opportunity to be deceitful in order to marry money. Lily flirts with the role Bertha enacts. Scruples keep her from adopting it.[19] But the many parallels between Bertha and Lily, which become overt in Lily's implication in the Dorsets' marital imbroglio, emphasize how much Bertha represents Lily's alter ego, the distorted spirit of female sexuality that Lily might be were she to fulfill society's expectations.

Given the "volcanic" quality of Bertha's letters, it is disorienting to think of them as going to the impassive Lawrence Selden. Indeed, his asexuality and passivity are just two of the many characteristics Selden shares with Lily in the novel. The parallels suggest the characters' potential unity as feminine and masculine parts of a single self in contrast to the stark gender distinctions of the Gothic short stories. Yet Selden and Lily also play out those Gothic gender roles. Like male characters in the Gothic short stories, Selden perceives Lily as a piece of art, something for men to look at and purchase, and Lily will, in spite of her spirit and energy, *become* the lifeless art that he visits, just as Lombard visits his painting and the Duke his sculpture. The Gothic subtext in *The House of Mirth* accentuates the horror of the manners plot.[20]

In many ways Selden is the male version of Lily, described much as she is. As the poor "sallow-faced girls in preposterous hats" walk by Lily and Selden at the novel's beginning, Selden muses to himself, "Was it possible that she belonged to the same race? The dinginess, the crudity of this average section of womanhood made him feel how highly specialized she was" (6). Lily's specialization, the "modelling of her little ear," and her "straight black lashes" are echoed in the description of Selden as having "keenly modelled dark features which, in a land of amorphous types, gave him the air of belonging to a more specialized race" (6, 7, 104).

Although Selden is ostensibly part of the novel's high society, he is portrayed as an outsider, much like Lily, one too "specialized" to fit in with those around him. He has "a certain social detachment," we are told by the narrator, an "air of friendly aloofness" (86, 104). It appeals to Lily that "everything about him accorded with the fastidious element in her taste, even to the light irony with which he surveyed what seemed to her most sacred. She admired him most of all, perhaps, for being able to convey as distinct a sense of superiority as the richest man she had ever met" (104).

Lily admires Selden's notion of success in life as freedom from all of life's exigencies in a "republic of the spirit" because she has similar pretensions to life without responsibility and vulnerability. Their philosophical interchange about the republic, society, and values sounds like a single voice engaged in point/counterpoint. Indeed, it may well be an allusion to Plato's *Republic*. But to be absolutely free "from money, from poverty, from ease and anxiety, from all the material accidents," as Selden describes *his* republic, is impossible, unless one is dead (108). Lily alludes to such a realization in her subsequent cutting observation to Selden that he spends a great deal of time in the monied society he scorns as unfit for his republic. Seventeen years later, in *The Age of Innocence*, the more self-confident and mature Ellen Olenska will summarily reject Newland Archer's equally ideal place where nothing on earth matters but their love with the retort: "Oh, my dear—where is that country? Have you ever been there?" (293).

The high ideal of the republic of the spirit is emphasized by the lofty setting of Lily's and Selden's conversation about it on an "open ledge of rock" overlooking a valley (*HM* 101). Mountains and other more metaphorical heights—of enthusiasm, of sexuality, of intellect—are a common motif in Gothic fiction, representing "intensity of sensation and expansion of vision, inflation of the self and ascension to omnipotence" (Bayer-Berenbaum 140). Like Gothic characters before them, Lily and Selden are enthralled by the heights. Selden feels "a lazy sense of pleasure, veiling the sharp edges of sensation as the September haze veiled the scene at their feet" (*HM* 102). Lily is even more aroused, feeling a "sense of buoyancy which seemed to lift and swing her above the sun-suffused world at her feet" (102). As in a later episode, after Gus's attempted rape, Lily feels herself two beings, but this time the loftier one dominates: "drawing deep breaths of freedom and exhilaration . . . the free spirit quivered for flight" (102, ellipsis mine).

In a Romantic merging of scene and sensation worthy of Ann Radcliffe, Lily and Selden toy with the idea of marriage while "the soft isolation of the falling day enveloped them: they seemed lifted into a finer air. All the exquisite influences of the hour trembled in their veins, and drew them to each other as the loosened leaves were drawn to the earth" (116–17). After Lily's bold declaration that she could adapt to penuriousness, the two stand "smiling at each other like adventurous children who have climbed to a forbidden height from which they discover a new world. The actual world at their feet was veiling itself in dimness, and across the valley a clear moon rose in the denser blue" (117).

But "a radical shift from ectasy [sic] to dejection—augmentation followed by drastic reduction—is the Gothic progression" (Bayer-Berenbaum 140). The sound of a car, a reminder of the society they have imagined escaping, brings Lily and Selden down with a thud from their heights of ideality. "Let us go down!" Lily murmurs (*HM* 118). After lighting a cigarette to proclaim "his recovered hold on the actual" and to show Lily that "their flight over, he had landed on his feet," Selden repeats, "Let us go down" (118, 119). Selden, like Lily, cannot "breathe long on the heights" (422). Neither has the moral or emotional strength to try to live or even to explore their vision of another kind of life.

Selden's and Lily's similar family backgrounds provide some explanation of their similar responses to experience. Though Lily's family comes across as the crasser of the two, both families have high aspirations and tastes that exceed their means to pay for them. In Lily's there is never a time when there is enough money; Selden's parents are always "spending a little more than was prudent," yet "they never quite knew how it was that the bills mounted up" (245). Both have dominant mothers. Lily's is lauded for "the unlimited effect she produced on limited means," and she strikes her acquaintances as "heroic" for "living as though one were much richer than one's bank-book denoted" (46). Selden's mother exemplifies elegance with her "knack of wearing her old velvet as if it were new" and is the one from whom Selden gets "his sense of 'values' " (245, 246).

Though Lily's mother conspicuously consumes while Selden's practices a "detachment from the sumptuary side of life," both Lily and Selden learn a love of the beautiful and the dramatic from their mothers (246). Lily is proud of her mother's aptitude with affect, which helps her develop her own "lively taste for splendour" (47). Selden, too, learns from his mother the "Epicurean's pleasure" with material things (246). Lily's "dramatic instinct" is matched by Selden's enjoyment of "spectacular effects" (211, 212). In fact, just as Lily is "the victim of the civilization which had produced her," Selden is, we are told, "as much as Lily, the victim of his environment" (10, 245).

Part of their victimization derives from their emotional reserve, their inability to feel fully and to express feeling. Scenes between them "operate with the intensity of suppression" (Lidoff 531). Lily's love of beauty, the narrator tells us, "made up for certain obtusenesses of feeling of which she was less proud" (*HM* 314). Selden, in turn, has a finely tuned ability for "spectatorship" that blunts his ability to empathize (109). Nowhere is this disastrous shared trait more evident than at the end of the novel when Selden visits Lily at Mrs. Hatch's. Though he cares earnestly about her welfare and she yearns for his concern, reserve is their common response. "The situation between them was one which could have been cleared up only by a sudden explosion of feeling; and their whole training and habit of mind were against the chances of such an explosion" (449). As Joseph Wiesenfarth observes, in *The Novel of Gothic Manners*, "respectability is transmuted into the equivalent of Gothic horror by denying validity to strong feeling. . . . In forbidding emotional explosions, respectability invites emotional implosions" (118, ellipsis mine).

That Lily *does* self-destruct, does become fatally overwhelmed by intense despair while Selden doesn't, is, on the one hand, an ironic recognition of her fuller humanity, her greater sense of self. On the other hand, Lily's temptation to be a beautiful object, coupled with Selden's persistent objectification of her throughout the novel, places them both in restraining Gothic roles recognizable from the short stories.

In Selden's perception of her, Lily finds the perfect reflection of the male-centered view of herself learned from her mother. From his first impression of her, that "she must have cost a great deal to make, that a great many dull and ugly people must, in some mysterious way, have been sacrificed to produce her," to his later perception that, in her *tableau vivant* pose, he is seeing "the real Lily Bart," Selden diminishes Lily's womanhood by emphasizing that she is an art piece to be gazed at (*HM* 7, 217). Reading *The House of Mirth* in the context of "The Duchess at Prayer" and "The House of the Dead Hand," where women's lives are metaphorically transfixed into statuary and painting, makes Selden's response to Lily the more chilling.

The Gothic stories remind the reader of *The House of Mirth* of the psychological as well as social pathology at work in the characters' lives. For Selden's role as a "gentleman" and Lily's role as a "lady" in a society of restraining manners and cruel customs are not alone in dooming them to their respective lives as spectator and object. Selden and Lily also share a mutual (Gothic) horror of the feminine/maternal and the "vicissitudes of natural things" it embodies (de Beauvoir 148). Objectification of the female Other (in Selden's case) and of oneself (in Lily's case) is a way to simulate control over vulnerability, loss, isolation, death, in short, one's mortality. As de Beauvoir explains, "Because he fears her contingent destiny, because he fancies her changeless, necessary, man seeks to find on the face of woman, on her body and limbs, the exact expression of an ideal . . . man, wishing to find nature in woman but nature transfigured, dooms woman to artifice" (148, ellipsis mine). And as Dinnerstein adds, "What we deny or ignore at our peril is that women share men's anti-female feelings" because "we, like men, had female mothers" (90). The "sunny summits" of idealization and aesthetization are temporary escape for both women and men from fear of the "maternal shadows—cave, abyss, hell," or what I am calling the Gothic darkness (de Beauvoir 137).[21]

Though they share a mutual horror of their inner darkness, Lily and Selden obviously fare differently as a result of it. In this sense the Gothic reading extends the "manners" one, for while the result for Lily of objectification by others and by herself is as deadly as poison and imprisonment are for the Duchess and Sybilla, Selden's objectification of Lily results in, we are lead to believe, male life as usual in the house of mirth. Social codes and behavior, Wharton suggests, valorize Gothic gender roles.

Though Lily shares a similar fate with her counterparts in the Gothic short stories, she differs in that she eventually recognizes and acknowledges the fears that aesthetization attempts to quell (although she doesn't recognize the connection between them). Simon Rosedale's overt admiration of her rather than Selden's silent assessments encourages this realization. Rosedale has the kind of "collector's passion for the rare and unattainable" that Professor Lombard has in "The House of the Dead Hand," and Lily is acutely aware of the "steady gaze of his small stock-taking eyes, which made her feel herself no more than some superfine human merchandise" (*HM* 183, 412). What frightens Lily most, however, is that Rosedale admires her as a woman, not just as a spectacle, and that she will be a sexual possession if she marries him: "She had learned, in her long vigils, that there were certain things not good to think of, certain midnight images that must at any cost be exorcised—and one of these was the image of herself as Rosedale's wife" (400). Like the noise of the Furies that torments her during her dreadful, sleepless nights, the thought of marrying Rosedale haunts Lily with her own femaleness.

Despite his similarity to the villains of the Gothic short stories, Rosedale is a complex deconstruction of that role. Of all the people who come in contact with Lily, he is the most compassionate, the most aware of and forthright about her financial distress and her precarious future. When he visits her in the boardinghouse near the end of her life, Rosedale expresses an outrage about her situation and an urgent desire to help that speaks of authentic concern for her as a human being. As a Jew and a self-made man, Rosedale is an "outsider" to the high society of *The House of Mirth*, in spite of his money, just as Lily is because of her penurious orphancy. His engagement with Lily's predicament may well derive from his having known such difficulty himself. Rosedale is, in a sense, a successful male version of what Lily tries to be: practical, ambitious, morally expedient, humane. But his maleness, of course, gives him the option of making his fortune rather than having to marry for it or wait to inherit it, without risking his chance of eventually buying his way into society. In the nexus of manners and Gothic, Rosedale both deconstructs and perpetuates the role of male villain.

Because Lily lacks Rosedale's attributes, her monetary disinheritance by her aunt accentuates her physical disinheritance from the life she had expected. She seeks safety in the womblike environment of Mrs. Hatch, which initially gives her "the sense of being once more lapped and folded in ease, as in some dense mild medium impenetrable to discomfort," but she flees when its ghostliness reminds her of her own corporality (440). Through the "pallid world" of the Emporium Hotel move "wan" beings who drift and float in a life "outside the bounds of time and space" (442, 443). Lily soon realizes that she has entered a disorienting, "dimly-lit region" peopled by beings with "no more real existence than the poet's shades in limbo" (441, 442). While in "the outer twilight," the "vast gilded void of Mrs. Hatch's existence," Lily develops "an odd sense of being behind the social tapestry, on the side where the threads were knotted and the loose ends hung" (444, 445). Her disquietude increases when she suspects that a sexual/financial trap is being set for one of society's young heirs. The experience is a metaphorical version of Alice Hartley's when her satisfaction with Brympton Place turns to uneasiness about its ghost and suspicion about the sexual wrongdoing the house secretes.

The ghostly denizens of the "underworld of toilers" in the hat shop where

Lily briefly works represent what the ghost Emma does in "The Lady's Maid's Bell" or even what the ghostly Bertha does, the untold story of sexuality, of un-spoken experience beyond the pale of social acceptability (461). The women are all sallow-faced; "the youngest among them was as dull and colourless as the middle-aged" (455). In fact, "in the whole work-room there was only one skin beneath which the blood still visibly played," and that is Lily's flushed face as she attempts to become one of these ghostly workers (455). In the claustrophobic workroom, the women's talk of men and illness has "the incoherence of a dream" for Lily, except when social names from the past "floated to the surface" and she saw "the fragmentary and distorted image of the world she had lived in reflected in the mirror of the working-girls' minds" (460, 461). That she has fallen from the world of "vanity and self-indulgence" the others discuss further alienates her from the women she views as "unpolished and promiscuous" (461, 463). Lily's physical, emotional, and mental frailty at this point makes her less capable than she has ever been of facing these ghosts and their story.[22]

At the end of the novel Wharton has Lily and Selden use several almost identical phrases about their respective situations, just as earlier she has drawn parallels between their appearance, demeanor, and background. Now, however, Lily's intense awareness of her inner darkness and the actions she takes as a result of it make her words resonate with sincerity, while Selden's evasive, non-committal behavior turns the same words into "bathetic sentimentality" and arrogant self-deception (Wolff 132).

By the end of her life, Lily perceives that "she had saved herself whole from the seeming ruin of her life" because she has preserved her essential morality by burning Selden's letters rather than selling them (*HM* 497). Wharton has Selden use almost identical words in his thought that the moment of love he and Lily shared "had been saved whole out of the ruin of their lives" (532). But while Lily, by burning the letters, has *acted* to save what she considers the best part of herself from a life that is, as a result, only a "seeming" ruin, Selden rationalizes that he has been heroic. Though he believes that he "*had* loved her—had been willing to stake his future on his faith in her," that "this moment of love . . . had kept them from atrophy and extinction," the novel and Lily's silent dead body suggest otherwise (532, ellipsis mine). Indeed, the novel doesn't make it at all clear that Selden "*had* loved" Lily, and it is even less clear about whether he had been "willing to stake his future on his faith in her." Instead, there are several examples of his lack of faith in Lily, including when he sees Trenor's name on an envelope Lily had addressed just before her death. Selden's supposed "mo-ment of love" has perhaps kept *him* from "atrophy and extinction," but Lily is dead. It is doubtful, too, that his life is a "ruin" as he dramatically asserts.

Lily's belief that she has preserved her essential morality, her essential self, is closer to the truth, for by the end of her life she has had the quintessential Gothic experience of looking into the abyss, the nothingness that yields awareness. Eventually what she sees so frightens her that she permanently closes her eyes to it, but she has seen herself the way Selden never does, she has gone beyond what reason can reveal.

When Lily visits Selden's library for the second and last time, she has begun the process of understanding that characterizes Wharton's Gothic. This process is much like that experienced by mystics, involving an intense awareness of one's nothingness and a "dark night of the soul," a time when ties with conventional sources of value are broken and an awakening of new understanding usually follows (Christ 14ff.). Like so many others in Wharton's Gothic who face essential, often startling, realizations in libraries, Lily becomes lucidly aware of who she is and what she needs while in Selden's library. Words rise to her lips "spontaneously," and she feels "an intense longing to dispel the cloud of misunderstanding that hung between them" (493). Rather than engaging in the usual repartee with Selden, Lily is now in a state of "extra-lucidity, which [gives] her the sense of being already at the heart of the situation" and makes word-play unacceptable (494). When he resorts to lightness she feels it "incredible that any one should think it necessary to linger in the conventional outskirts of word-play and evasion" (494). With a "passionate desire to be understood" driving her, Lily is finally attempting to tell her story rather than to hold her tongue like the ghostly Alice and Mrs. Brympton or to stare silently like the ghost Emma (494).

Now, Lily is painfully honest about feeling like a "very useless person," without "an independent existence (498).[23] At the same time, and this point is crucial, she accepts what she has been as part of her: "She understood now that she could not go forth and leave her old self with him: that self must indeed live on in his presence, but it must still continue to be hers" (500). How different this is from the Lily who has hated the dark side of herself, who has said "I can't bear to see myself in my own thoughts" (265).

When Lily encounters Nettie Struther in Bryant Park and is taken home by her, she goes through another stage of awareness. Nettie's sympathy and her warm kitchen seem to offer Lily the nurturant mothering she so desperately needs and the intimacy missing between Alice and Mrs. Brympton in "The Lady's Maid's Bell." Indeed, Nettie's role in Lily's experience is usually read heroically. Elaine Showalter, for instance, sees their encounter as "the strongest moment of female kinship in the novel" ("The Death" 144). Gloria Erlich, too, sees Nettie's role as wholly positive, in that she is the one who enables Lily to experience the "continuity of life" (65).

But Nettie's warmth is deceptive, for she can't really hear Lily, and so she can't really help. "I have been unhappy—in great trouble," Lily confesses "involuntarily" to Nettie, but the young woman invalidates Lily's words. *"You* in trouble? I've always thought of you as being so high up, where everything was just grand" (*HM* 505). She never does ask Lily why she is "in great trouble."

Instead she continues to relate how much she has admired Lily's past social achievements and, oblivious to the irony, gushes to Lily about her baby daughter, "Would n't it be too lovely for anything if she could grow up to be just like you?" (511). As Nettie wistfully and unfortunately confesses, "I only wish I could help *you*—but I suppose there's nothing on earth I could do" (510). She has been lucky enough to meet someone who knows about her affair with another man and yet loves her unconditionally: "George cared for me enough to have me as I was" (509). This acceptance by another allows Nettie to victoriously accept herself, "I did n't see why I should n't begin over again—and I did," but she can offer no such unconditional therapeutic love to Lily.

The baby girl Lily holds in Nettie's kitchen and later imagines she holds as she dies has been called by one critic the symbol of Lily's "potential rebirth"; by another a symbol of the future "New Woman," a blend of the leisure and working class; and by a third the "emblem" of Lily herself, infantilized by society's image of women (Wershoven 53, Ammons 43, Wolff 130). I suggest that this baby makes Lily intensely, debilitatingly aware of her own vulnerability and need for love and nurture as well as her fear of becoming the sexual, childbearing mother. What appears at first to be a positive experience, the baby thrilling Lily with "a sense of warmth and returning life," becomes ominous, threatening: "At first the burden in her arms seemed as light as a pink cloud or a heap of down, but as she continued to hold it the weight increased, sinking deeper, and penetrating her with a strange sense of weakness, as though the child entered into her and became a part of herself" (510). The phallic verb "penetrating" suggests sexuality that overcomes Lily. The life force and nature that the baby on the one hand represents, with its instinctive movements and its "tendrilly motions of the folding and unfolding fingers," have, because of Lily's desperation and emptiness, her intense fear of her own physicality, the destructive potential to overwhelm her (510). This scene reminds us that conflict with and ambivalence about the mother is at the heart of the female Gothic. To become a sexual being like one's mother and bear children is "to become the passive and perhaps unwilling victim of one's own body" (Fleenor 16).[24]

Overwhelmingness has been called crucial to the Gothic, a genre that communicates the "special understanding of how *much* this fact matters, for the individual, the race, even the species of man—that the deep truth of life is overwhelming, that it cannot be managed or fully assimilated" (Wilt 118). However much Lily has grown in self-awareness since the beginning of the novel, her feeling of "weakness" in this maternal situation reflects her inability to live with the "deep truth of life" she is encountering about her female self.

When Lily returns to her room to read the story of her life in her dresses and checkbook, she passes into the dark night of the soul, becoming increasingly aware of her "inner destitution." She is, she knows now, "rootless and ephemeral, mere spin-drift of the whirling surface of existence, without anything to which the poor little tentacles of self could cling before the awful flood submerged them," without "any real relation to life" (*HM* 515–16).

She then has a period of "vivid wakeful fatigue," "a multiplication of wakefulness" (518, 520). This "separate wakefulness" of every nerve, "as though a great blaze of electric light had been turned on in her head," oppresses and terrifies her, for she now understands that she is alone with herself: "she felt as though the house, the street, the world were all empty, and she alone left sentient in a lifeless universe" (520, 519). Like all who travel through the dark night of the soul, Lily has broken her ties with "conventional sources of value" but has not yet discovered new values (Christ 14). "She had never hung so near the dizzy brink of the unreal" (*HM* 519–20). Christ points out that "to one who has 'awakened,' conventional notions of reality seem as unreal and illusory as the world of dreams does to a person abruptly aroused from sleep. To one 'enlightened,' it is as if she had been trying to make out clear shapes in a dark room and suddenly the lights were turned on. . . . Awakening implies that the ability to see or to know is within the self, once the sleeping draft is refused" (18, ellipsis mine).

But Lily's "poor anguished self" craves rather than refuses the sleeping draft, since she is too weakened to stay awake and continue the journey of self-discovery. "She must take a brief bath of oblivion. . . . Her mind shrank from the glare of thought as instinctively as eyes contract in a blaze of light—darkness, darkness was what she must have at any cost" (*HM* 520–21, ellipsis mine). The light of knowing is brighter than Lily can face.

Like the ghost Emma Saxon "peering dreadfully down into the darkness," Lily now looks down "into the dim abysses of unconsciousness." The chloral, however, makes the experience not dreadful but "delicious" (521). A sense of "complete subjugation" overcomes Lily, and she no longer feels alone because Nettie's baby is lying on her arm, with its "gentle penetrating thrill of warmth and pleasure" (522).

Then Lily, like Selden later, fantasizes that "there was something she must tell Selden, some word she had found that should make life clear between them. She tried to repeat the word, which lingered vague and luminous on the far edge of thought—she was afraid of not remembering it when she woke; and if she could only remember it and say it to him, she felt that everything would be well" (522–23). Lily's childlike trust that "some word" will make life clear between Selden and her, so that all is well, add poignant irony to her situation.

Selden, too, believes that "in the silence there passed between them the word which made all clear" as he kneels over Lily's dead body, "draining their last moment to its lees" (533). *His* use of "the word" as an assurance of clarification in what is instead a welter of self-deception emphasizes his reliance on rationalization, on the patriarchal symbolic to find closure on Lily's death, to make it acceptable and understandable. Selden's presumption of clarity, when so much about Lily's life and death, including her relationship with Selden, isn't clear, puts him in the company of the "rational" men who people Wharton's Gothic short stories and exemplifies the tragic limitation of such reason.[25]

At the same time Wharton redefines the power of the patriarchal symbolic. The verbal medium that surrounds the "word" in these two mirrored scenes reconstitutes it as supernatural. The word "that should make life clear" between Selden and the dying Lily "lingered vague and luminous on the far edge of thought" and "the word which made all clear" passes between Selden and the dead Lily "in the silence" (522–23, 533). This is the word as ghost, as spirit, lingering "vague and luminous" beyond thought, beyond the rational.

When awareness, "a dark flash of loneliness and terror," jolts Lily momentarily just before she dies, she fears she had "lost her hold of the child," but then "the recovered warmth flowed through her once more, she yielded to it, sank into it, and slept" (523). The sleeping drug permanently frees Lily from assimilating her sense of vulnerability with her adulthood, allowing her to be overwhelmed without having to "awaken" to her new knowledge. Completely identifying with the dream child is to become an object, engendering what Margaret Homans calls "the threat that hides within all losses of identity, all self-duplications, all kinds of objectifications of the self: no longer to be oneself is to die" (278).[26] The horror and dread that permeate Wharton's Gothic texts can yield enlightenment, but seldom are those who look into the abyss strong enough to face what they have seen and learned from the experience. Ellen Olenska and Vance Weston, in *The Age of Innocence* and *The Gods Arrive*, will be the exceptions, but usually only the reader sees what might be learned if the gazer into the abyss were more able to endure.

3 | Confronting the Limits of Reason

WHARTON'S LOVE AFFAIR with Morton Fullerton, which began in 1908, made her realize that "all one side of me was asleep" (Gribben 30). Common to the Gothic stories written during this time of erotic discovery—"Afterward," "The Eyes," "The Triumph of Night," and "Kerfol"—is a strong emphasis on the limitations of rationality as well as on the fearfulness of nonrational experiences. The Gothic stories are trenchant portrayals of the difficulty of understanding and accepting what one has observed of the inner life of the soul. Unlike the earlier stories, however, where characters are unwilling or unable to understand the mystery they are engaged in, the main characters in these stories are eventually well aware of the ghosts they have seen, even if they then hide from the discoveries in fear. It is particularly apparent now that an arrogant, exclusive reliance on intellect that denies spiritual, emotional, and intuitive ways of knowing is morally reprehensible. The Gothic texts of this period, from 1906 to 1916, make clear that facing one's inner darkness, the source of awareness, takes fortitude that intellect alone cannot provide.

The narrator of *Ethan Frome,* published in 1911, is the most courageous of the male characters in that he allows himself to face his vision of his paralyzed feminine and masculine selves. Wharton's passionate affair with Fullerton, which so tested her sense of her controlled, intellectual, "masculine" self, no doubt provided the impetus for her creation of an educated male character, an engineer, who tells a story about his fearful yet alluring inner life.

Fullerton had been a student of Charles Eliot Norton, the father of her friend Sara Norton, at Harvard and was the Paris correspondent for the London *Times* when he met Wharton. As she wrote Sara, he seemed to her "very intelligent, but slightly mysterious" (Lewis, *Biography* 183). Fullerton began visiting Wharton regularly, both in Paris, on the Rue de Varenne where she was now living when in Europe, and at the Mount. By mid-1908 they were lovers, and Wharton faced "the whole dark mystery" of love and sexuality for the first time at the age of forty-six. In describing her response to the experience in a letter to Fullerton, she notes that the discovery of her eroticism had made her realize the dominance of self-control and repression in her life: "You woke me from a long lethargy, a dull acquiescence in conventional restrictions, a needless self-effacement.

If I was awkward & inarticulate it was because, literally, all one side of me was asleep" (Gribben 30).

The sexual experience immerses Wharton in *jouissance,* a totality of sensuality: "And if you can't come into the room without my feeling all over me a ripple of flame, & if, wherever you touch me, a heart beats under your touch, & if when you hold me, & I don't speak, it's because all the words in me seem to have become throbbing pulses, & all my thoughts are a great golden blur—" (Gribben 22). The "masculine" control recedes as she sees that "I, who dominated life, stood aside from it so, how I am humbled, absorbed, without a shred of will or identity left!" (Lewis, *Biography* 211).[1]

Before becoming involved in a physical relationship with Fullerton, Wharton wrote "Ame Close," the "closed soul," a poem in which she compares her soul to a ghost in a haunted house:

Yet one stray passer, at the shut of day,
Sees a light trembling in a casement high.

Even so, my soul would set a light for you,
A light invisible to all beside,
As though a lover's ghost should yearn, and glide
From pane to pane, to let the flame shine through.
Yet enter not, lest as it flits ahead,
You see the hand that carries it is dead. [Lewis, *Biography* 206]

In making the connection between female body and a haunted house, Wharton plays on one of the most prominent images of her Gothic fiction. The warning "Yet enter not" suggests the fear that the Gothic expresses of confrontation with nonrational understanding.

Wharton's two spheres surfaced prominently for her during this time of intense new awareness, the ones that her Gothic fiction exaggeratedly presented in male and female characters: the self that prized order, control, and intellect and the self that sought sexual freedom and disorderly emotional intensity. In a letter to Sara Norton dated July 7, 1908, she expressed her admiration for Nietzsche's treatment of the ancient issue of the mind/body split in his "Jenseits von Gut und Böse" ["Beyond Good and Evil"]: "I think it is salutary, now & then, to be made to realize what he calls 'die Unwerthung aller Werthe [the unworthiness of all values],' & really get back to a wholesome basis of naked instinct. There are times when I *hate* what Christianity has left in our blood—or rather, one might say, taken out of it—by its cursed assumption of the split between body & soul" (Beinecke).[2]

Her anticipated adultery, which was making her feel "beyond good and evil," in a private world of pleasure, was also a cause for moral questioning. Like George Eliot, Wharton believed that personal acts had social consequences, but she also sensed danger in the split between the sensual and social selves. In a review of Leslie Stephen's *George Eliot*, Wharton writes that Eliot's choice of a life of passion over outward social respectability had led to a sacrifice of creative liberation: "It is, perhaps, not a paradox to say that if George Eliot had been what the parish calls 'respectable,' her books would have been less a continuous hymn to respectability" (251). In Wharton's view, Eliot's following through publicly with her personal desires and breaking social law by living unmarried with Lewes entailed harmful isolation from the human community that inspired her: "She retired from the world a sensitive, passionate, receptive, responsive woman; she returned to it a literary celebrity; and in the interval ossification had set in. Her normal relations with the world ceased when she left England with Lewes. All that one reads of her carefully sheltered existence after she had become famous shows how completely she had cut herself off from her natural sources of inspiration" (251).

Later George Sand provided a more salutary example of how passion might be integrated into an artist's life. In *A Motor-Flight Through France*, published in 1908, the year Wharton began her affair with Fullerton, she describes her pilgrimage to Nohant, George Sand's home. She is surprised to find the house so "dignified and decent, so much more conscious of social order and restraints, than the early years of the life led in it" (45). Somehow, she admits, she expected that the house would bear some mark of that "dark disordered period" when Sand was writing her passionate fiction and becoming a literary celebrity (46). Instead, "one beholds this image of aristocratic well-being, this sober edifice, conscious in every line of its place in the social scale" (47). Rather than adapting to the changes in Sand, the house represents "those grave ideals" to which Sand "gradually conformed the passionate experiment of her life" (47). Wharton seems relieved that a woman writer can have both the "dark, disordered" creative and emotional life within and social engagement without and that these selves can coexist in one woman.

In fact, in a late uncompleted story called "Miss Moynham," Wharton depicts a woman who is both "Georges," with literally two conflicting sides. Miss Moynham has "reached her apogee a few years before the Depression," and she is now both handsome and ugly,

> a large powerful sarcastic woman, with black hair, heavy brows and chin, a stately angular figure dressed with careless art, and one profile like George Eliot's and the other like George Sand's. Yes—literally: she had two faces. . . . It came of her mouth, I think, which, without seeming uneven when one faced her, yet contrived, when seen sideways, to show a fuller, warmer curve on the left, a harsher flatter line on the right. I can see her right hand mouth flattening into irony, the left rounding into mirth at the idea that, viewed from different angles, she evoked two images so eminent and so unlike. I don't suppose she had read a line of the works of either George, for she was not a reader; but she

knew enough about them, about their private histories and their place in literature, to find the suggestion intelligible and amusing. [Beinecke]

Wharton's Gothic, of the stories and within the realistic novels, fictionally allows for the tension between internal emotional drama and outward social order that she observed in Eliot's and Sand's life and felt in her own, with the Gothic giving credence to the disruptive emotions that otherwise have no language in realistic fiction as she perceived it.

"The Hermit and the Wildwoman," written in 1906, though not obviously a Gothic story, has many Gothic elements and is thus worth examining as a transitional work between the early and middle periods. The story allegorizes a key trait of Wharton's Gothic, the conflict between "masculine" reason and "feminine" sensuality, but it also complicates the gender portrayals. As such "The Hermit and the Wildwoman" is an intriguing piece in Wharton's evolving study of the integrated self that she explores in the Gothic.

The Hermit has become such because of a grotesque experience in which his family has been among the victims of a vicious attack on his walled town by a marauding army. He runs for his life, "through the slippery streets, over warm twitching bodies, between legs of soldiers carousing, out of the gates, past burning farms, trampled wheat fields, orchards stripped and broken, till the still woods received him and he fell face down on the unmutilated earth" (*HW* 4). This highly symbolic description emphasizes the savage destruction of (female) nature by male violence that the orphaned Hermit escapes. The female iconography is further emphasized in the nurturing home he creates for himself in the woods, in a cave in the hollow of a hill high above a valley.

A sensitive young man who loved to sit at his mother's feet watching her embroider flowers or to watch the artist painting the chapel, and who had nightmare visions of gargoyles climbing down from the Gothic church, he now longs "to live hidden from life" (4). His desire "to be perfectly good" requires that he live apart from human community, in a womblike sanctuary safe from life's daily temptations and pressures. He strips all that might be considered indulgence from his life, including copies of lauds he has created and had printed by a priest on sheepskin in honor of Christ and the saints (6). He has vowed not to look at these beautiful creations until he is dying, fearing "the sin of vanity" (8). The Hermit is thus like other Gothic villains—the Duke in "The Duchess at Prayer," the father in "The House of the Dead Hand"—for whom art is a weapon of repression, although emotional trauma has clearly driven him to this repression.

His longing for a compatriot in the life he has chosen leads him to seek out the "Saint of the Rock," whose extreme asceticism has taken him to a hollow in a barren hillside. The Hermit's journey through the wilderness up treacherous mountain ranges bears the mark of a traditional Gothic experience in which the traveler leaves the unfamiliar and is tested in the climb to foreign and threatening heights. Two key events occur on the Hermit's journey. First, he views the sea for the first time, and at the sight of this surging feminine power, "fear seized him then, for it was terrible to see that great plain move like a heaving bosom" (11–12). Second, the "Saint of the Rock" turns out to be a decrepit, fly-bestrewn old man who ridicules the Hermit for seeking him out to share his solitude. For the reader the grotesqueness of the Saint, whose "holy practices" involve sitting motionless in the hollow of a rock without shade or water and with rheum spilling from his two red eye sockets, emphasizes the failings of patriarchal Christianity (13). As a result of the visit to the Saint, the loneliness of the Hermit's life is reinforced, because he has not only not gained a comrade but also fears that his garden, his one hold on beauty and fertility, will have dried up during this absence.

The young Wild Woman, "brown as a nut and lean with wayfaring," who has nourished his garden while he was away and whom he finds sleeping in his cave, becomes the companion he has sought (16). The parallels between them suggest that she is the "wild" feminine self with which he can now live peaceably. Like the Hermit she is an orphan who has ended up in the cave attempting to escape the violence of marauding drunken soldiers. Like him as well she is a Christian who has chosen to live apart from society, having escaped her restraining life as a nun.

Though the Wild Woman's assertion that "I was once a cloistered woman, but I will never willingly be one again" initially disturbs the Hermit, as does her reason for escaping—her sensuous desire for bathing—she reminds him of his sister, and his response to her is loving: his heart "melted" at her story and he "yearned to save her" (17, 18). He empathetically accepts "his sister's fault" by recalling his own desire for his lauds (26).

The Wild Woman is eroticism incarnate, a part of the Hermit that has gone untended until now. Imprisoned as a girl in a convent like a Gothic heroine, she yearned for a bath in the garden tank, but bathing, like sex, was "an indulgence forbidden to cloistered virgins" (20). As the Abbess explained to her, "this desire to indulge the despicable body is one of the lusts of the flesh, to be classed with concupiscence and adultery" (23). When the Wild Woman manages to break out and enter the water, the experience is an erotic delight, a merging with a lover: "the water . . . seemed to crave me as I craved it. Its ripples rose about me, first in furtive touches, then in a long embrace that clung and drew me down; till at length they lay like kisses on my lips" (24, ellipsis mine). Her punishments for human desires—"fasting, scourging, imprisonment, and the privation of drinking water"—are clearly meant to be considered as barbaric as the self-induced inflictions of the Saint of the Rock (25).

The Wild Woman brings the Hermit knowledge of non-Christian peoples she encounters after escaping from the convent, whose gentleness and spirituality counter the inhumane cruelty of the wandering monks who threatened both her and the "mild and merciful" people she comes to know (27). She also introduces the Hermit to her skill of healing, learned from a "wise woman" (29). While at first distrusting this power, the Hermit then accepts the Wild Woman as part of a tradition of "holy women," though he makes her promise that she will not bathe (30). They live "side by side," as partners in piety, he encouraging religious structure in her, she encouraging respect for alternative spirituality in him (32).

The Hermit, however, has always feared the Wild Woman's desires for bathing, her sensuality. Just before they are both to be honored by the Bishop for their role in banishing a plague, he finds her face up in a stream pool. Before he realizes she is dead, he reacts with fury, then with shame that he will be found by the church hierarchy to have just touched a naked woman. The Hermit seems at first like other male characters in the Gothic stories of the middle period, unable to accept what he has learned about female power. He curses the Wild Woman as a demon—only to realize that she now wears a halo around her floating head and that he has cursed a saint. That the words to his lauds, "so long hidden in the secret of his breast," come to him while he himself is dying and that he soars on the chant "to the seat of mercy" suggest a tempering of his rigidity (39). Like the Wild Woman, he dies immersed in sensory pleasure.

This tale has been called an allegory of the conflict between sacred and profane love as well as a veiled story about Wharton and Walter Berry or Wharton and Henry James. I read it as a conflict between Wharton's two selves, the one who must always be "good" and rule-abiding and who fears sensuality, the other who is wild and unconventional and craves bodily pleasure and freedom (Lewis, *Biography* 470; Tintner 32).[3] Here, as in many of the Gothic stories of the early and middle periods, sensuality is killed off by restraint, even though it is proven more "saintly" in the end. Later, in *The Age of Innocence* and *The Gods Arrive*, sensuality and freedom as they are embodied by Ellen Olenska and Halo Spear are allowed to live, though not without these characters struggling with social rules just as the Hermit does.

"Afterward," published in 1910, four years after "The Hermit and the Wild Woman," and adapting elements of that story, is a stunning portrayal of a woman's process of coming to awareness about her husband's immorality and her own collusion in the lie they live together. Brilliantly crafted, the story uses several aspects of Gothic fiction: the nested story, whereby a past event is framed by a present one and suggesting that the reader is entering a state of mind; light and dark contrasts suggesting degrees of awareness; a mysterious house that symbolically encourages the merging of conscious and subconscious thought; a climb to heights that brings a revealing perception. The story bears traits of Wharton's distinctive revision of the Gothic as well: the intellectual man who tries to seclude his wife and himself from the human community; the childlike woman who at first accepts her seclusion and perceptions of life provided by her husband but then faces terrifying awareness; the limitations of the rational figured by the spectral library and the ghostly abduction of the husband. Wharton also associates water imagery with feminine/maternal knowledge and experience in this story, an element she uses in "The Hermit and the Wild Woman" and frequently in subsequent stories, as she becomes more comfortable with female iconography.[4]

As in earlier Gothic stories, Mary Boyne and her husband Ned are distinctly gendered, the passive and nurturing nonintellectual female and the emotionally distant and controlling male intellectual. Unlike earlier heroines, however, Mary probes her way into awareness, even though such understanding is threatening and terrifying. She faces the kind of self-knowledge that Lily Bart won't allow herself to see. Because the limited-omniscient narrator privileges Mary's perceptions, we observe her learning to read the subconscious and uncanny in her experience, putting pieces together that bring her new understanding, albeit at great cost.

When Mary and Ned Boyne negotiate for a country house in England, they share the belief that "they could not get far enough from the world, or plunge deep enough into the past" (G 72). That the house's name, "Lyng," is one letter shy of "lying" prepares us for the disruptive results of lying that take place within it. At first the Boynes expect not only utter seclusion but also total control over their lives. They have planned in advance all the daily details, intending to "give themselves only to harmonious activities" (72). Ned, in particular, intends to have a "Benedictine regularity of life," driven by "recurrences of habit," a protected life much like the one the Hermit lives, the one Selden aspires to in his republic of the spirit, and the one Newland Archer later succumbs to in *The Age of Innocence* (95). Monotonous regularity is a common hiding place from awareness for characters in Wharton's Gothic fiction. The Boynes' deluded attempt to avoid and control the vicissitudes of life sets them up for psychological upheaval because it also entails attempting to escape from moral accountability.

The house in which the psychic discord occurs is aptly Gothic, "hidden under a shoulder of the downs," without modern conveniences, and possessing "the charm of having been for centuries a deep dim reservoir of life" (73). The conjunction of (female) water with the metaphoric "reservoir" and the house's uncanny power is borne out in the repeated mention of the fish pond between the yews on the grounds and the narrator's comment that "these back-waters of existence sometimes breed, in their sluggish depths, strange acuities of emotion" (73).

Since Mary senses the house's "ghost-seeing faculty, that communed visually but secretly with its own past," it is worth remembering Wharton's own convergence of water, femaleness, and ghost sight expressed in her belief that it is in "the warm darkness of the pre-natal fluid far below our conscious reason that the faculty dwells with which we apprehend the ghost we may not be endowed with the gift of seeing" (75, vii). Like the maternal body, the house is a keeper of secrets that Mary feels one might surprise out of it if one "could only get into close enough communion with the house . . . and acquire the ghost sight on one's own account" (75, ellipsis mine).

Early in the story Mary is repeatedly described as having "short-sighted eyes" (77, 89, 96). In sharpening her ghost sight Mary is able to see her husband and her marriage to him more clearly than she ever has and so defines her identity apart from him. Ned has this ghost sight from the start, indicating that it isn't solely a female ability, but he tries to ignore the message it conveys, a common predilection of men in Wharton's Gothic.

The first ghost sighting takes place, aptly, from the roof of the house, which Mary reaches by pressing "(like a novel heroine) a panel that opened on a flight of corkscrew stairs leading to a flat ledge of the roof" (76). Like Jane Eyre hearing Bertha Rochester's "preternatural" laugh for the first time from the roof of Thornfield Hall, Mary has a perception on the rooftop of Lyng that eventually changes her life (Brontë 108).[5] When her husband joins her they both see the figure of a man approaching the house, which they later both realize is a ghost; while Mary has a "blurred impression" of the man, her husband "had apparently seen more," because he rushes downstairs, leaving Mary to climb down cautiously and then lean "over the banister to strain her eyes through the silence of the brown sun-flecked depths" (77, 78).

Mary will spend the rest of the story looking into the depths of her husband's nefarious business dealings and her own naivete about them during their marriage. But immediately after the event, "which had no mark of the portentous," she tells us later, Mary and Ned climb to another height, Meldon Steep, a mountain near their house; the narrator explains the psychology of memory at work in the story, that the pleasure of the second climb hides the disturbance of the first until "afterward," when the detail becomes significant because it fits into a larger context (79).

When Mary experiences another piece of her husband's mysterious past, by receiving a newspaper article in the mail about a suit brought against Ned by a man named Elwell, she vacillates between a childlike need for reassurance and an adult need to question persistently in order to understand. "You knew about this, then—it's all right?" she asks her husband (84). She is reassured by the composure of his face, asks more questions, feels "a quick thrill of relief," asks more questions, then repeats, as a child might, "It's all right—it's all right?" (85, 86). "Afterward" she recalls that one of the strangest things "out of all the next day's strangeness" was how completely secure she felt (86). As she gazes at the house while she works in the garden the next day, she senses it as "a mind slowly ripened on a sunny wall of experience" and feels a sense of intimacy with it, "a conviction that its secrets were all beneficent, kept, as they said to children, 'for one's good' " (88–89). Readers of Wharton's Gothic know that houses hold few beneficent secrets and that only harm will come from Mary's willingness to stay unaware. Maturity requires that one explore one's inner life and uncover secrets kept "for one's good."

It takes another series of "afterwards" for Mary to realize that the gentleman who comes to her in the garden and whom she sends into the house to see her husband is the man with whom he leaves, the man whom he has cheated in a business deal, the man who has died and returned as a ghost. All of these realizations occur in the library, an apt site in Wharton's terms, given the emotional and intuitive as well as rational process of Mary's awareness.

Indeed, when the Boynes are considering whether to live in Lyng, they learn that the library is "the central, the pivotal 'feature' " of the house (69). When the readers first learn that, by reading her husband's face and mood, Mary suspects that he is keeping a secret, she is in the library, standing among the shadows of the hearth. It is here that Ned spends his days, working on his book. Mary senses that "the room itself might have been full of secrets. They seemed to be piling themselves up, as evening fell, like the layers and layers of velvet shadow dropping from the low ceiling, the rows of books, the smoke-blurred sculpture of the hearth" (74). Cloaking the secret between them in supernatural form, she concludes, "Why, of course—the house is haunted!" (74).

A conversation with her husband in the library takes place in an eerie play of light and shadow. The parlor maid's light "struck up into Boyne's face" as he bends over a tray of letters; he moves into the shadow of the hearth as they discuss ghosts; his profile, which startles Mary, is "projected against the circle of lamplight" (81, 82). Only with the arrival of another lamp does Mary feel "less oppressed by that sense of something mutely imminent which had darkened her afternoon," in great part because she now reads relaxation on Ned's face; that relief lasts only until another "shadow of apprehension" covers his face after she opens the envelope containing the newspaper clipping about Elwell and is filled with "undefinable terror" (82, 83, 84). Just as surely as a Gothic heroine fearfully exploring the halls of a ruined castle illuminated by flickering candles casting shadows, Mary is apprehensively exploring her fears, reluctantly yet persistently trying to find their source.

It is to the library that Mary sends the strange gentleman who has come to find her husband. Later, when she tries to determine where her husband has gone, it is in the library that she is "seized by a vague dread of the unknown . . . as she stood alone in the long silent room, her dread seemed to take shape and sound, to be there breathing and lurking among the shadows" (96, ellipsis mine). There she spends "her long lonely evenings" after Ned's disappearance, feeling that "the intense consciousness of the old dusky walls seemed about to break out into some audible revelation of their secret" (104). It is in the library that Mary learns about Elwell's suicide as a result of her husband's cutthroat business dealings, and she realizes Elwell's revenge, taking Ned with him. Her dread as her knowledge grows is a key emotion of the Gothic experience.

Mary's earlier childlike lack of awareness about her husband's affairs has made her an unwitting participant in his demise, and at the thought, she "felt the walls of books rush toward her, like inward falling ruins" (112). Full awareness is a crushing blow, the metaphor tells us, but the process of getting to it is as much psychological and emotional as intellectual. Eventually, Mary realizes that her first sighting of Elwell's ghost had been "stored away in the fold of memory" and that questions she didn't ask her husband at the time "all along have been there, waiting their hour" (79, 80). Only as she grows psychologically strong enough to examine her fear is she able and willing to put the memory pieces together.

In "The Eyes," as in "Afterward," Wharton uses Gothic elements such as the story within a story, the eerie house, the dark library, and the untrustworthy intellectual to take the reader into a psyche. In both stories Wharton makes overt what her earlier Gothic stories had only suggested, that the Gothic experience is a vehicle for disorienting discovery that alters what characters have assumed about themselves and their lives. Characters in earlier Gothic stories go through traumatic events but seem not to understand their significance. They are simply victims, victimizers, or observers. In stories after 1909, the Gothic experience brings characters awareness even if they then deny it.

Andrew Culwin, in "The Eyes," is just such a denier. Unlike Mary Boyne, who struggles to accept the disastrous ramifications of her unawareness, Culwin resists accepting his culpability in the destruction of others. Like Ned Boyne, Mary's husband, and like Doctor Lombard in "The House of the Dead Hand," Culwin lives the life of a detached intellectual: "His carefully guarded hours had been devoted to the cultivation of a fine intelligence . . . and none of the disturbances common to human experience seemed to have crossed his sky" (G 40–41). Indeed, he believes that, as a writer, "sustained intellectual effort could engage a man's whole activity" (45). Yet despite his intent not to understand the "ghosts" he sees, in the form of two sneering red eyes, he eventually assimilates the horror he has attempted to keep at an aesthetic distance from his self-satisfied vision of himself.

The story calls attention to its Gothic setting, as if to satirize superficial trappings but confirm the Gothic context. A group of companions is sitting in Culwin's dark library, lit only by the gleam of a hearth fire, telling ghost stories. They are a sophisticated lot, the narrator suggests, not usually given to seeing ghosts. Culwin is presumably the most removed from the supernatural, since science and reason are his métier. A Positivist, he is "essentially a spectator, a humorous detached observer of the immense muddled variety show of life," with a mind "like a forum . . . somewhat cold and draughty, but light, spacious, and orderly" (40, 41, ellipsis mine).

Then come the clues that Culwin's nature is more murky than we have been led to believe and that the dark library may well be the setting of a Gothic encounter with discomforting personal discovery, just as it was for Ned and Mary Boyne in "Afterward." A new member of the group, Phil Frenham, is the latest example of Culwin's fascination with young men. As another member has crudely put it, he "liked 'em juicy" (41). It is Phil who twits Culwin that he must have a ghost story to tell, as Culwin, "his little eyes glimmering over a fresh cigar . . . cowered gnome-like among his cushions, dissembling himself in a protective cloud of smoke" (43, ellipsis mine).

Culwin's story, nested within the framing one as is typical in the Gothic stories, begins in his old aunt's "damp Gothic villa, overhung by Norway spruce, and looking exactly like a memorial emblem done in hair" (45). There, he plans to write a great book in her Gothic library and is "lent" his cousin Alice Nowell as a copier. Culwin gradually reveals his baseness, to his listeners and eventually to himself. We enter a person's consciousness as haunted as any house; the traditional Gothic setting yields to a modern psychological Gothic that reveals the potential for cruel egotism in the writer's life.

The story Culwin tells shows that he experiments with the feelings of people over whom he has power, as a scientist with an insect specimen. In addition to Phil, who is, the narrator tells us, "a good subject for experimentation," Culwin tells his listeners that earlier he has tried to "find out the secret" of Alice's "content," so he toys with her until she falls in love with him (42, 45). Then he puts her cousin Gilbert, an aspiring writer whom he admires for his "slender and smooth and hyacinthine" body, "under the microscope" and toys with his ambitions until the youth despairingly figures out the truth about his lack of talent (53, 54). When Culwin reasons about how he may supposedly avoid hurting both of them, by asking Alice to marry him when he doesn't care about her and lying to Gilbert about the quality of his writing, he hurts them most, for he really avoids only his own discomfort by his deliberate lying. As he tells one of his friends, "You know how I hate to be uncomfortable!" (44).

So it is that when he begins to see two grotesque red eyes staring at him in the middle of the night after each time he has undertaken to "promote the moral order of the world" with his "good action," he can't explain them (47).[6] Reason enables him only to discount any cause and effect between his actions and the appearance of the eyes, to deny that his "inner consciousness" has anything pathological about it, and to dismiss the eyes as an "insane irrelevance" (58). All he knows for sure is that they don't appear after he undoes his acts of "grace," by fleeing to Europe without even a note to Alice and by laughing at Gilbert when he finally realizes that his writing is no good.

The reader has learned earlier that Culwin has changed from "a charming little man with nice eyes" to "a phosphorescent log," with "the red blink of the eyes in a face like mottled bark" (40). So we see the connection between Culwin's transformation and his realization that these were eyes "which had grown hideous gradually, which had built up their baseness coral-wise, bit by bit, out of a series of small turpitudes slowly accumulated through the industrious years" (59). The more we learn about Culwin, the more connection we see between the apparitional "swollen lids dropped across the little watery bulbs rolling loose in the orbits" and his decadent, leering nature (59). With their "expression of vicious security" and "base astuteness," the ghostly eyes are a disgustingly appropriate symbol of Culwin's traits, to which he is consciously blind yet of which he is viscerally aware (49). Like Ned Boyne, who is haunted by his guilt in the form of Elwell's ghost, Culwin is haunted by his decadence and "vicious security" in the form of these supernatural eyes. "Their red lids were the edge of my abyss," he recalls presciently at the same time that he denies knowing why they haunt him (51, ellipsis mine).

Then Culwin's external and internal awareness merge, his dissociation disappears. Ending the story he has been telling, he notices how silent Frenham has been and sees that he flings his arms on the table and hides his face in them after meeting Culwin's eyes in a long look. Assuring Frenham in a bantering but quivering laugh that the eyes haven't appeared in years, Culwin catches a reflection of his "congested face" in a small mirror on the table (66). After some momentary lack of recognition, "he and the image in the glass [confront] each other with a glare of slowly gathering hate" (66). Frenham doesn't stir. Both men have made a shocking discovery about themselves, Culwin that he and the hideous eyes are one, Frenham that he is the next victim of Culwin's viciousness.

"The Triumph of Night," written in 1910, the same year as "The Eyes," has elements recognizable from that story as well as from "Afterward" and "The House of the Dead Hand." Wharton extends her handling of the Gothic experience in "The Triumph of Night," however, by portraying the deleterious effects on a weak individual of looking "too deep down into the abyss" (X 278). Incrementally, in her Gothic fiction, Wharton is defining the kind of person who is capable of facing the darkness within.

The protagonist of "The Triumph of Night," George Faxon, eventually realizes his culpability in a traumatic experience resulting in another's death, just as Mary Boyne does in "Afterward." At the heart of the traumatizing experience in both stories is an immoral business deal that sacrifices one individual to the greed of another. George and the young man he comes to know, Frank Rainer, are like Sybilla in "The House of the Dead Hand" in that they are too passive, too psychologically fragile, too scared to act when action is called for. George's observation of Frank, that he has "a healthy face but dying hands," which are "so long, so colourless, so wasted," also recalls Sybilla, symbolized by the limp, dead hand over the entrance to her father's house (248). Frank Rainer's uncle, John Lavington, recalls Sybilla's father—powerful, dominating, and dangerous to the health of his charge. The evil eyes with which John Lavington's double,

seen only by George, glares at Frank are much like those in "The Eyes," signifiers of a dark soul.

The Gothic setting of "The Triumph of Night" prepares us for the psychological journey of its protagonist into the abyss that yields awareness. Northridge, the town to which George has gone to become secretary for one of the
wealthy residents, is appropriately high in altitude, clinging as it does "to an
exposed ledge over the valley from which the train had lifted him" (241). The
most ubiquitous Gothic symbol is the weather, representing the vicious phallic
power waged by John Lavington against his nephew Frank. When George arrives at the Northridge station the blast of cold is "sharpening its edge" against
the "bitter black-and-white landscape. Dark, searching and sword-like, it alternately muffled and harried its victim, like a bull-fighter now whirling his cloak
and now planting his darts" (241). Later, when George tries to escape Lavington's house and is followed by Frank, the icy snow "seemed to be driving a
million blades into his throat and lungs," and he falters from the "stealthy pene-
tration of the cold" (271). As the snow continues to fall "out of a pall of inscrutable darkness," the wind lashes the faces of both men with "barbed thongs"
(272, 274). The weather eventually overcomes them as surely as Lavington's evil
power does.

Frank's and George's weaknesses make them potential victims. We learn of
George's vulnerability first; he has a temperament that "hung on lightly quivering nerves." Later we learn of his "rootless life," his hopelessness, his "haunting sense of starved aptitudes," his several near breakdowns (243, 270). Frank
is weakened from TB and a trusting, childlike innocence that prevents him
from suspecting his uncle of jeopardizing his health in order to be the bene-
ficiary of his inheritance. Good-humored and sincere, Frank is the emotionally
sensitive soul victimized by steely intellectual cruelty, as in most of the Gothic
short stories. When he tells George that "my uncle has such an eye on me!" he
has no sense of the irony in that metaphor, no sense that his uncle is training
on him an eye of hatred, not concern (247).

Lavington's house, where Frank takes George when George realizes that his
prospective employer has forgotten to pick him up at the station, is another obviously Gothic element in the story. As they approach it, the place looms up at
the end of a long avenue. In spite of its many amenities, the house is, George
senses, "oddly cold and unwelcoming," and he posits that Lavington's "intense
personality—intensely negative, but intense all the same—must, in some occult
way, have penetrated every corner of his dwelling" (250). The house/body
meant to be comforting and nurturing holds, instead, threat and fear.

Lavington himself is the type we have met before, with a difference. He
hides his greed and cruelty from everyone but the hapless George, who becomes
the conduit of the supernatural by being the only one who sees Lavington's evil
other self, glaring demonically at Frank. By reputation a man of money, hospi-

tality, generosity, and artistic taste, he appears to George to have a "contracted frame and manner," with "a sort of dry and stilted cordiality that exactly matched his narrow face, his stiff hand, and the whiff of scent on his evening handkerchief" (250). With his demonstrable interest in flowers, which fill the room George occupies, his big house, his charities, his wealth, his small frame, and his controlled, cold demeanor, he shares enough of Wharton's own traits to suggest that he represents, as do other male Gothic characters like him, the potential danger to which Wharton sensed she might succumb: starving one's humanity by wielding patriarchal power gained through money, intellect, and steely efficiency.

In seeing Lavington's double, with its look of "pale hostility" and "deadly menace" directed at Frank, in contrast to Lavington's own look of "untroubled benevolence" and "half-amused affection," George is overcome with horror that drives him from the house and into the snowstorm (255, 264). His incipient understanding that a destructive power is overwhelming Frank overwhelms him, bringing him "to the perilous verge over which, once or twice before, his terrified brain had hung" (270).

George has already inadvertently become an agent of Frank's demise by providing the stamp that legalizes his will and by fleeing without speaking to him about the danger he senses. Frank's chasing after him into the storm is the final assault on a frail body. Provided with an opportunity to live heroically, George is too psychologically fragile to seize it. With "no personal life, no warm screen of private egotisms to shield him from exposure," he is as weak as Frank (270). Rather than considering his ghost sight a power, he thinks of it as an "abnormal sensitiveness to the vicissitudes of others" (270). He tries to save Frank from the brutal winter storm; had he been stronger he could also have tried to save him from his brutal uncle.

After suffering a nervous breakdown, George concludes that he had "looked too deep down into the abyss" (278). He has been incapable of absorbing and acting on understanding gained from beyond the rational, a trait that later male gazers into the abyss in "The Young Gentlemen" and "Miss Mary Pask" will share. When he learns for certain that Lavington has encouraged Frank's death in order to obtain his money and save himself from financial ruin, George fully realizes, like Mary Boyne, what he has mentally hidden away rather than deal with, that "the powers of pity had singled him out to warn and save, and he had closed his ears to their call, and washed his hands of it, and fled" (280). Wharton makes clear that the "sensitive," docile person in conflict with the cruel, dominating one bears some responsibility for accepting the victim's role urged on him or her.

Ethan Frome is a pivotal work in the development of Wharton's Gothic. While characters in the Gothic stories written around the time of this novel, like George in "The Triumph of Night," fearfully hide from the awareness gained in entering the darkness of the suprarational, *Ethan Frome*'s narrator enters fully and freely into the dark world of his fears and fantasies. With its absorption in sexuality and gender merging, the tale the narrator tells prepares us for Wharton's later Gothic fiction emphasizing assertive female eroticism and the development of a conjoined fe/maleness that culminates in *Hudson River Bracketed* and *The Gods Arrive*.

Wharton prepares us to read the Gothic in *Ethan Frome* by referring, in her introduction to the 1922 edition, to Balzac's Gothic short story "La Grande Bretèche." Just as the narrator of that story says of La Grande Bretèche, "I tried to penetrate the mystery of this dwelling as I searched for the clue of the solemn story, the drama that had killed three people," so Wharton's narrator tries to penetrate the mystery of the Frome house and the story of the three metaphorically dead lives within it. Ostensibly Wharton uses "La Grande Bretèche," and Browning's *The Ring and the Book*, as models for her novel's narrative method, whereby the story accretes through the versions of various storytellers. This is of course also one of the most common characteristics of the Gothic, a narrative technique that stresses ambiguity and the psyche of the narrator, who binds the whole together in his own act of creativity.

The narrator of *Ethan Frome* is an educated professional not unlike the writers and readers who are the key male characters in the Gothic short stories preceding it. An engineer, he might be expected to have little interest in the dark mysteries of Ethan Frome's life, but instead he is immediately drawn to the "ruin of a man" he first sees on the street in Starkfield, Massachusetts, and avidly embraces his story (*EF* [1911]: 3). In addition to the powerful attraction the narrator feels for Frome, parallels between them suggest that the narrator is entering, in his "vision" of Frome's story, his own psyche.[7]

Like the narrator, Frome has studied, if only briefly, to be an engineer, and he maintains his interest in learning enough to read the narrator's science book. The narrator's chaffing at being "anchored" in Starkfield, followed by his submission to the "hypnotizing effect of routine," mirror Frome's itch to leave Starkfield followed by his succumbing to his life's routine (8).

The most significant parallel binding the two is that just as the narrator becomes immersed in a "vision" of Frome's story, so he describes Frome as immersed in a dream state. Frome lets "the vision" of lying in a grave with Mattie at his side "possess him" as they walk by the family graveyard (55). When Mattie touches his side, the warmth that floods through him is like "the prolongation of his vision" (56). When he and Mattie reach the house, Ethan's head is "heavy with dreams," and the sight of his spectral wife in the doorway has "the intense precision of the last dream before waking" (56, 58). Later, sharing dinner alone with Mattie is "just as he had dreamed of it," and he reminds himself that "I've been in a dream" that will end (95, 103). When he tells Mattie she has to leave, her response makes him feel as if he "saw her drowning in a dream"

(130). After their first sled ride he becomes immersed in the illusion that he is free to marry Mattie, and he is "only half-roused from his dream" when she tells him they must leave (168). "The hated vision of the house he was going back to—of the stairs he would have to go up every night, of the woman who would wait for him there," combined with Mattie's allure, which "made the other vision all the more abhorrent," drive Ethan to take the dark descent to death (180, ellipsis mine). The narrator, while listening to Ruth Hale tell about the accident, is vicariously "plunged in the vision of what her words evoked" (194).

In their dream states, Ethan and the storyteller who creates his story plunge into the dark maternal abyss of sexual passion and death. Ethan tries to have a great tree take his life, a primary symbol of the Great Earth Mother.[8] While Ethan's is a literal attempt to return to the mother, to submergence in oblivion, the narrator's imaginative act of submergence in Ethan's story allows him to face fear, desire, and loss, primal emotions engendered by the maternal. He thereby enriches his life rather than loses it as Ethan does.

The narrator's plunge into his vision is triggered by his entry into Ethan's house. True to form as a site of Gothic recognition, the house is set on a hill. The disabling snowstorm driving the narrator there, which seems like "the winter night itself descending . . . layer by layer," is another device signaling that we, the readers, along with the narrator, are in a world separated from the daily routine one (25, ellipsis mine). "Two or three times," the narrator reports, "some ghostly landmark sprang up to warn us that we were astray, and then was sucked back into the mist," a disorienting experience much like the one faced by the main character in the fog of the later short story "Miss Mary Pask" (25). Snowstorms also appear in "The Triumph of Night," "Bewitched," and "All Souls' " as signifiers of isolation and death.

Like the houses in "The Duchess at Prayer" and "Afterward," Ethan Frome's is personified by the narrator, who describes its walls as shivering in the wind (22). Its "forlorn and stunted look" he attributes to its lack of a warm center, caused by the absent connection between the house and barn usually found in New England farm dwellings (22). That Ethan is the one who removed the **L** connection leads the narrator to see "in the diminished dwelling the image of his own shrunken body" (23). In entering Ethan with the narrator, we are prepared to know a man who, for reasons unknown, has removed his maternal center, his connection to warmth and nourishment. Though he says that "I had to take down the '**L**,' a while back," suggesting an unspoken reason, the fact remains that he has done this by his own volition (22).[9] The narrator will vicariously experience the traumatizing effects on a life without this connection to the nourishing maternal when he imagines Ethan's life in the cold little house.

Through her narrator's immersion in his/Ethan's psyche that entering the cold house enacts, Wharton encourages us to see Ethan, Zeena, and Mattie Silver as elements of a single self, projections of the narrator's fears about femininity and masculinity.[10] She does this also by referring to them all as "my *granite outcroppings; but half-emerged from the soil, and scarcely more articulate*" and by drawing crucial parallels among them in their portrayal (*EF* [1922]: ii). Each is defined in good part through nature images. Mattie is the most definitively "natural": the motion of her mind was "as incalculable as the flit of a bird in the branches" and her hands are compared to a pair of birds (*EF* [1911]: 51, 101); her lashes are like "netted butterflies" (130); she droops before Ethan like "a broken branch" (131); "the call of a bird in a mountain ash was so like her laughter" (152); her hair is "like certain mosses on warm slopes" and "smelt of the woods" (158, 168). After the crash Ethan mistakes her for "a little animal twittering" (185).

Zeena is less appealingly but no less naturally portrayed as "a shape of stone" wearing "a stony image of resentment" and bearing "hollows and prominences" on her high-boned face (139, 138, 58). During Ethan and Mattie's tête-à-tête over dinner Zeena is personified by her cat, jumping between the two onto Zeena's chair at the table and later onto her rocker and breaking the incriminating pickle dish. Ethan, with his "great height," his "powerful look," his stiffness, his lean brown head, and his "brown seamed profile," is an image of the trees he cuts down, makes into lumber, and hauls into town (3, 15). The narrator's first impression of him is that "he seemed a part of the mute melancholy landscape" (15). All three characters are only slightly more articulate than the bird, moss, cat, and trees to which they are compared.

More striking and significant are the passivity and paralysis of spirit they share, their inability to live lives of fulfilled love, and the allure they each find in death. Mattie, like Lily Bart, is an orphan with no particular life skills who has apparently played no role in determining her own future. Though attracted to Ethan, she has no plan to act on her attraction other than to suggest that they commit suicide together. Her eventual physical paralysis figures her internal passivity.[11]

Ethan has had the eagerness to travel and live in towns "where there were lectures and big libraries and 'fellows doing things,' " but he marries a woman who serves as a mother substitute and submits to her preference for stasis (76). Having chosen a mate out of neediness rather than love, he is paralyzed by guilt when he tries to extricate himself and attempts suicide rather than acting on his desire for Mattie. A "despairing sense of his helplessness" seizes him when faced with his wife's intent to send Mattie away (126). That he chooses death as an expression of desire is prefigured by the "warm sense of continuance and stability" the family graveyard gives him and by his dream of lying in it next to Mattie (55).

Zeena's absorption in her ailments, whether real or imagined, is her chosen form of physical gratification. Unhappy with her life and strong willed, she has nevertheless done nothing about her unhappiness other than dwell on it and her ever-impending death. With her "drawn and bloodless face" she is a living ghost, a spectral presence in the kitchen, which has "the deadly chill of a vault" (70, 58). Probably little loved herself, she is now as an adult incapable of showing or receiving love. As she says reflectively of her geraniums and no doubt of herself, "they pine away when they ain't cared for" (150).[12]

Another element encouraging us to see Ethan Frome, Zeena Frome, and Mattie Silver as elements of a single self is their alternating roles as caretaker and the one taken care of. Ethan cares for his parents and then is cared for by Zeena, who helps him tend to his mother. Zeena becomes the one in need of care until Mattie is disabled, at which point Zeena becomes the one who tends to her. Mattie is unwanted until she is taken in by Ethan and Zeena. She tends to their needs until she becomes like Zeena—gray haired, bloodless of face, and helpless. "I guess it's always Ethan done the caring," Harmon Gow says of him, but as the narrator comments, "there were perceptible gaps between his facts" (7).

Ethan and Zeena also alternately exchange dominance in their relationship with one another. Zeena's "hard perpendicular bonnet" and Ethan's "helmet-like peak" on his cap suggest their common strength, to the point of rigidity (67, 15). Ethan wields power by not listening to Zeena, while she wields it with her silence. Like the Duke in the earlier story "The Duchess at Prayer" and like the Duke de Ercole in the later story "Kerfol," Zeena's "fault-finding was of the silent kind, but not the less penetrating for that" (65). She has the same stealthy, suspicious alertness to her husband's habits that both men in the short stories have to their wives' ways.

Despite his potential strength, Ethan is rendered immobile by the dread common to those who face primal emotions characteristic of the Gothic experience. Since the previous night when Zeena had come to the door to let Ethan and Mattie in after their intimate walk home, "a vague dread had hung on his sky-line" (65–66). Then "his dread was so strong that, man-like, he sought to postpone certainty," reminding us that in Wharton's Gothic it is usually men who resist confronting their fear (66). Yet both Zeena and Ethan end up with the halting gait of broken spirits; she has a "dragging down-at-the-heel step," while he drags himself across the brick pavement, with a "lameness checking each step like the jerk of a chain" (133, 4). Though it is Ethan who feels himself "a prisoner for life," Zeena, and eventually Mattie as well, are no less imprisoned in their lives (146). Masculinity and femininity blend and waver in the narrator's vision, a horrifying yet potentially restorative insight into his worst fear, of inarticulate, immobile, impotent existence.[13] His courage in plunging imaginatively into the abyss prepares the way for characters in Wharton's subsequent Gothic fiction to claim their eroticism and their will.

"Kerfol," like *Ethan Frome*, is a pivotal work in the development of Wharton's Gothic but for a different reason. This is the first Gothic story in which a woman held a virtual prisoner by her husband acts to save herself. In attempting to escape she is a forerunner of the heroines in *The Age of Innocence* and "Dieu d'Amour." In "Kerfol" Wharton also emphasizes, more than she has done in Gothic stories to this point, the unreliability of the male narrator who rejects his empathy and intuitive knowledge for sole reliance on control and rationality.[14]

"Kerfol," published in 1916, is enough like "The Duchess at Prayer," published in 1900, to suggest that it is a deliberate revision of it. Like the Duke in the earlier story, Yves de Cornault in "Kerfol" is a brooding, domineering man who regularly abandons his young wife in his cavernous villa while he goes off for long periods of time. He has essentially purchased Anne from her bankrupt father; then, once he has married her, he buries his "treasure" by not allowing Anne to leave the prisonlike Kerfol (*X* 174).

Like the Duchess in "The Duchess at Prayer," Anne appears "happy enough"; at least "no one asserted that she was unhappy," although a servant had found her crying about her loneliness (168). Less animated than the Duchess, Anne nonetheless also has a young admirer in her life, whom she sees secretly. Like the Duchess as well, Anne receives a veiled threat from her husband that she will be killed into art. The Duke brings home a "kneeling figure wrapped in deathclothes" that resembles his wife, and Cornault tells Anne that, with her dog at her feet, she reminds him of a carved marble effigy of his great-grandmother (*CI* 22). Unlike the Duchess, Anne will see her husband avenged, although revenge doesn't bring her freedom.

Similar, too, in both stories is the narrator who comes upon the ruined villa and learns its story, filtered through layers of storytellers. Wharton makes more clear in "Kerfol," however, that the narrator shares a significant trait with the bully Cornault and the patriarchal judicial system that condemns Anne to imprisonment in the keep of Kerfol for supposedly killing her husband. Like Cornault, the narrator has an "unsociable exterior" and is "solitary-minded" (*X* 153). Like the judges, he dismisses Anne's story of her husband's death by refusing to take seriously the suprarational knowledge he has gained while visiting the ruined Kerfol. With his arrogant judgment of Anne, the narrator joins the cast of Gothic characters who deny intuitive understanding and take refuge solely in reason.

Kerfol has the most typically Gothic setting thus far. Remotely situated, it is reached by a long avenue, lined with "grey-trunked trees" which "sprang up straight to a great height and then interwove their pale grey branches in a long tunnel through which the autumn light fell faintly" (154). The sexual iconography of this entrance, the trees which "sprang up straight" and the long tunnel, is supported by other such imagery later on and by the story's sexual conflict between the jealous Cornault and his lonely wife, whose friendship with

Hervé de Lanrivain and love for her pet dogs enrages him. Surrounded by an overgrown moat, Kerfol resembles the ruined castles of traditional Gothic fiction. Like Lyng, in "Afterward," it seems human to the narrator, looking down on him and embodying "a long accumulation of history . . . that sheer weight of many associated lives and deaths which gives a majesty to all old houses" (155, ellipsis mine). This personification supports a similar maternal/body reading of the house as possessor of experience and knowledge transcending the intellectual.

That the narrator sees the ghostly dogs, loved by Anne and killed by her husband, while visiting Kerfol suggests that he has the ghost (in)sight that he will use in understanding Anne's story. Significantly he wants to know more about the house, "not to *see* more—I was by now so sure it was not a question of seeing—but to feel more: feel all the place had to communicate" (156). He feels the "pressure of the invisible" at Kerfol and has the sense that it is "the loneliest place in the whole world" (161). Yet he ignores all this supporting evidence when he reads the proceedings of Anne's trial, taking stock in the judicial over the intuitional.

The many layers through which Anne's story is filtered riddles it with ambiguity and emphasizes, as do the concentric stories of other Gothic fiction, the sense that the reader is entering a psyche. The narrator is lent, by an ancestor of Hervé de Lanrivain, a history book written about a hundred years after the Kerfol affair that he believes "is transcribed pretty literally from the judicial records" (164). The narrator in turn translates it and, though he says he adds nothing of his own, interprets Anne's story from his own perspective. We learn as much about his unwillingness to sympathize with Anne and his fear of the dark knowledge he has gained about her life as we do about Anne's story.

With their passive silence, suggesting emotional neglect and abuse, the ghostly dogs clearly speak for the passive Anne, whose husband does not talk to her for days. In strangling the pet dogs her husband is strangling her, choking off her source of love and liveliness. When we the readers learn of Anne's testimony that the dead dogs have killed her husband, the story rings true, in spite of its occultness, because we want to believe that Anne's legitimate rage has found an outlet and taken revenge where it is due. The physical detail of Anne finding her dead husband "at the head of a narrow flight of stairs leading down from his wife's rooms to a door opening on the court" where Hervé de Lanrivain is waiting to help her escape accentuates the sexual threat her husband has been (170–71). The vaginal image of the "narrow flight of stairs," with her husband at the top and another man at the opening, embodies the terrifying sexual tension Anne has endured with a jealous husband.

The narrator makes no such connections, however. In spite of having seen the ghost dogs, having felt the intense loneliness of Kerfol, and having gathered ample evidence of Cornault's cruelty to Anne, the narrator doesn't even entertain the possibility that the ghost dogs might indeed have been the murderers. Near the end of the account he interjects that the judges were plainly surprised by the "puerility" of Anne's explanation for her husband's death, and he suggests that he agrees with them: "It did not help the accused in the eyes of the public. It was an odd tale, certainly; but what did it prove? That Yves de Cornault disliked dogs, and that his wife, to gratify her own fancy, persistently ignored this dislike. As for pleading this trivial disagreement as an excuse for her relations—whatever their nature—with her supposed accomplice, the argument was so absurd that her own lawyer manifestly regretted having let her make use of it, and tried several times to cut short her story" (181).

We might give the narrator the benefit of the doubt, by acknowledging the stretch of faith it takes to believe that dogs can return from the dead to retaliate against the husband who has bullied their loving mistress. But the narrator expresses no sympathy at all for Anne, handed over to her husband's family and kept a prisoner in Kerfol until she "died many years later, a harmless madwoman" (188). Instead he expresses envy for the outcome of Hervé de Lanrivain, who had become a Jansenist, a sect known for its extreme rigidity in matters of morality, discipline, and dogma. "In the course of his life two great things had happened to him," the narrator says in his detailed discussion of this minor character in the preceding drama; "he had loved romantically, and he must have talked with Pascal" (188).

As for Anne, the narrator's abrupt dismissal of her with "And so ends her story" contradicts the connection the reader has established with her and suggests that the narrator can't or won't face what he has learned about Anne's life and fate. For the reader of Wharton's Gothic, Anne's vicariously expressed rage and her failed attempt to escape victimization are precursors of Ellen Olenska's fearless anger and determined rejection of an abusive husband in *The Age of Innocence* and the Princess's heroic escape from a coercive marriage before it begins in "Dieu d'Amour."

4 | Reclaiming the Feminine

WHARTON'S DECISION, like Ellen Olenska's in *The Age of Innocence,* to live as an expatriate in Paris, beginning in 1910, marked a period in her life of triumphant independence, achievement, and emotional growth. These qualities are also reflected in Ellen Olenska, who becomes the aware feminine self Wharton's Gothic has helped her create, a woman comfortable with autonomy, with her body, with self-knowledge. At the same time, Newland Archer is the tempered masculine self that evolves in the Gothic text during this period, unwilling to repress the feminine self or freeze it into art, aware of the patriarchal system that oppresses men and women alike, trying to open himself to emotional fulfillment.

With the sale of the Mount in 1911, Wharton ended her life in America and began what R. W. B. Lewis calls a time of "hectic traveling and aimless loitering," but which might also be read as the exhilarating stimulation her energetic intellect so craved (*Biography* 318). In the words of her reserved friend Henry James in a 1912 letter, "Her powers of devastation are ineffable, her repudiation of repose absolutely tragic and she was never more brilliant and able and interesting" (323).

In her relationships with men, Wharton was untangling herself from constraint and forging new bonds. She had ended her affair with Fullerton in 1910, yet not without having been enriched by the sexual awakening it provided. Not coincidentally the Gothic stories written during the period from 1917–1926—"The Young Gentlemen," "Miss Mary Pask," "Bewitched," and "Dieu d'Amour"—are more assertive about female eroticism and about male fear of it than previous stories have been. Wharton's separation from Teddy in 1911 and their divorce in 1913 gave her considerable freedom from years of conflict and trauma. Walter Berry, whom Wharton would call, at his death, "the love of all my life," became a more constant, intimate companion once Wharton was divorced and had moved permanently to France (Notebook 1924–34).

The upheaval in Wharton's life during this time and the immense energy it freed in her was a reflection in microcosm of the inherent paradox of World War I. On the one hand it was a horrific plunge into the darkest abyss of human destruction; on the other, it was a source of immense energy as people struggled to fight off annihilation and maintain social continuity. For Wharton the war was the impetus for stunningly courageous social and creative achievement.

Within two weeks of the war's beginning in 1914, Wharton had organized a sewing establishment employing hundreds of seamstresses. She became an indefatigable fund raiser for the many support services she organized. In addition, in 1915 alone she made five tours to the front, arranged a benefit concert in France and promoted others in America, and organized sales and fund-raising exhibits. Wharton confronted the war with ferocious energy; her awesome achievements gained her the Chevalier of the Legion of Honor and the devotion of the French people (Lewis, *Biography* 378, 386). But the constant activity was not purely altruistic. Without it, she knew, "her awareness of the horror would be too much for her" (378).

That the war was "almost unbearably agitating," suffusing people with "an unmistakable sexual intensity" (Wolff 266), is reflected in Wharton's sexual language as she describes the war's effect on her creativity: "The noting of my impressions at the front had the effect of rousing in me an intense longing to write, at a moment when my mind was burdened with practical responsibilities, and my soul wrung with the anguish of the war. Even had I the leisure to take up my story-telling I should have had no heart for it; yet I was tormented with a fever of creation" (*BG* 355).

One result of the fever was *Summer*, "written at a high pitch of creative joy" and published in 1917 (356). Though created amid "a thousand interruptions, and while the rest of my being was steeped in the tragic realities of the war," Wharton notes that "I do not remember ever visualizing with more intensity the inner scene, or the creatures peopling it" (356). *Summer* has been called both "the most erotic fiction that Wharton ever published" and a confrontation with "the most furious and lawless impulses that lie buried in human nature" (Wolff 267; Lewis, *Biography* 397).

The Gothic subtext in *Summer* begins the new emphasis on assertive female eroticism and on female characters confronting the Medusa, the terror and power of their inner feminine/maternal self.[1] Charity both confronts and reclaims this self in her journey to the Mountain and her mother. Most critics consider Charity's experience on the Mountain as one of total renunciation. For instance, Waid believes that in rejecting the "animal body of the mother Mary who must be buried," Charity escapes reliving her mother's life (122). Gilbert writes that "there is no salvation from or for her mother's 'vile body,' " and Elbert states that Charity sees her mother as "the horrible destroyer" because her mother manifests her own limitations ("Life's" 370; "Politics" 7).

Reading Charity's story as part of the continuum of Wharton's developing Gothic, however, helps us see the restorative function of confronting the mother's distorted, grotesque body. In facing her worst fears about her primal female body, Charity is engaged in the "coming-to-awareness" process crucial to Wharton's Gothic. To confront "her relation to the maternal body that she shares, with all its connotations of power over and vulnerability to forces within and without" is to tap the secret center of "that knowledge which is power" (Kahane, "Gothic Mirror" 338, 339). Thus the confrontation with her mother on the Mountain allows Charity to reclaim this shameful, wild, sexual maternal self as part of her and, ultimately, to be empowered by that act.

Charity resembles Wharton's earlier Gothic short story heroines in the confinement of her liveliness and sexuality in a restrictive house by an older man, her collusion in that confinement, and her ambiguous "rescue." Like Lily Bart, Charity is an orphan who faces sexual experiences unguided and unprotected. Unlike Lily, however, she faces the abyss—the dark knowledge of her sexuality, rage, shame, and potential death—in reclaiming her mother on the Mountain. Rather than face the terror of the inner life vicariously through the narrator's vision as she does in *Ethan Frome*, Wharton courageously has Charity confront firsthand her greatest terrors and accept as part of herself the ugliness she finds within. At the same time, through subtle parallels between Charity Royall and Lucius Harney, Wharton suggests the potential unity of gender strengths in a single individual, a unity toward which she is striving in the Gothic subtexts of her realistic novels.

Charity is doubly constrained within a house within a town, both of which metaphorically emphasize her restrained situation. The name of Charity's "weather-beaten sunburnt village of the hills," North Dormer, suggests not only its lethargy (the French *dormir* meaning "to sleep," "to be stagnant") but also its confinement as a small appendage to a house's roof. Though lying "high and in the open," the town is a deserted ruin, "abandoned of men, left apart by railway, trolley, telegraph, and all the forces that link life to life in modern communities" (*S* 7, 10–11). Its smallness intensifies the attention the residents pay to one another, which exacerbates Charity's sense of constraint. The cold, moldy, vaultlike Honorius Hatchard Memorial Library in which she works further imprisons her, as does the faded red house Charity lives in with Lawyer Royall, surrounded by overgrowth and an "adjoining wilderness of rock and fern" (23).

The suggested allusion of the red house to the red room in which Jane is locked in Charlotte Brontë's *Jane Eyre* accentuates the Gothic quality of *Summer*'s setting. Like Charity, Jane is an orphan, brought to Gateshead Hall by her uncle just as Charity is brought to North Dormer and the red house by Mr. Royall, who is old enough to be her uncle/father. Jane, like Charity, feels herself to be "a heterogeneous thing" in her environment, out of place and unhappy (Brontë, *Jane Eyre* 12). Charity's "How I hate everything" as she leaves the house and her wish throughout the novel to flee North Dormer echoes Jane's intense resentment about her victimization in the Reed household and her resolve to "escape from insupportable oppression" (*S* 9; *Jane Eyre* 12).

Most significant is that the red room, where Jane's uncle died and lay in state, with its "Freudian wealth of secret compartments, wardrobes, drawers, and jewel chest," bears a "deadly and bloody" association with the female body, as well as providing a representative vision of the patriarchal society in which Jane is trapped (Showalter, *A Literature* 114–15; Gilbert and Gubar, *Madwoman* 340). This amalgam of sexuality and patriarchal control is true for the red house as well, for there Charity sleeps in the bedroom of Mr. Royall's dead wife and has had to fend off the sexual advances of her surrogate father. There she develops an increasing sexual attraction for Lucius Harney while knowing that Mr. Royall is scrutinizing her movements and trying to keep her from seeing Lucius. It is to the red house that the pregnant Charity is brought after being overtaken and led into marriage by Mr. Royall.

Complicating her constraint, however, is her past decision to agree with Royall that she won't go away to boarding school because he is "too lonesome" (*S* 26). Although only fifteen, she is strong willed and experienced enough to know the potentially dangerous personal consequences of her decision. When Miss Hatchard's fumbling allusion to the dangers ends with "You're too young to understand," Charity harshly retorts, "Oh, no, I ain't" (26). In spite of her early frustrating sense of confinement, she doesn't have enough self-identity to leave what confines her. No doubt it is *she* who would be "too lonesome" away from the familiar constraints.

As it has been for the main characters in "The Eyes" and "Afterward," a library is the scene of recognition for Charity, beginning her process of self-awareness. When Charity meets and then confronts Lucius Harney in the Honorius Hatchard Memorial Library, she becomes aware of sexual attraction, she sees her life as something more than "too desolate, too ugly and intolerable," and she regards herself as an attractive, likable person (45). When Lucius gently and straightforwardly asks that Charity trust him to correct the precarious situation he has created for her by criticizing the library, "All the old frozen woes seemed to melt in her" and she is primed to become someone other than the angry, resentful young woman she has been (52).

Just as Lily Bart and Lawrence Selden are not only potential lovers but also female and male versions of a person who might ideally blend the lives of both, so the shared traits of Charity and Lucius suggest that Wharton sees them as female and male aspects of one person, the sensual and the intellectual. Charity's courageous Gothic confrontation with her mother and herself that the love affair with Lucius precipitates allows her to develop internal strength she has not earlier possessed. As such, she is a precursor of the unification of gender traits that Ellen Olenska will so handsomely exhibit in *The Age of Innocence*.

Some of the similarities between Charity and Lucius are minor—they both have sunburnt hands, they both wear straw hats—but such small details prepare the reader to see other, more substantial parallels. For instance, Charity's thought of Annabel Balch when she sees Lucius for the first time might be read simply as a coincidental narrative device to prepare us for the part this "other woman" will play. But when one reads the roles of Charity and Lucius as female and male parts of a single self, their mutual attraction to this representative of respectable society carries additional weight.

For Charity and Lucius both, Balch is all Charity can never be: "she represented all the things that Charity felt herself most incapable of understanding or achieving" (220). Charity's initial thought, once she knows she is pregnant, is that "compared to her sovereign right Annabel Balch's claim seemed no more than a girl's sentimental fancy" (228). But once she reads Lucius's letter this bravado is quickly overcome by the vision of "the indestructible figure of Annabel Balch" standing "fixed and upright" between them (230). Balch's silent yet powerful place in the text emphasizes her role as the patriarchal ideal, the "fixed and upright" phallic womanhood that both Charity and Lucius want to possess. Nonetheless Charity subsequently realizes that the love experiences she has shared with Harney "had passed into her blood, and become a part of her, they were building the child in her womb; it was impossible to tear asunder strands of life so interwoven" (231). Her acceptance of her pregnancy allows her to acknowledge that she does not have to be Annabel Balch or Lucius's wife to feel herself joined with him, and to feel herself a worthy woman.

Lucius's and Charity's mutual familiarity with old houses, his because he studies them and hers because they are part of her heritage, prepares them both for the disorienting experiences that entering old houses in Wharton's Gothic entails. Lucius is already predisposed, if only intellectually, toward the asocial world that the dilapidated houses around North Dormer contain. He refers to the Mountain community as an "independent kingdom" composed of people with "a good deal of character," apparently because they "don't give a damn for anybody" (65). His implied admiration extends to Charity, whose Mountain ancestry makes her "different" in his eyes and, he suggests, special (67). The praise provides Charity with an alternative self-view to the disparaging one her community has given her about her heritage.

Lucius and Charity represent the dualities of intellect and sensuality, yet they both possess a sense of power that other characters in the novel lack. Charity is initially bewildered by Lucius's "unintelligible" remarks in the library and lets much of what he says slide over her without bothering to comprehend it (17). Her métier is nature, "all that was light and air, perfume and colour," to which "every drop of blood in her responded" (21). Lucius is the architect, the reader, the researcher. Charity realizes even before meeting him that he has "the air of power that the experience of cities probably gave" (51).

But Charity too has power in her life, for after Royall's attempted seduction and the consequent hiring of Verena Marsh, she knows that "nothing now would ever shake her rule in the red house" (38). She "knew her power, knew what it was made of, and hated it" (23). Indeed, although the assertion is contradicted by other parts of the text, we are told, as Charity hunches outside Lucius's bedroom window, that "she had never in her life been afraid" (105).

Charity initially dreams of being sweetly dependent on Lucius, but the "happy comradeship" that precedes love between them is based in good part on their mutual personal strength (129). When they kiss for the first time, "an unknown Harney had revealed himself, a Harney who dominated her and yet over whom she felt herself possessed of a new mysterious power" (149). This interchanging power reiterates the sense of Charity and Lucius as parallel characters, female and male.

At the same time, a crucial gender difference between them is that Lucius has the confidence builders of money and education to help him eliminate unwanted constraints on his physical and emotional freedom. Charity, with neither money nor education, is beset by the characteristic Gothic emotions of fear and dread caused by Mr. Royall, who is a sexual threat and an ugly restraint on her just as the Duke, Professor Lombard, Mr. Brympton, and Yves de Cornault are on the young women in their lives in "The Duchess at Prayer," "The House of the Dead Hand," "The Lady's Maid's Bell," and "Kerfol." An educated professional and a part of the social power structure, as many of the Gothic tyrants are, Royall is "harsh and violent" and prone to watching Charity in brooding silence (24). Her reaction to him is usually disgust mingled with fear. During his first marriage proposal to Charity he stands before her "unwieldy, shabby, disordered, the purple veins distorting the hands he pressed against the desk . . . like a hideous parody of the fatherly old man she had always known" (34, ellipsis mine). The incest threat prevalent in much Gothic fiction and strongly suggested in Wharton's short stories is redolent in *Summer,* as this description and Royall's subsequent pressure of the weakened Charity into marriage reveal.

So although Charity has felt powerful in Royall's house, she feels afraid too. After getting him to hire Verena Marsh, "a belated sense of fear came to her with the consciousness of victory" (30). As she becomes more involved with Lucius, she doesn't fear the neighbors' talk.

> What she most feared was that the inevitable comments should reach Mr. Royall . . . she had always felt that, on the day when she showed too open a preference, Mr. Royall might, as she phrased it, make her "pay for it." How, she did not know; and her fear was the greater because it was undefinable. If she had been accepting the attentions of one of the village youths she would have been less apprehensive: Mr. Royall could not prevent her marrying when she chose to. But everybody knew that "going with a city fellow" was a different and less straightforward affair: almost every village could show a victim of the perilous venture. And her dread of Mr. Royall's intervention gave a sharpened joy to the hours she spent with young Harney. [62–63, ellipsis mine]

This passage vividly captures Charity's amorphous apprehensiveness, felt by most Gothic heroines—her sense of pervading danger which she can't identify and the contradictory attraction to danger and fear of its consequences with which she flirts.

Charity's erotic involvement with Lucius Harney creates a need to know herself and a willingness to plunge into the threatening dark abyss of her inner life that yields self-knowledge. At first, much as Lily is unwilling to face herself, Charity, before Lucius, feels "only a sullen reluctance to explore the corner of her memory where certain blurred images lingered" about her early life (59). Sexual feeling for Lucius, however, "had stirred her to the sleeping depths," making her "become absorbingly interesting to herself"; now "everything that had to do with her past was illuminated by this sudden curiosity" (59).

The Independence Day celebration at Nettleton, where Charity and Lucius share their first kiss, is a precursor of the disorienting experience Charity will later have on the Mountain, which will so essentially change her sense of herself. The intense heat, the smells, the cacophony of sounds, the startling contrasts of light and darkness transport Charity into an altered state. Her reaction to the movie she sees with Harney encapsulates her disorientation, for after it "everything was merged in her brain in swimming circles of heat and blinding alternations of light and darkness" (139).

Most affecting, however, is Charity's confrontation with the grotesque, drunken Royall: "His face, a livid brown, with red blotches of anger and lips sunken in like an old man's, was a lamentable ruin in the searching glare" (151). As he stands staring at her, "trying to master the senile quiver of his lips," and then slowly curses, "You whore—you damn—bare-headed whore, you!" she is struck by shame, not only for herself, but also for him (151). Her sympathetic reaction to this "new and dreadful" Royall, "You come home with me—you come right home with me," is as transformative as the loathing she feels the next day, when she realizes that Royall's is a "debauched and degraded life" (152, 158). She now understands the "horrible moment when he had tried to force himself into her room" as "a vulgar incident" in a vulgar life rather than as a "mad aberration" (158). It is fitting that she now looks at the familiar sights of North Dormer as if "from the other side of the grave," for she has begun a Gothic process of realization that will take her into another kind of consciousness than she has known (156).

The journey into herself involves a climb to the heights as do the revelatory experiences of Lily Bart, the Hermit, Mary Boyne, George Faxon, and the narrator in *Ethan Frome*. Charity climbs the hill path behind the house and then climbs "into the heart of the forest" (162). Along the way she shudders with what she remembers later as "involuntary terror" when an evangelist with a round white face emerges from a large white tent and exhorts her that "your Saviour knows everything" and that she should "lay your guilt before Him" (238, 161). This frightening encounter with a ghostly man of God conflates the Gothic with the religious, an emphasis Wharton develops further in her last completed novels, *Hudson River Bracketed* and *The Gods Arrive*.[2]

The little deserted house in which Charity seeks refuge, and where she will fall into the abyss of passion with Lucius, sits above the road on "a slope in one of the lonely rifts of the hills" (162). The house is appropriately ruined,

> its wooden walls sun-bleached to a ghostly gray . . . the broken gate dangled between its posts, and the path to the house was marked by rose-bushes run wild and hanging their small pale blossoms above the crowding grasses. Slender pilasters and an intricate fan-light framed the opening where the door had hung; and the door itself lay rotting in the grass, with an old apple-tree fallen across it.
>
> Inside, also, wind and weather had blanched everything to the same wan silvery tint; the house was as dry and pure as the interior of a long-empty shell. [166, ellipsis mine]

Said to be haunted, the house is "like some frail shell," Charity's shell, within which she becomes a changed person in the experience of passion (179).

After making love to Lucius for the first time in the deserted house, Charity returns to North Dormer, feeling "as if she were suspended in the void," and she goes into "a kind of trance" when his name is mentioned (174, 176). In giving up the self she was, a courageous act that Wharton equates with the uncanny Gothic experience, Charity enters an altered state of consciousness. Charity's experience in the deserted house resembles Wharton's sense, expressed in her sonnet "Ame Close," that her soul is like an abandoned, haunted house. Wharton makes the allusion after Fullerton apparently urged physical consummation of their increasingly intimate relationship, eight years before she began writing *Summer*. Once immersed in the love affair, like Charity and Lucius together in their abandoned house, Wharton felt that she and Fullerton were isolated in their own other world, "behind the scenes together . . . —*on the hither side*" (Lewis, *Biography* 222, ellipsis mine).

Likewise, loving Lucius has carried Charity away "into a new world, from which, at stated hours, the ghost of her came back to perform certain customary acts, but all so thinly and insubstantially that she sometimes wondered that the people she went about among could see her" (*S* 182). In essence her earlier self dies and she recreates herself: "Everything unrelated to the hours spent in that tranquil place was as faint as the remembrance of a dream. The only reality was the wondrous unfolding of her new self, the reaching out to the light of all her contracted tendrils" (180). The language of "her contracted tendrils" is reminiscent of the scene in *The House of Mirth* in which Lily holds Nettie Struther's baby girl and watches "the vague tendrilly motions of the folding and unfolding fingers" (*HM* 510). While the baby represents Lily's infantile self that she cannot acknowledge and nurture, Charity submits to the vulnerability that consummated passion brings and finds joy in it.

Because the shell of the new self is frail, though, the experience of vulnerability is also fearful. "The first fall of night after a day of radiance" when she is in the house "often gave her a sense of hidden menace: it was like looking out over the world as it would be when love had gone from it" (*S* 183). Mr. Royall's unannounced intrusion into the house and his violation of its intimacy, with his allusions to Charity's mother's promiscuity and, by extension, her own, illustrates how fragile the borders of Charity's self are. Nonetheless, after he leaves, she allows herself to be "sucked down" with Lucius, "into some bottomless abyss" (211). She willingly loses herself in a way no character before her in Wharton's fiction has done.

Charity has already had a sense of the dangerous fragility of her new self, when the crashing down of the makeshift maple branches at the Old Home Week ceremony revealed Lucius sitting with Annabel Balch. "In a flash," the vision of their two faces "had shown her the bare reality of her situation. Behind the frail screen of her lover's caresses was the whole inscrutable mystery of his life" (197). She feels not jealousy but "a terror of the unknown, of all the mysterious attractions that must even now be dragging him away from her, and of her own powerlessness to contend with them" (198). That terror is compounded by a sense of "deadly apprehension" and "a glare of fear" as she realizes that the suffocating heat and the nausea overwhelming her are probably because she is pregnant (198). That these reactions are expressed in the language of the Gothic—"terror," "deadly apprehension," "powerlessness," "glare of fear"—emphasizes the connection Wharton is making between the Gothic and fundamental psychological/spiritual/emotional realizations. Charity's culminating faint reinforces this sense of dying to the old self as realizations occur.

Having opened herself to these fundamental realizations about herself, Charity feels intense shame when she doesn't measure up to the standard that Lucius and his imagined world—a world of learning and social status—have become for her. Royall's intrusive accusations about Lucius and Charity in the deserted house cause Charity to feel "a leaden weight of shame," and she feels mortified and despairing that she can't find the words to respond to the letter Lucius sends her (212). After she violently tears Annabel Balch's blouse in two when she hears that the girl is engaged to marry Lucius, she feels that "she had never known how to adapt herself; she could only break and tear and destroy" (220–21). The similarity of this act to Bertha Mason's tearing of Jane's wedding veil in two in *Jane Eyre* suggests that Charity, like Jane, is still incapable of accepting the raging, inarticulate, wild part of herself. As a result she feels herself at the mercy of power beyond her control, "passively awaiting a fate she could not avert" (214). "The sense of fatality weighed on her," and "she felt herself too unequally pitted against unknown forces" (220, 221).

A second recognition Charity experiences in the library changes everything. As the books begin to "spin around her" and the dizziness is followed by nausea, she is shaken, terrified, and sure now that she is pregnant (221). That this intensely physical experience occurs in the library carries the same ironic force that the transformative experiences in libraries of other characters in

Wharton's Gothic fiction do. Book knowledge is emphatically not the sole kind. Understanding that changes people's lives derives as often from physical, emotional, and spiritual experience as from the intellectual.

Charity now understands that "she would never again know what it was to feel herself alone," that "it was impossible to tear asunder" the interwoven strands of life which link her to Lucius, that she will never marry him, and that she must escape to the source from which she came, the Mountain and her mother (228, 231). The Mountain is "the only answer to her questioning, the inevitable escape from all that hemmed her in and beset her," just as mountains have provided "intensity of sensation and expansion of vision" for characters in traditional Gothic novels (236; Bayer-Berenbaum 140).

Instinctively Charity knows that the Mountain will provide her with knowledge, with answers to her questions about herself. She wants to know the wild sexual self who can't "adapt" to a life that demeans and disparages her. In the past Charity has been "not very clear about the Mountain," but she has learned from her North Dormer society that "it was a bad place, and a shame to have come from" (12). The Mountain, casting its shadow over North Dormer, is Charity's birthplace, her mother, her femaleness about which she has been taught to be ashamed. As Royall says to Lucius about Charity, "They all know what she is, and what she came from. They all know her mother was a woman of the town from Nettleton, that followed one of those Mountain fellows up to his place and lived there with him like a heathen. . . . I went to save her from the kind of life her mother was leading—but I'd better have left her in the kennel she came from" (207–208, ellipsis mine).

About to be a mother herself, Charity now wants to know her mother for herself rather than as Royall has defined her, to understand the femaleness, the sexuality that she shares with her: "She herself had been born as her own baby was going to be born; and whatever her mother's subsequent life had been, she could hardly help remembering the past, and receiving a daughter who was facing the trouble she had known" (240). A mountain is a potent archetypal symbol of maternal protection, worshiped as the Great Mother, the "female godhead" (Neumann 99). Wharton's capitalization of the "Mountain" in *Summer*, her description of it as "swarthy" just as Charity is described, her emphasis on it as Charity's home and the place where Charity finds her dead mother, as well as Charity's fleeing to it when she becomes aware of her sexuality and pregnancy, all suggest that Wharton was aware of the archetypal potency of the Mountain as a symbol of femaleness (182, 8).[3]

As Charity makes the ascent up the Mountain, first on foot and then in Mr. Miles's buggy, she is physically and psychologically leaving the world she has known. Mr. Miles's information that her mother is dying gives Charity a sense of "unescapable isolation" as "the world [is] dropping away below them in great mottled stretches of forest and field, and stormy dark blue distances" (242, 244).

Like traditional Gothic heroines before her, climbing mountains into deep forests and entering ruined castles, Charity is entering the dark, threatening world of the mother, the source of birth, death, and sexuality, the source of herself. As Claire Kahane writes, "What I see repeatedly locked into the forbidden center of the Gothic which draws me inward is the spectral presence of a dead-undead mother, archaic and all-encompassing, a ghost signifying the problematics of femininity which the heroine must confront" ("Gothic Mirror" 336).

Charity finds a grotesque mother on the dark Mountain: "She did not look like a dead woman; she seemed to have fallen across her squalid bed in a drunken sleep and to have been left lying where she fell, in her ragged disordered clothes. One arm was flung above her head, one leg drawn up under a torn skirt that left the other bare to the knee: a swollen glistening leg with a ragged stocking rolled down about the ankle. The woman lay on her back, her eyes staring up unblinkingly at the candle that trembled in Mr. Miles's hand" (248). As Charity helps the minister "compose" her mother's body for the funeral, "she looked at her mother's face, thin yet swollen, with lips parted in a frozen gasp above the broken teeth. There was no sign in it of anything human: she lay there like a dead dog in a ditch" (250).

In confronting her mother's physical degradation, Charity, and Wharton with her, confronts her own shameful sexuality, her self-hatred, her vile female body. Giving "*visual* form to the fear of self" has been called a distinctive trait of female Gothic (Moers 163). Often, in Gothic by modern women writers, "when the unseen is given visual form, when we lose the obscurity of the Gothic darkness, the Gothic focuses on distorted body images and turns into the grotesque," grotesque female bodies in particular, visualizing the "problematics of femininity" (Kahane, "Gothic Mirror" 343). In "composing" her mother's body Charity is involved in the act of creating this grotesque image of the mother as well as reconciling it with her sense of herself, claiming it as her own. She thereby accepts her mother's and, by extension, her own ugly self-hatred and shame, and faces her worst fears about the wages of female sexuality.[4]

Charity's first triumph is that she accepts her mother and realizes that she needs to reclaim their relationship, in spite of the pain it causes. She reconsiders her earlier hatred of her mother for abandoning her: "was her mother so much to blame? Charity, since that day, had always thought of her as destitute of all human feeling; now she seemed merely pitiful. What mother would not want to save her child from such a life?" (*S* 260). In accepting her mother, Charity accepts herself and her past while at the same time she realizes the paralyzing limitations and degradation of her mother's primitive world. A brown song sparrow perched in an upper branch of a thorn tree above her mother's grave singing "his small solitary song" images Charity's idealistic resolve to live her life differently by finding a quiet, clean place to bear and keep her child by herself (263).

Charity's second triumph is that she stays alive. In spite of the "mortal lassitude" that weighs her down, she leaves her mother's house (261). Climbing the mountain again, she "felt herself a mere speck in the lonely circle of the sky. . . . In her fagged and floating mind only one sensation had the weight of reality; it was the bodily burden of her child. But for it she would have felt as rootless as the whiffs of thistledown the wind blew past her" (264–65, ellipsis mine). The description recalls Lily Bart's sense, near the end of her life, that she is "something rootless and ephemeral, mere spin-drift of the whirling surface of existence" (*HM* 515). But Lily blots out awareness of her physicality, her terror, her aloneness, with chloral. Rather than coming to know her sexuality, she loses herself in the "gentle penetrating thrill of warmth and pleasure" given her by the imagined child/self lying on her arm as she dies (522). Though Charity is utterly desolate after leaving her mother's house, her sense of her pregnant body keeps her alive and moving. Loving Lucius and reclaiming her mother and her past makes Charity more aware of herself, including her physical body, rather than becoming other than herself as Lily does in yielding to the "tender pressure" of the baby and to death (523). Charity, like Jane Eyre on the heath, knows instinctively that to become part of the "nature" of her mother's world on the Mountain is to die (Homans 269).

Charity's "rescue" by Mr. Royall is an ironic, ambiguous turn on the traditional Gothic heroine's return to the safe and socially acceptable world of marriage and home with her hero. The inequality of wills involved and Charity's total exhaustion in the face of Royall's patriarchal pressure revise traditional Gothic texts in which the heroine willingly and happily abandons her dark journey into the self for the sake of romantic love. Charity accepts Royall's help initially because she feels relief that "someone was near her in the awful emptiness" (*S* 265). From there on, until she wakes up in the hotel room, married, she is described as silent and apathetic. "Half unconsciously" she enters Mrs. Hobart's kitchen, surrendering to "complete passiveness . . . conscious only of the pleasant animal sensations of warmth and rest" (268–69, ellipsis mine). When Royall asks Charity to marry him and she struggles weakly to speak, he silences her by providing the patriarchal answer, "Do you know what you really want? I'll tell you. You want to be took home and took care of. And I guess that's all there is to say" (271).

Reading *Summer* in the context of Wharton's Gothic short stories makes it difficult to see Royall as simply a benevolent patriarch who saves Charity from prostitution (Waid 116,114). With his drinking, his brooding silences, his dominating restraint on Charity's actions, and his threatening sexuality, he has been and may well continue to be a Gothic tyrant whose "rescue" of Charity is just another act of domination.

Charity's submission to Royall's will at this point echoes Lily's submission to chloral, infancy, and death. As Charity and Royall descend from the Mountain into the valley, Charity slides into a kind of death:

> as they descended through the bare woods there were moments when she lost the exact sense of things, and seemed to be sitting beside her lover with the leafy arch of summer bending over them. But this illusion was faint and transitory. For the most part she had only a confused sensation of slipping down a smooth irresistible current; and she abandoned herself to the feeling as refuge from the torment of thought.
>
> Mr. Royall seldom spoke, but his silent presence gave her, for the first time, a sense of peace and security. She knew that where he was there would be warmth, rest, silence; and for the moment they were all she wanted. She shut her eyes, and even these things grew dim to her. [S 273]

Charity's regression and deathlike oblivion are emphasized when, arriving in Nettleton, "the sense of unreality grew more overpowering" for her, and "she followed Mr. Royall as passively as a tired child" (274). She feels herself to be in a "confused dream," and "everything else in her consciousness grew more and more confused and immaterial, became more and more like the universal shimmer that dissolves the world to failing eyes" (274–75). Although "Mr. Royall's presence began to detach itself with rocky firmness from this elusive background" and she momentarily feels close to him, "these feelings were only brief streaks of light in the grey blur of her physical weakness" (275, 276). That the words of the minister who marries her to Royall have "the same dread sound of finality" as those read at her mother's funeral reiterates that the Charity to whom "something irreparable and overwhelming had happened" before she is overtaken by Royall seems now to be dying (278, 274).

Yet at the same time Charity doesn't die, as Lily does and as she might have had Royall not found her. His "rescue" of her, overpowering though it is, allows Charity the opportunity to continue changing. She neither totally succumbs to passive victimization, thereby negating her Gothic journey to the Mountain/mother, nor becomes a fully realized woman. She becomes only as much as Wharton can manage for her at this point in her fiction. In choosing to use Royall's money to reclaim Lucius's brooch from Dr. Merkle, rather than using it to buy the new clothes that would make her his decorated possession, Charity reasserts her choice to keep her child and chooses to maintain a link "between Harney's child and its unknown father" (288). Even more significantly, when she writes to Harney:

> I'm married to Mr. Royall. I'll always remember you.
> Charity. [289]

the words "flowed from her pen irresistibly" (289). Unlike her earlier struggle with the blank page, when she had no language for her story, these words communicate the "truth" as she now understands it, that she both accepts her marriage to Royall and yet she will not invalidate her past, the memories that she has thought of as "ripening in her blood like sleeping grain" (228).[5] It is also worth noting that Charity doesn't write Harney about her pregnancy. Deliberately staying silent about this information is "an act of defiance," since Charity "makes her statement by not writing what she is expected to write" (Gubar 89).

In keeping her baby—the outcome of her past sexual joy—in taking "the opposite way" from Royall down the street to reclaim her brooch, in finding words for her version of her life that mingle acceptance with assertion, Charity saves herself from oblivion (285). As mother and writer, she is empowered by her courageous plunge into the dark abyss of self-knowledge, because these choices evolved out of her confrontation with overwhelming uncertainties and fears about herself.[6]

Nonetheless, in returning to the red house as Royall's wife, a role she has not willingly chosen, Charity remains a trapped Gothic heroine. The feminine self she represents for Wharton is still restrained by the masculine self, representative of the patriarchal social system. This contradictory ending will be answered by Ellen Olenska's story in *The Age of Innocence*, for Ellen's wise maturity has come in good part from leaving a bad marriage with an overbearing husband and facing the dark terrors of self-awareness, acts that enable her to become her own caretaker.

The year *Summer* was published Wharton traveled to Morocco with Walter Berry and others, a trip indicative of her attraction to "the unexplored, the precivilized, and the dangerous" that her biographers associate with *Summer* (Wolff 268, 270; Lewis, *Biography* 397). Wharton considered the trip a journey beyond the pale of civilization, into "*a country without a guidebook,*" as she puts it in *In Morocco* (3). Her European group was the first to visit the country since the savage massacre of foreign residents only five years before, the first to see a "primitive" society that would soon, Wharton writes contemptuously, be open to "the banalities and promiscuities of modern travel" (viii).

This trip to the "vast unknown," as she referred to Morocco, reinforced by her emotional and psychological breakthroughs around this time, may well have been incentives for Wharton to go deeper into her internal "unknown" in the "Beatrice Palmato" fragment, written between 1918 and 1919.[7] "Beatrice Palmato" does not at first glance appear to be a Gothic tale. The unpublished piece has two unassimilated parts: a matter-of-fact plot summary telling of the tragic effects of incest on a woman and her daughters and an erotic description of oral sex between the woman's husband and their youngest daughter.

Tellingly, Wharton planned to include the work in a collection of short stories entitled *Powers of Darkness*, for "Beatrice Palmato" is quintessentially Whartonian Gothic in its portrayal of a woman drawn sexually to male power and of the calamitous results when she submits to it. As in the early Gothic tale "The

House of the Dead Hand," a key element in "Beatrice Palmato" is the entrapment of a woman's spirit and sexuality in art, her being made into art by patriarchal control. But the danger to Beatrice is more complicated, less obvious than it was to Sybilla in "The House of the Dead Hand," because the stylized, erotic encounter between father and daughter in the fragment seems so glowingly pleasurable, with no readily apparent "victim" and "villain." Biographer Wolff even argues that the incest is "in *no way* abhorrent" until social injunctions are invoked in the summary and that Wharton, finding incest "irresistibly attractive," thereby understood the need for social repression (307). The suicides of the women in the family Wolff explains as "violent authorial retaliation for behavior that offends our sense of 'decency' " (308).

Yet Beatrice Palmato, unnurtured by her mother, her erotic powers "owned" by her father, is no less a Gothic victim than the earlier Sybilla Lombard. Reading "Beatrice Palmato" in the context of the early Gothic story, we can see how masterfully Wharton uses her artistry to show the dangerous potential of artistic power, for she so vividly describes female passion that readers are tempted to forget or even dismiss its context. The plot summary shows us that Beatrice's incestuous merging with her wealthy, art-collecting father, however arousing, doesn't develop her own artistic and intellectual powers; rather, it devours them in destroying her autonomy. Even the erotica, when read within the context of Wharton's Gothic, reveals more verbal links to the female victimization in the plot summary than one might otherwise see.

"Beatrice Palmato" is a "found" manuscript, labeled "unpublishable" by Wharton and discovered among her papers by her biographer Cynthia Griffin Wolff. Found manuscripts are a common Gothic device, "remains from the past" that counteract the obliteration of time, distance the manuscript from the "real" world, and imbue it with mystery and ambiguity (Bayer-Berenbaum 89). Wharton used this device earlier in "Kerfol" to preserve Anne de Cornault's story, and with "Beatrice Palmato" she puts her future readers in the vicarious role of Gothic narrators as they attempt to make sense of a summary and pornographic fragment that don't easily fit together into a unified story.

The formlessness of the manuscript, the fragment related to but seemingly unassimilable into the summary, creates a sense of "unease and uncertainty" in the reader, a disorientation characteristic of Gothic narration.[8] Such reader unease is apparent in R. W. B. Lewis's comment that Wharton "could not conceivably have intended the fragment to be part of 'Beatrice Palmato,' had the story ever been sent to press. It does not really accord with the outline (which planned to *conceal* the incest until the last page), and in any event, no respectable magazine in the world would have published it" (*Biography* 544).

Lewis is probably correct about the unpublishability of "Beatrice Palmato" in Wharton's time, but the patronizing tone of the comment is reminiscent of the condescension of "respectable" North Dormer toward the disreputable

Charity and her "individual adventures" that find no place in her society. As in earlier fiction, especially in Charity's journey to the Mountain in *Summer*, Wharton uses the Gothic in "Beatrice Palmato" to explore the self-knowledge with which respectable members of society, including herself, are uncomfortable. Casting these journeys into the self in the dramatic language and symbolic setting and characterization of the Gothic frees Wharton to enact her deep unease about her life as a woman and the role of art in it.

What is conspicuous about the summary when the reader is alert to Wharton's Gothic motifs is her description of Mr. Palmato as a rich and cultivated collector of art and his daughter as "a musical and artistic child, full of intellectual curiosity, and at the same time very tender and emotional" (Lewis, *Biography* 545). Combine this with Wharton's typical use of the weak mother, in this case one who, despite her concern for her daughter, suffers two nervous breakdowns, spends time in a sanatorium, and then succumbs to madness, and the scene is set for the daughter's absorption by the socially prominent father as an extension of his art collection.[9] The metaphorical sexual control of Professor Lombard over his daughter Sybilla via the Leonardo painting in the early Gothic story "The House of the Dead Hand" has now become literal.

The plot summary tells us that Mr. Palmato is a "half-Levantine, half-Portuguese banker," Wharton's descriptors for the sensual, slightly sinister outsider (Wolff 411). By contrast, his home and the women in his life are consistently "agreeable." He lives in "an agreeable artistic-literary house" in London and in Brighton, his wife is "handsome, shy, silent, but agreeable," and the governess whom Palmato engages for Beatrice and eventually marries after his wife's death is also "good-looking and agreeable" (Lewis, *Biography* 545). What is the artistic and intellectually curious young Beatrice to do in such a family matrix? She does the socially acceptable thing by marrying a "simple-minded country squire with a large property and no artistic or intellectual tastes" and having children (545). But she is clearly not fulfilled by the marriage, either intellectually or, as the erotic fragment reveals, sexually. Having sex with her "handsome, cultivated and accomplished" father is how Beatrice tries to fill her emptiness and achieve his identity (545).

Rather than having her own artistic and intellectual abilities cultivated by this incestuous relationship, the erotic fragment reveals that Beatrice is devoured by the sexual attention of her powerful father and becomes art rather than creates it. The description of the setting for the assignation with her father is stylized erotica: pink-shaded lamps, a fire in the fireplace, a "lustrous black bear-skin rug" spread in front of it scattered with purple velvet cushions (547). Stylized too are the vibrating fibers, the burning lips, the fiery kisses.

When the fragment is read with the plot summary and the earlier Gothic stories in mind, however, the suggestion of victimization in the repetition of "pressing" and "forcing" becomes disturbing. Mr. Palmato is pressing the "secret bud" of his daughter's body, "forcing its tight petals softly apart," first with his fingers, then with his tongue, "pressing apart the close petals, and forcing itself in deeper and deeper." Then her lips are thrust open, her knees "pressed apart," the "secret gates" pressed open (548).[10]

Just as disturbing as the suggestion of force is the description of Beatrice's body as "thirsting." Needy women are in danger of trying to "lose their sense of impotence in worship of the man who gives sexual joy and the possibility of blissful merging" (Perera 162). But in her hunger to "merge with the masculine," such a woman is unable to distinguish between "her unmothered need for the mother and her need for a male partnership" (162, 163). Clearly Beatrice is just such a needy woman, attempting to fill the powerless void of mother love and artistic stimulation with patriarchal authority.

"What is it, my own?" Palmato asks his daughter when she expresses distress at one point during their sexual liaison (Lewis, *Biography* 548). He does indeed "own" his daughter as much as he owns the paintings and tapestries bought on their trip to Paris together. For Beatrice, like Sybilla, cannot escape the destructive power her father has over her, even after Palmato dies and after she bears two children. When, several years later, she one day sees her husband kissing their daughter, who, we are told, is "exquisite, gay, original, brilliant, like her mother," Beatrice screams out, "Don't kiss my child. Put her down! How dare you kiss her?" and grabs the child from his arms. In a mutual epiphany, husband and wife realize the "hidden power" of incest controlling Beatrice that has perpetually come between them (546). Beatrice puts the girl down, goes to her bedroom, and shoots herself.

In collusion with the art connoisseur Mr. Palmato, the artist Edith Wharton makes Beatrice Palmato and her passion into art in the erotic fragment. At the same time, in the plot summary, Wharton shows that such a "need to be filled with patriarchal authority" costs Beatrice her autonomy, her spirit, and eventually her life (Perera 163). The reader/narrator who understands the Gothic story of Beatrice Palmato by putting the fragment and summary together and reading both in the context of Wharton's other Gothic fiction learns that when a woman allows herself to be contained by art and by the "masculine" authoritative self who controls it, she loses everything.

Ellen Olenska, in *The Age of Innocence,* deliberately and consciously resists being made into art, just as she resists being sexually "owned" by a man. Rather than being objectified, she actively sees; rather than being acted upon she acts. Ellen is the woman Charity Royall has the potential to become, a "different" woman, as Newland Archer refers to her at the end of the novel, who has confronted the "Terrible Mother" within and has escaped entrapment by male power. Having survived the abyss, Ellen is richly and lovingly portrayed as a woman coming to accept her maturation.

That Ellen lives as comfortably in a home of her own as she does with her sexuality no doubt reflects Wharton's establishment of two beloved homes of her own as a single woman. Wishing to leave a Paris that she now regarded as "a kind of continuous earthquake of motors, busses, trams, lorries, taxis and other howling and swooping and colliding engines," Wharton found Pavillon Colombe in St. Brice-sous-Foret, outside Paris, in 1917 (Lewis, *Biography* 419–20). She was delighted that the estate had been named after two actress sisters of erotic fame "installed there" by their lovers around the mid-1700s, and she immediately returned its name to Pavillon Colombe from the more prosaic "Jean-Marie," as it had later been called (420). Enthusiastically claiming its female past and making it her own, Wharton built, shaped, and planted her own environment out of "the pathetic wilderness" that the house and grounds had become (Lubbock, "Memoirs"). "I saw the house, and fell in love with it in spite of its dirt and squalor," she reminisces in *A Backward Glance*. "As soon as I was settled in it peace and order came back into my life" (363).

Ste. Claire du Vieux Chateau, overlooking Hyères and the Mediterranean, was equally dear to Wharton. Like Pavillon Colombe, it had a female past, as a convent for nuns of the order of Ste. Claire, built within the walls of an old château (Lewis, *Biography* 421). Upon leasing Ste. Claire in 1919, Wharton began a massive renovation project of the long-abandoned house and its "tangled wilderness," just as she had with Pavillon Colombe (Lubbock, "Memoirs"). The home quickly became a part of herself. As she wrote to her close friend Royall Tyler, "I am thrilled to the spine . . . *Il y va de mon avenir;* and I feel as if I were going to get married—to the right man at last!" (Lewis, *Biography* 421, ellipsis mine). Wharton had found, and claimed, her own ruin. Complete with crenelated walls, the gray stone castlelike structure jutting out from the rocky hillside became the locus for her embrace of the ancient past. Robert Norton, her frequent companion at Ste. Claire, writes that on a car trip down from Paris, as they neared Hyères, Wharton conveyed "her own sense of being on holy ground. For her no corner of Mediterranean lands, with such blessings of climate, fertility and scenery, had played so continuous a role in European history. Phoenicians and Greeks had come to trade and settled; the Romans had made it the richest province of their Empire—this was the Provincia par excellence, the true Provence, living still as it had lived for two thousand years and more, taking no heed of the artificial life of its coast-line, the cosmopolitan Riviera, the very name of which she hated" (Lubbock, "Memoirs").

At the same time that the chateau embodied an ancient past, it was also her "beloved Ste. Claire," her "blessed place," her "funny house," as much her own claim of self as Ellen Olenska's "funny little house" on West Twenty-third Street. Just as Ellen values the gift of being alone there, so Wharton now relished that gift: "Back again after eight months away. Oh, the joy of being alone—alone; of walking about in the garden of my soul!" (Notebook 1924–34). Pavillon Colombe, too, provided rich solitude: "How it clears my soul to be alone, as I have been now for a week. The sediment deposited by others sinks to the bottom, and leaves me with myself" (Notebook, 1924–34). It is just such an ability to face and even relish her aloneness, gained from facing the Medusa, her dark inner life, that most characterizes Ellen Olenska.

In the evolution of Wharton's Gothic, *The Age of Innocence* contains several triumphant revisions of the Gothic paradigm. Ellen is the most obvious revision, a woman who confronts, as Lily cannot and Charity partially does, her inner darkness and then has the maturity and strength to control her own life rather than being controlled. Another revision is that the "villain" is eviscerated, his power canceled by a wave of Ellen's angry hand. The last and equally daring change is the journey of the masculine self, Newland Archer, into the abyss of self-understanding. In coming to a degree of peace with femininity in her portrayal of Ellen, Wharton also evolves a masculine self who goes from controlling representative of social structure and possessor of art and women to a questioner of those values. Most critics of the novel focus primarily on Archer. Wolff, for instance, believes Ellen is just a catalyst in the process of Archer's development to become authentically himself (314). Consideration of the palimpsestic Gothic text in *The Age of Innocence* reveals that Ellen's process of individuation is equally significant.

When Ellen Olenska arrives in America, she has already looked at the Gorgon, the terrifying monster/woman within who "dries up one's tears" (*AI* 291). She has "opened my eyes too," Ellen adds, as she explains to Newland why she will not run away with him (293). "It's a delusion to say that she blinds people. What she does is just the contrary—she fastens their eyelids open, so that they're never again in the blessed darkness" (293). The implicit contrast between Ellen's "powerful female gaze" at the Medusa and Perseus's evasive mirrored glance is a tribute to her courage (Showalter, "American Female" 135).

Yet Ellen's rhetorical comment about her transformative experience—"Isn't there a Chinese torture like that? There ought to be"—captures her understandable ambivalence about self-honesty and awareness (*AI* 293). Having once faced the abyss, the terrifying loss of self and support as one has known it, and the evolving new understanding of oneself and one's place in the world, one can't be innocently, unknowingly blind again.[11] Wharton had earlier acknowledged, in "The Letters," a short story written in 1910, the strength and maturity it takes to face the awareness signified by the Medusa: "It was horrible to know too much; there was always blood in the foundations. Parents 'kept things' from children—protected them from all the dark secrets of pain and evil. And was any life livable unless it were thus protected? Could anyone look in the Medusa's face and live?" (Lewis, *CSS* 2:204).

Because such awareness gained from looking the Medusa in the face is so threatening and alienating, Ellen initially tries to cast off the responsibility of being the cultured, sexual, knowing woman she has been in Europe. She returns home to New York City, she tells Newland, because "I want to forget everything else, to become a complete American again." "I want to feel cared for and safe." "I want to cast off all my old life." "I want to wipe out all the past" (*AI* 62, 72, 106, 107). Her return to her family is, she hopes, a lapse into oblivion, a state of pre-Oedipal childhood in which she can shed the independent self that has caused her isolation and pain. She hopes to "escape from freedom," to live in what Existentialists would call "bad faith," exchanging self-realization for a less authentic existence as "en-soi," an object-self, defined and directed by those collected around her (Donovan, *Feminist Theory* 22).[12]

The ramifications of Ellen's decision to return to New York society are immediately clear to the reader. Our first view of her is as an object studied through the opera glasses of Lawrence Leffert. Upon his exclamation she is studied by all the men in the opera box, the disapproving town fathers.[13] Being other-defined, which is implicit in Ellen's wish to cast off her old self, means being seen as a Lacanian Other, an object of fantasy (Lacan 50). Ellen will henceforth continue to be watched and pointed to. Her dark blue velvet gown, her stroll with Julius Beaufort on Fifth Avenue, and her honesty are all evidence that she is the objectionable and objectified Other.

Unlike Sybilla and the Duchess in Gothic situations before her, Ellen has already escaped from being made into an art object when she leaves her marriage to her "awful brute" of a husband Count Olenski, "a half-paralyzed white sneering fellow" who "when he wasn't with women . . . was collecting china. Paying any price for both" (*AI* 13, ellipsis mine). Ellen was surrounded by art at the Olenski mansion, and the fact that "her portrait has been painted nine times" is an eerie reminder of Browning's "My Last Duchess" and the Duchess in "The Duchess at Prayer," whose equally "noble" husband replaces her with a plaster replica (161). Indeed, the rumor is that Count Olenski kept Ellen "practically a prisoner" until she leaves his control (38). She maintains her independent mobility in New York by living where she chooses, going to parties at Mrs. Lemuel Struther's as she chooses and, when she becomes too uncomfortably the center of attention, leaving New York when she chooses. Compared to Lily's and Charity's dependence on others, and the ramifications of that vulnerability on their ability to act, Ellen's independence and freedom of movement give her control over her life that Lily and Charity never possess over theirs.

Beaufort is potentially the bully "villain" to Ellen that Count Olenski has been. Dominating others with "his easy arrogant way" and his "usual half-sneering smile," "his habits were dissipated, his tongue was bitter, his antecedents were mysterious" (28, 211, 17). "Tall and red-faced, scrutinizing the women with his arrogant stare" or striding around with a floridness that seemed "heavy and bloated," Beaufort recalls earlier Gothic bullies, Mr. Brympton in "The Lady's Maid's Bell," the Duke in "The Duchess at Prayer," the Count in "Kerfol," Trenor in *The House of Mirth* (181–82, 210). His villainy is neutralized by Ellen, however. Unlike Mrs. Beaufort, who, "dressed like an idol, hung with pearls," seems to have acquiesced to being a bought woman and a piece of decorated art, Ellen never allows Beaufort to be more than an entertaining diversion (17). Newland considers Ellen to be Beaufort's "victim," who will be charmed by him "even though it were against her will," because "his view of life, his tone, his attitude, were merely a coarser reflection of those revealed in Count Olenski's letter" trying to lure back his wife (137). But Newland doesn't yet understand the strong core of self Ellen has that gives her the cool self-assurance to dismiss Beaufort when he pushes to be more than entertainment and that helps her evade the restraint of counts and dukes who have kept women in the Gothic stories powerless.

Ellen's willingness and ability to speak honestly about those who impinge on her are another way in which she avoids becoming a passive object. The leering New York society members appear to her to be in "knickerbockers and pantalettes" (15); the van der Luydens' Duke, who thinks she is "the handsomest girl in the room," she calls "the dullest man" she has ever met (64, 61); Beaufort's "extraordinarily large bouquet of crimson roses, with a knot of purple pansies at their base," Ellen angrily calls "ridiculous" (157, 163). Of her female "protectors," who want her to stay silent about her life and within the strict parameters of socially acceptable behavior, she cries out, "The real loneliness is living among all these kind people who only ask one to pretend!" (75).

Ellen's self-possession derives from having gone into the depths of herself and having experienced the death of the unaware person she was before the journey. Unlike Lily Bart, whose stationery says "Beyond!" but who can't get there without literally dying, Ellen has experienced the nothingness that precedes awakening in the spiritual quest and has returned to life with "a deeper, resonant awareness" of herself and her relationship to others in her life (*HM* 249; Perera 143). She has, in a sense, given birth to herself and become her own mother. Carol Christ discusses the "*new naming* of self and world" that often accompanies this rebirth, this awakening, a naming that reflects "wholeness, a movement toward overcoming the dualisms of self and world, body and soul, nature and spirit, rational and emotional" (13).

In a first edition copy of *The Age of Innocence* presented to Katherine Cornell, who played Ellen in the 1928 stage rendition of the novel, Wharton wrote, "With admiration and gratitude to Katherine Cornell, whose art has given new life to the wistful ghost of Ellen Olenska. EW July 1929." Wharton's reference to Ellen as a ghost supports the character's own comments about herself as having died and returned to a spirit life. When Newland mentions that she has been away a long time, Ellen answers "Oh, centuries and centuries; so long . . . that I'm sure I'm dead and buried, and this dear old place is heaven" (*AI* 15, ellipsis mine). Later, before they are reunited, Newland remembers Ellen as simply "the most plaintive and poignant of a line of ghosts" (208). When she subsequently tries to explain her inner journey confronting the Gorgon to Newland, her explanation "seemed to come from depths of experience beyond his reach" (291). As she acknowledges, "You've never been beyond. And *I* have. . . . And I know what it looks like there" (294, ellipsis mine).[14]

It is just such an internal strength that strikes Newland about Ellen, a quality both mysterious and enthralling. There is about her, not youthful prettiness, but "the mysterious authority of beauty, a sureness in the carriage of the head, the movement of the eyes, which, without being in the least theatrical, struck him as highly trained and full of a conscious power" (*AI* 58). She looks at him with "eyes so deep," "meditative eyes," and possesses, he feels, the "mysterious faculty of suggesting tragic and moving possibilities outside the daily run of experience," possibilities he yearns to know but can't (70, 113).

Ellen's "passionate honesty" and "conscious power," the by-products of having faced her fundamental being, allow her, while she is back in New York society, to stay receptive to values not her own while remaining strong against the absorbing pull of collective standards (315, 58). Having experienced nothingness, she is also able to be alone, in fact relishes it. As she explains to Newland, part of "the blessedness" of her "funny house" is being alone in it as long as her friends keep her from feeling lonely (71, 70). The mature self-acceptance implied by this feeling, that one enjoys oneself *and* the company of others, is echoed by Wharton's own comments to Mary Berenson after Berenson's nervous breakdown. The "only cure," Wharton wrote her, is "to make one's centre of life inside of one's self, not selfishly or excludingly, but with a kind of unassailable serenity—to decorate one's inner house so richly that one is content there, glad to welcome any one who wants to come and stay, but happy all the same in the hours when one is inevitably alone" (Lewis, *Biography* 413).

Ellen's story in *The Age of Innocence* is of her realization that she *cannot* cast off the mature self she has become, cannot "wipe out all the past" and live in blissful oblivion as she initially thinks she wants to (*AI* 107). Unlike the motherless Lily Bart in *The House of Mirth*, who never loses her longing for oblivion, the motherless Ellen is supported in her transitional period of neediness by two surrogate mothers, her Aunt Medora and her grandmother Catherine. Their attentiveness and affection enable her to reclaim her mature role as "pour-soi," a changing, self-defining individual, and to avoid seeking self-worth and power through a man (Donovan, *Feminist Theory* 119–22). The two older women provide her with a strong female heritage, for they are models of untraditional, even eccentric womanhood. They encourage self-reliance and intriguing individuality in Ellen rather than the restrained "factitious purity" typical of Old New York women (*AI* 43). And as in the best mothering, Medora and Catherine allow Ellen to outgrow them, to surpass them in self-knowledge and initiative. Until Ellen reaches this point they provide the financial and emotional support that allows her to nurture herself. In terms of the Gothic text as Wharton is developing it, the two women are living, humorous amalgams of the mythical mothers, Medusa and the "Great Mother."

Ellen has acquired her individuality in part from her eccentric aunt Medora Manson, who raises her after her parents die. On the one hand it is ironic that Medora's name is only two letters shy of being Medusa, for she is a deflated, enfeebled version of that fierce, snake-headed woman, a Medusa *manqué*: "long, lean, and loosely put together . . . clad in raiment intricately looped and fringed, with plaids and stripes and bands of plain colour disposed in a design to which the clue seemed missing. Her hair, which had tried to turn white and only succeeded in fading, was surmounted by a Spanish comb and black lace scarf" (156, ellipsis mine). On the other hand, like the Gorgon, Medora has been a powerful influence that Ellen has both learned from and escaped.

Medora provides Ellen with "an expensive but incoherent education, which included 'drawing from the model,' a thing never dreamed of before, and playing the piano in quintets with professional musicians" (57). Under her influence Ellen became "a fearless and familiar little thing, who asked disconcerting questions, made precocious comments, and possessed outlandish arts, such as dancing a Spanish shawl dance and singing Neapolitan love-songs to a guitar" (57). It is an "education" that frees Ellen from expectations and restraint and encourages her to speak fearlessly.

Medora's idiosyncrasies keep her from being trapped by the domestic social system, and she has educated Ellen to be as free. "Repeatedly widowed," Medora is "always coming home to settle down (each time in a less expensive house), and bringing with her a new husband or an adopted child" from whom she invariably becomes estranged; then she "set out again on her wanderings" (56). Her witty advice to her adopted daughter attests to her lifestyle: "Beware of monotony; it's the mother of all the deadly sins" (209).

Medora provides a refreshing antidote to the "domesticity at any cost" of old New York. Yet her wanderings also speak of an inner emptiness, the search of the "incorrigibly romantic," as Ellen calls her, for security outside herself (165). "Poor Medora," Ellen remarks sadly to Newland, "there's always some one she wants to marry" (166). Such romantic dependence makes Medora dangerous. Her predilection for nobility (she uses her first husband's name because he made her a Marchioness) may well have been what influenced Ellen to marry "an immensely rich Polish nobleman of legendary fame," much to her misfortune (57). That same predilection for security and nobility makes Medora believe that Ellen should consider the plea of "poor, mad, foolish Olenski" to return to him and his riches (160).

Ellen's other teacher and surrogate mother is the mammoth living icon Catherine Mingott. Matriarch of the family, Catherine is distinguished by a history, a house, and a body that remove her from society's constraints at the same time that their "difference" grants her social power. Catherine's power in the family and their society derives as much from her inaccessibility as from her personality. She is literally the "Great Mother," her "monstrous obesity" freeing her from the ritual activities of society (3). "The immense accretion of flesh which had descended on her in middle life like a flood of lava on a doomed city had changed her from a plump active little woman with a neatly-turned foot and ankle into something as vast and august as a natural phenomenon. She had accepted this submergence as philosophically as all her other trials, and now, in extreme old age, was rewarded by presenting to her mirror an almost un-wrinkled expanse of firm pink and white flesh, in the centre of which the traces of a small face survived as if awaiting excavation" (25). The image is grotesque but evocative, the matriarch as living mountain, symbol of the "female god-head," the "immobile, sedentary symbol that visibly rules over the land" (Neu-mann 99).

Ellen's authority and independence—when she wants to live alone, when she visits her cousin Regina Beaufort, when she refuses to return to her hus-band—are encouraged by her "Great Mother" Catherine. For Catherine is a renegade, breaking the unwritten rules of her society when she wishes, and she supports her granddaughter Ellen in the same kind of behavior. As she tells Newland, while complaining of the Mingott fear of being different, "I thank my stars I'm nothing but a vulgar Spicer; but there's not one of my own children that takes after me but my little Ellen" (153).

In keeping with Wharton's career-long association of houses with the fe-male body/self, Catherine's cream-colored stone mansion in "an inaccessible wilderness near the Central Park" *is* the woman in that she has designed it to suit herself, not fashion (10). Rather than a threatening, gloomy dwelling, as a house is apt to be in the Gothic stories, Catherine's is threatening only to her New York society. For she has replaced the typical Victorian furniture with Mingott heirlooms and Second Empire frivolity, and she has put her reception room upstairs and her bedroom downstairs, "in flagrant violation of all the New York proprieties" (25).

It is Catherine who takes Ellen into her maternal refuge (Gimbel 134). Cath-erine also supports Ellen when she rents her own home and then provides the money that allows Ellen to return to Europe yet live independently rather than with her husband. When the family pressures Catherine to cut off Ellen's allow-ance and so force her to accept her husband's bribes to return to him, Catherine first capitulates, but then, she tells Newland, "the minute I laid eyes on her, I said: 'You sweet bird, you! Shut you up in that cage again? Never!' " (302).[15]

Like Catherine's home, Ellen's home, which she rents from Medora with Catherine's money, also represents herself, and it too threatens old New York with its eccentricity. But Ellen's "funny house," as she refers to it, is part of the maternal realm that nourishes her (70). With its dilapidation and its location on

West Twenty-third Street beyond social boundaries, the house recalls the dilapidated brown house where Charity and Lucius have their world apart in *Summer*.

We learn through Newland's response to the home that it is intimate and sensuous, like Ellen herself. During his first visit there he is led through a narrow hall into a low firelit drawing room that has a "faded shadowy charm" and a "vague pervading perfume" in the air like "the scent of some far-off bazaar, a smell made up of Turkish coffee and ambergris and dried roses" (67, 69). The female iconography of the narrow hall opening into low firelit room captures Ellen's comfort with her physical body, a quality that befuddles old New York society. The house, for her, is "like heaven," its "blessedness" deriving from the freedom she feels in it to see whomever she pleases, to speak freely, to weep, to be alone (70, 71). Books are scattered about the room, Newland notes, "a part of the house in which books were usually supposed to be 'out of place' " (102). Unlike the many characters before her, and like Newland himself, who have startling revelations about themselves in libraries, Ellen doesn't split off the intellectual part of herself from the emotional/spiritual/physical parts, as the casual scattering of books in the drawing room suggests.

Newland Archer, who begins his journey into the abyss of self-awareness as a result of knowing and loving Ellen, has several epiphanies in the Archers' Gothic library and in his study "with its rows and rows of books" (40). These realizations play on the mind/heart distinction Newland tries futilely to maintain. The first epiphany in the Gothic library is when he finds himself retorting to Sillerton Jackson that he is "sick of the hypocrisy that would bury alive a woman of her age if her husband prefers to live with harlots" and that women "ought to be free—as free as we are," the latter a comment he later calls a "mad outburst" (39, 80). In the process he is "making a discovery of which he was too irritated to measure the terrific consequences," for like Alice Hartley in "The Lady's Maid's Bell," who finds herself, as if possessed, speaking words she is surprised by, Newland is voicing sentiments distinctly out of character (39). The Gothic language in his comment, "hypocrisy that would bury alive a woman of her age," and in later realizations in his study reminds the reader that Newland is engaged in the same kind of unsettling, frightening Gothic journey into himself that takes the narrator into Ethan Frome's house and Charity to the Mountain.

Later that evening in his book-lined study, Newland realizes that "the case of the Countess Olenska had stirred up old settled convictions and set them drifting dangerously through his mind" (40). One of these convictions is about the nature of marriage itself, for he now understands, "with a shiver of foreboding," that, rather than "passionate and tender comradeship," his marriage would become "a dull association of material and social interests held together by ignorance on the one side and hypocrisy on the other" (41). After spending time with Ellen at her home and then failing to convince May that they should marry quickly, "a haunting horror of doing the same thing every day at the same hour besieged his brain" later in his study (82). It is here also that Newland reads Rossetti's *The House of Life,* which affects him as Ellen and her home do, with its "atmosphere unlike any he had ever breathed in books; so warm, so rich, and yet so ineffably tender, that it gave new and haunting beauty to the most elementary of human passions" (138). *The House of Life* then inspires him to pursue "the vision of a woman who had the face of Ellen Olenska" in his dreams (138). Newland is beginning to unlearn the distinctions between mind and body, intellect and passion.

After his marriage Newland continues to make unsettling discoveries in libraries: that he has been excluded from family discussion about Ellen's destiny; that the self he was before loving Ellen is dead; that, unknown to him, Ellen has been persuaded by the family to return to Europe; that May's pregnancy will prevent him from following Ellen; and that May's deceptive announcement of it to Ellen before she was sure persuaded Ellen to leave New York and him (267, 298, 327, 346). His library is, Newland ruminates years later, "the room in which most of the real things of his life had happened," but by this point Newland remembers only the happy events of family life that have occurred in it rather than the earlier wrenching emotional and psychological discoveries (347).

The ending of *The Age of Innocence* confirms that although Newland has felt as imprisoned by his life as Charity Royall has, and although he comes perilously close to losing his convention-bound self, he steps back from the abyss and sacrifices "the flower of life" that such a transformative experience promises (350). Nonetheless the masculine self that Newland represents in the novel is fundamentally changed by the realizations he has while standing on the edge of the abyss.

Not unlike the possessorship over their art/women claimed by men in the Gothic short stories, Newland initially feels a "thrill of possessorship" about his fiancee May, who is often referred to as an art piece (4–5). He is "proud of the glances turned on her," and the "simple joy of possessorship" he feels about her at first clears away the confusion Ellen is causing him (79). The sight of May, her face wearing "the vacant serenity of a young marble athlete," temporarily soothes his growing sexual agitation (141). It is her unawareness, he realizes, that gives "her face the look of representing a type rather than a person; as if she might have been chosen to pose for a Civic Virtue or a Greek goddess. The blood that ran so close to her face might have been a preserving fluid rather than a ravaging element" (189).

When, after they are married, May becomes a representative for Newland of "the steadying sense of an unescapable duty," he again feels "the glow of proprietorship that so often cheated him into momentary well-being" as May's "Diana-like aloofness" and "classic grace" bring murmurs of appreciation from onlookers (208, 212, 211). Newland still realizes, however, that the price of May's visual "perfection" is that "not a thought seemed to have passed behind her eyes or a feeling through her heart" (211). Such awareness of the perils of women's role as possessed art is what makes Newland so different from the flat male characters in the Gothic short stories or the men who leer at Lily Bart as the portrait of Mrs. Lloyd in *The House of Mirth*.

Newland's questioning of patriarchal control over women, which begins in the Gothic library with his comment about Ellen's right to freedom, carries him again and again to the edge of a precipice into which he never leaps. Nonetheless, the feelings and thoughts he allows himself about the power-structure conventions he has heretofore taken for granted carry him further in the journey to the feminine/maternal within than any male character before him has gone. When he opens himself to Ellen's spiritual power, he feels "like a wild animal cunningly trapped" as he travels with May from one house to another after their engagement is announced (66). Increasingly his thoughts about his future are expressed in Gothic language: he feels his "fate was sealed" in having to live in a conventional New York house, and he has "a haunting horror of doing the same thing every day at the same hour" when May refuses to alter any of the matrimonial conventions (69, 82). Days after returning home from his interchange with Ellen at Skuytercliff, Newland feels that "the taste of the usual was like cinders in his mouth, and there were moments when he felt as if he were being buried alive under his future" (138).

Such dire observations about his life alternate with moments when he takes refuge in the conventional. As he talks with Ellen about her wish to be free of her marriage, her refusal to explain finds him "pouring out all the stock phrases that rose to his lips in his intense desire to cover over the ugly reality which her silence seemed to have laid bare. . . . Better keep on the surface, in the prudent old New York way, than risk uncovering a wound he could not heal" (110, ellipsis mine). The "reality" he has earlier sought to make others face about Ellen's right to live her own life he now fearfully finds "ugly." When May questions whether he loves someone else but assumes it is his former lover rather than Ellen, Newland is "dizzy with the glimpse of the precipice they had skirted" (149). Though feeling trapped, he can't dive beneath the surface of the conventional.

Once Newland admits his love for Ellen, however, the unaware, habitually conventional man he was dies. When he realizes that his lack of forthrightness has led Ellen to give up the idea of divorce because of his plea that she do so, "the silence that followed lay on them with the weight of things final and irrevocable. It seemed to Archer to be crushing him down like his own gravestone" (170). Newland's marriage ceremony intensifies this suggestion of his death. During it he finds himself several times "adrift far off in the unknown," thinking of Ellen, and then, facing his new wife, "suddenly the same black abyss yawned before him and he felt himself sinking into it, deeper and deeper, while his voice rambled on smoothly and cheerfully" (186, 187).

The description of the wedding is scattered with death images. A spring wind "full of dust" blows, and the scent of lilies on the altar is "almost smothered" by the smell of camphor from old furs (179). Most glaring is Wharton's having used, in the first edition of the novel, the words to the Episcopalian funeral service, "Forasmuch as it hath pleased Almighty God—" rather than those of the marriage service, "Dearly beloved, we are gathered together here—," which she unfortunately corrected in subsequent editions (186). For just as Charity's love affair with Lucius, her journey up the Mountain, and her marriage to Lawyer Royall are laden with images of death because the child self she was has died, and just as Ellen talks of having been "beyond" and being a ghost after giving up the restrained self she was with her husband, so the single Newland, who is "free" to marry the woman he really loves, dies, and a more conflicted and complex man begins a new life.

That Newland's relationship with Ellen has taken him beyond the self he used to be, in spite of his apparently becoming the model society husband, is clear when he sees her again after his wedding. He feels, when he is asked to fetch her from the beach, that he is in a dream, and he senses later that the hypnotically systematic environment of the Welland house is now "unreal and irrelevant," while the brief scene at the beach is "as close to him as the blood in his veins" (219). These responses recall Charity's sense, after making love to Lucius and returning to North Dormer, that she is in "a kind of trance" and "suspended in the void" (*S* 176, 174). Like the dilapidated, deserted house where Charity meets Lucius, with its "rose-bushes run wild" and reminders of a classical past, the seemingly deserted Blenker house to which Newland goes to find Ellen is "a long tumble-down house with white peeling from its clapboards" (*AI* 225). The overgrown box garden full of "rusty rose-bushes encircled a ghostly summer-house of trellis-work that had once been white, surmounted by a wooden Cupid who had lost his bow and arrow but continued to take ineffectual aim" (225).

When Newland finds, not Ellen, but the giggling, flirtatious Miss Blenker in "this [Gothic] place of silence and decay," the painfully ironic contrast between the romantic reunion he expects and the disappointment he experiences, imaged by the unarmed Cupid, is intensified by the reader's memory of the sexual passion Charity and Lucius share in their deserted house (225). In this context Newland's epiphany, that "his whole future seemed suddenly to be unrolled before him; and passing down its endless emptiness he saw the dwindling figure of a man to whom nothing was ever to happen," is profoundly sad, but the realization pushes him to act on what he wants in a way he has never done before (228).

Like Charity journeying up the Mountain to claim the self that has always heretofore been defined by others, Newland journeys to the "wilderness" of Boston, seeking Ellen and the self who loves her (232). Appropriately he has "such a queer sense of having slipped through the meshes of time and space" when he arrives, for his is as much an internal journey as an external one (231). This sense is accentuated by the boat ride with Ellen, which is like "drifting forth into this unknown world" while "everything in the old familiar world of habit was receding" (239). Newland speaks more directly with Ellen during this meeting than he has ever spoken, and he realizes a passion for her that, unlike those "superficially satisfied" with caresses, is "closer than his bones" (245). He experiences a loving self who isn't playing the conventional lover role but instead is "stirred and yet tranquillized" by the balance Ellen has maintained "between their loyalty to others and their honesty to themselves" (248). In Ellen he finds not artful calculation but "unabashed sincerity" (248).

The renewal Newland undergoes during this inward journey fundamentally affects how he responds to his world upon his return to it. Monsieur Rivière's announcement that Newland's family believes Ellen should return to her husband gives Newland "the sense of clinging to the edge of a sliding precipice" as he realizes the "deep tribal instinct" excluding him from family counsel about Ellen's future (254). Now considered an "Other" like Ellen, he perceives his family in a way he has never done before. His disjunction from their way of perceiving Ellen and her decision to remain in America, created by his love for her, now makes him more comfortable living inside himself, where he has built "a kind of sanctuary in which she throned among his secret thoughts and longings" (265). Like Charity's sense, during her relationship with Lucius, that she has been carried away "into a new world, from which, at stated hours, the ghost of her came back to perform certain customary acts, but all so thinly and insubstantially that she sometimes wondered that the people she went about among could see her" (*S* 182), Newland finds his inner world to be the authentic one: "Little by little it became the scene of his real life, of his only rational activities; thither he brought the books he read, the ideas and feelings which nourished him, his judgments and his visions. Outside it, in the scene of his actual life, he moved with a growing sense of unreality and insufficiency, blundering against familiar prejudices and traditional points of view as an absent-minded man goes on bumping into the furniture of his own room. Absent—that was what he was: so absent from everything most densely real and near to those about him that it sometimes startled him to find they still imagined he was there" (*AI* 265).

The more intensely Newland desires Ellen, the more intensely he feels himself "beyond" the life he has lived and the self he once was. "I *am* dead—" he imagines himself saying to May when he experiences the claustrophobia of their life together. "I've been dead for months and months" (298). When he and Ellen decide to consummate their love, Newland looks at the familiar objects in his house "as if he viewed them from the other side of the grave" (316). Aptly, this decision is made in the antiquities section of the Metropolitan Museum, where the guard walks listlessly by like "a ghost stalking through a necropolis" and vanishes down "a vista of mummies and sarcophagi" and where the shelves hold small broken objects of domesticity, for both Ellen and Newland are in an emotional world that is, as Wharton explained her own affair, *"on the hither side"* (314; Lewis, *Biography* 222).

Though Newland realizes, because of his love for Ellen, the soul-crushing limitations of his life in old New York society with a wife he only marginally loves, he remains a captive of the system he represents. He feels both horrified and imprisoned by his realization that Ellen has been persuaded by his wife to return to Europe and that he must, at a family dinner, cordially celebrate her leave-taking. Newland's state of mind at the dinner recalls Lily's delirious terror the night before her death, punctuated by flashes of recognition about her destitute situation, and Charity's terrified flashes of realization about her tenuous relationship with Lucius before she leaves for the Mountain. Newland feels himself "assisting at the scene in a state of odd imponderability, as if he floated somewhere between chandelier and ceiling"; it comes over him "in a vast flash made up of many broken gleams," that his family has presumed he and Ellen are lovers who must be separated (*AI* 338). The deadly power of the social elite he has been part of, "the way of people who dreaded scandal more than disease, who placed decency above courage," makes him feel like "a prisoner in the centre of an armed camp" (338).

The Gothic language suits Newland's intense sensitivity to the nuances of his plight, that he is losing what he knows he wants in his life and that he is paralyzed by the system's power: "a deathly sense of the superiority of implication and analogy over direct action, and of silence over rash words, closed in on him like the doors of the family vault" (339). The determined friendliness of everyone is "as if the guard of the prisoner he felt himself to be were trying to soften his captivity; and the perception increased his passionate determination to be free" (342).

A baby keeps Newland from being free just as it does Charity. But while Charity refuses to use her pregnancy as a means to force Lucius into marriage, Newland allows May to use hers as a weapon to prevent him from leaving her for Ellen. Wharton suggests that Charity's pregnancy helps give her a sense of rebirth, that she respects and understands herself and her past because of it. May, however, represents what Mary Daly calls "feminine antifeminism," the kind of woman whose internalized "patriarchal presence" leads her to look upon women like Ellen who threaten the power structure as a threat to herself (52). Daly's observation that "this divisiveness among women is an extension of the duality existing within the female self" captures well the role May serves for Wharton in *The Age of Innocence* as a representative of her past discomfort with female power (52). May is never as unaware and innocent as Newland believes she is, and her wish to save her marriage has to be respected, but she is not the frank, passionate, creative woman Ellen is.

Ellen and Newland are feminine and masculine selves that Wharton's Gothic has helped her create, willing to face the abyss of their inner darkness and to try to act on the awareness it brings. At the same time Wharton provides enough parallels between Ellen and Newland to encourage our seeing them as a unified fe/male self. They share a mutual impatience with old New York's avoidance of the "unpleasant," an interest in literature and art, an admiration for houses that deviate from the customary style, and similar views about a woman's right to freedom. Both also express the effect of their love for one another similarly, Ellen that "I shan't be lonely now" and Newland that "he should never again feel quite alone" (173, 245).

The most vivid parallels, however, are those between the characters and their creator, suggesting that they are *her* fe/male self at this point in her life.[16] Newland's old New York society, with its inarticulateness, its fear of the different and creative, is Wharton's society as a girl; his age, fifty-seven, is Wharton's when she wrote much of *The Age of Innocence*. His adult life as "a good citizen," dedicating himself to philanthropic, municipal, and artistic movements, reflects Wharton's own life in France (349).

Wharton is most reflected in Ellen, however. The young "bold brown Ellen Mingott," a "fearless and familiar little thing, who asked disconcerting questions, made precocious comments, and possessed outlandish arts, such as dancing a Spanish shawl dance and singing Neapolitan love-songs to a guitar," sounds like the young Edith Jones, who, with her energy, precocity, and verbal exuberance, was also a "fearless and familiar little thing" who even learned the shawl dance (*AI* 57; Lewis, *Biography* 17).

Ellen's home as an adult in New York City is a composite of Wharton's own homes. Ellen lives on West Twenty-third Street, as Wharton did as a child. Like Ellen's scattering of new books in her living room, Wharton's "petit salon" in her Rue de Varenne apartment in Paris had a "proliferation of books on tables, wherever they could be piled or ranked" (Lubbock, *Portrait* 80). Ellen's reference to the "blessedness" of her "funny house" and her joy in being alone in it echoes Wharton's comments about her home in Hyères as "my funny little house" and "this blessed place" in letters to friends Sara Norton and Margaret Chanler. After being away from Hyères she writes in her 1924–1934 Notebook, "Back again after 8 months away. Oh, the joy of being alone—alone" (Beinecke).

Ellen's plaintive description of the "miserable little country" of infidelity, "smaller and dingier and more promiscuous" than the world they leave, when Newland suggests they run away together, echoes Wharton's own plaintive outburst in 1911 to Charles du Bos about "the poverty, the miserable poverty, of any love that lies outside of marriage" (Lewis, *Biography* 317–18). Ellen's separation from her husband and her expatriation to Paris, with its "incessant stir of ideas, curiosities, images and associations" and, above all, "good conversation," were Wharton's choices (*AI* 362).

These similarities between Wharton's own biography and the details of Ellen's and Newland's life accentuate the pattern Wharton has been developing in the Gothic text of her novels, the main female and male characters as "feminine" and "masculine" parts of a self, struggling to understand one another and learn ways of being that repress neither. Wharton's last completed novels, *Hudson River Bracketed* and *The Gods Arrive,* with all their faults, nonetheless undertake the courageous task of creating a female and male character in Halo and Vance who attempt to deconstruct their gender identities.

No doubt her portrayals of Charity Royall and Ellen Olenska encouraged Wharton to create female characters in the Gothic short stories of this period whose sexuality is a force to be reckoned with. Allusions to witches and witchcraft in "The Young Gentlemen" and "Bewitched," as in the later "All Souls'," counter patriarchal ways of knowing with the matriarchal. The emotional timidness and fear of awareness of the male characters in "The Young Gentlemen," "Miss Mary Pask," and "Dieu d'Amour" are egregious and sometimes almost laughable. But Wharton builds on Newland Archer's courageous attempts, in *The Age of Innocence,* to face the lack of control and the disorientation that self-awareness brings by portraying Orrin Bosworth's comfort with the intuitive and mysterious in "Bewitched."

"The Young Gentlemen," written three years after *The Age of Innocence* was published, concentrates especially on the shame men feel about their feminine/maternal self and their rigid determination to keep suppressed the vulnerability that this self engenders. The story uses and revises elements common to Wharton's Gothic, perhaps the most familiar of which is the mysterious house. In "The Young Gentlemen" the house is an isolated "foursquare and stern" one owned by Waldo Cranch, "built of a dark mountain granite" and standing at "the far end of the green, where the elms were densest and the village street faded away between blueberry pastures and oak woods" (*HB* 38). The remoteness of the house in Harpledon, a small New England town that prides itself on its remoteness from modernity and change, encourages the reader to expect that the house hides a secret. The expectation is tickled by the detail that all the front doors in the town are kept unlocked except Cranch's, which his servant Catherine keeps "chained and bolted" (50). We know Cranch is suppressing his essential nature and is being supported in the suppression by his servant.

Another familiar element is the unaware male narrator, although this one is especially obtuse and supercilious about kinds of knowledge other than his own, particularly the intuitive.[17] This is quickly apparent when he discounts the observations of his old aunt Lucilla Selwick, who, he says, "remembered heaps and heaps of far-off things; but she almost always remembered them wrongly" (34). Though he concludes, "It will be seen that Aunt Lucilla's reminiscences . . . were neither accurate nor illuminating," we eventually learn that exactly the reverse is true (36, ellipsis mine). Lucilla's memory of Waldo Cranch moving into town with a black-and-white hobbyhorse on top of his belongings is accurate, just as her story of a woman's premonition of her husband's death is probably true. The narrator's "ancient relative," as he refers to her, "propped up in her bed and looking quietly into the unknown while all the village slept," is the town's "witch," the source of ancient female wisdom and (in)sight that the narrator can't or, more accurately, won't accommodate into his frame of reference (60).

Characteristically, the narrator is irritated and condescendingly scornful when Mrs. Durant, a close companion of Waldo Cranch, recounts Cranch's horrified anger at having a picture of the back of his house's wing appear in an illustrated magazine and when she empathizes with his response. "That there should be grown-up men who could lose their self-command over such rubbish, and women to tremble and weep with them!" he sneers. "The truth was, I had never thought of Cranch as likely to lose his balance over trifles. He had never struck me as unmanly" (55). The narrator's reaction neatly encapsulates his stereotypical views of men and women, views that the story undermines.

The narrator is also reticent about going to Cranch's house with Mrs. Durant, when she urges him to accompany her because she fears that Cranch has done something desperate. That the narrator is in his library among his books when she arrives at his house reminds us once again of this prevalent theme in Wharton's Gothic, the limitation of intellect that prevents one from respecting other kinds of knowledge. Not surprisingly the narrator recoils when he sees Waldo Cranch's two dwarf twin sons, the secret Cranch has been hiding in the wing of his house. Although the narrator is named one of the guardians of the twins when Cranch commits suicide, he never sees them again and hopes he never will, "certainly I shall not if I can help it," he tells us in the flashback that begins the story (33). He admits that "most men are cowards about calamities of that sort, the irremediable kind that have to be faced anew every morning." "It takes a woman to shoulder such a lasting tragedy," he concludes, but he discounts Mrs. Durant's doing just such accepting (72). "Would you have believed it? She wanted it—the horror, the responsibility and all," he recounts incredulously. "I believe she saw Cranch's sons every day. I never went back there" (77). The non sequitur with which he ends the story, "Women are strange. I am their other guardian; and I have never yet had the courage to go down to Harpledon and see them," clearly reveals his obtuseness about his emotional cowardice (78).[18] He both refuses to integrate emotional demands and "difference" into his life and refuses to credit women for their greater courage in doing so.

The narrator's fear of vulnerability, of the emotional engagement that the house interior elicits, is reminiscent of the narrator's in the earlier story "Kerfol" and is also a characteristic of Waldo Cranch, the protagonist of "The Young Gentlemen." Cranch shares the traits of the Gothic "villains" in earlier stories. Descended from a prosperous merchant family, he is now part of the social power structure in his town. As a painter, he is the socially prominent yet controlled artist. Though "hail and hearty and social," the cordiality is "studied" (36, 38). Most apparent are qualities he shares with his house: "aloofness," "isolation," and "remoteness" (41, 42). His punctiliousness and self-control are sternly self-imposed. Like the Duke in "The Duchess at Prayer" and Yves de Cornault in "Kerfol," Cranch is keeping the vulnerable and loving part of his life suppressed.

Rather than enacting this suppression by holding a woman captive, as the Duke and Yves de Cornault do, however, Cranch is hiding his dwarf twin sons, "two tiny withered men, with frowning foreheads under their baby curls, and heavy-shouldered middle-aged bodies" (64). Dressed in "old-fashioned round jackets and knickerbockers," they are building a house of blocks that falls to ruins when they are frightened by the appearance of the narrator and Mrs. Durant in the windowless wing of the Cranch house (63).

One of the pervasive motifs of modern female Gothic is "discovering a truth in 'a dark secret center' and giving it grotesque form," a form that in turn serves as a "monstrous image of self" (Kahane, "The Maternal Legacy" 244, 245). Wharton's use of hidden dwarf twins in "The Young Gentlemen" complicates both this motif and her evolving consideration of femininity and masculinity in her Gothic fiction.

Usually such "signifiers of negative identity—the freak, the dwarf, the cripple—that abound in Female Gothic" are expressions of women's "disturbed sense of self" and "feeling of lack or estrangement," a sense that they are "congenitally impaired" (Kahane, "The Maternal Legacy" 244). In having Cranch blame his Spanish great-grandmother for his sons' deformity, Wharton suggests that he is refusing to claim his own sense of impairment and lack.

His is a classic case of blaming the victim, for his great-grandmother, a rich merchant's daughter who was herself physically deformed, was jilted by one man who had been commissioned, sight unseen, to marry her, and then is essentially sold off to Cranch's great-grandfather, who receives a "big sum" for his shipping business in return. Cranch's maid Catherine tells the narrator and Mrs. Durant the story of the woman's miserable life in America: "the poor misbuilt thing, it seems, couldn't ever rightly get over the hurt to her pride, nor get used to the cold climate, and the snow and the strange faces; she would go about pining for the orange flowers and the sunshine; and though she brought her husband a son, I do believe she hated him, and was glad to die and get out of Harpledon" (HB 74–75). Significantly, the other person who has told this ancestor's story is the narrator's Aunt Lucilla Selwick, who, he says, always assumes an elegiac tone in talking about the "poor thing" who "never forgot the sunshine and orange blossoms" (37). Rather than being sympathetic like Lucilla, however, Catherine voices her master's misogynist rage about "that old Spanish she-devil" who "brought the curse on us" (71).

Only Lucilla the wisewoman, the purveyor of uncanny knowledge, recognizes the pain and anger of the woman who survives as a painting on Cranch's wall: "very short and thickset, with a huge wig of black ringlets, a long harsh nose, and one shoulder perceptibly above the other," the image of a "swart virago" in the narrator's words (37). Physically "unwomanly," even witchlike, in appearance, she is the ultimate "Other" in the patriarchy of Cranch's family. A foreigner used for her wealth, she is then despised and feared as an Eve-like originator of the family's "curse," their stunted progeny. Although Catherine says that Cranch despises his great-grandfather more than he hated "the Spanish woman," because the great-grandfather married "that twisted stick for her money, and put her poisoned blood in us!" the hatred is expressed in terms of the woman's body, "that twisted stick" and "her poisoned blood" (75).

In this powerful signification, the family history is built on the domination of a woman, treated as a commodity, whose rage, despair, and humiliation stunt her individuality. Such an "unwomanly woman" is considered evil incarnate. Yet ignoring her victimization results in the stunting of the men who carry on such a history. The two frail "little creatures" in their old-fashioned clothing tell us there is no future in such outmoded views of femininity and masculinity, just as their collapsed house of blocks visualizes the collapsed masculine self Cranch has tried to maintain by keeping his sons a secret and hating the female body they represent for him (65). The horror of grotesque beings, after all, is not that they are otherworldly but that they are "disturbingly familiar" (Bayer-Berenbaum 62).[19]

In keeping the door to the Cranch house bolted and promising to keep Cranch's secret, the servant Catherine upholds the patriarchal tradition, a culture that suppresses emotional reality, feels shame about vulnerability, despises femaleness.[20] Cranch's servant also provides the narrator and Mrs. Durant with the illogical reason for Cranch's suicide after the twins' existence threatens to become public knowledge: "He rushed out and died sooner than have them seen, the poor lambs" (*HB* 67–68). Of course rather than preventing the twins from being seen, Cranch's suicide only saves him the emotional pain of having to live with the experience. Like the narrator, Cranch is unable to face this assault on his sense of a coherent male self and world that the dwarfs represent.[21]

Mrs. Durant, who has been Cranch's close companion and would-be lover, also has, like Catherine, supported him in his accustomed role as unemotional town father. "I'm always sorry to see him lose his self-control," she tells the narrator after Cranch leaves her house furious because the architect who sneaks in to sketch the back of his house, and therefore intrude on his secret life, is the one she originally brought to meet Cranch (53). Still, she has the courage and will to enter Cranch's house after she gets a mysterious "good-bye" note from him and, like Catherine, responds to the dwarfs with sympathy rather than horror, as the narrator does. While the narrator plans never to see them again, admitting with inadvertent irony that "I hadn't the heart to go to that dreadful house again," Mrs. Durant devotes her life to their care (73). Although she seems to have played a traditionally compliant female role in her relationship with Cranch, her immediate sympathy for his deformed children suggests that she has sensed Cranch's vulnerability despite his attempt to hide it. Strong individuals, "The Young Gentlemen" suggests, incorporate their inner life and female heritage into their daily lives, while those steeped in the patriarchy turn from both in fear and horror.

The male narrator of "Miss Mary Pask" bears a strong resemblance to the one in "The Young Gentlemen"—emotionally timid, condescending toward women, determined to repress an encounter with his deepest fears. This gem of a Gothic story, however, humorously and incisively portrays masculinity incapacitated by a confrontation with the feminine/maternal within.

As in "The Young Gentlemen," the narrator frames his story in "Miss Mary Pask" with confessions of his emotional and psychological timidity, though he is more candid than the earlier narrator about his fearfulness and his attempts to repress his traumatic experience. "I could not have spoken of the affair before," he says of his inability to tell Grace Bridgeworth about seeing her sister Mary Pask, "not till I had been rest-cured and built up again at one of those wonderful Swiss sanatoria where they clean the cobwebs out of you. I could not even have written to her—not to save my life. The happenings of that night had to be overlaid with layer upon layer of time and forgetfulness before I could tolerate any return to them" (HB 1–2).

Like Waldo Cranch in "The Young Gentlemen," the narrator is an artist. While painting in Brittany, he remembers his friend Grace asking him to pay a visit to her older sister Mary, who lives alone there. The narrator is sensitive enough to perceive Grace's hypocritical concern for Mary, with whom she had been very intimate before her marriage but whom she has not bothered to see since then. As he sardonically puts it, between Mary and Grace lay "the inevitable gulf between the feelings of the sentimentally unemployed and those whose affections are satisfied," and now "Grace was one of the sweet conscientious women who go on using the language of devotion about people whom they live happily without seeing" (4–5). Yet the narrator is also brutishly condescending toward Mary, whom he recalls with "her round flushed face, her innocent bulging eyes, her old-maidish flat decorated with art tidies, and her vague and timid philanthropy" (4). He cruelly dismisses her as one of "hundreds of other dowdy old maids, cheerful derelicts content with their innumerable little substitutes for living" (4). His sensitivity takes him into his encounter with the feminine/maternal self that Mary represents, and his arrogance, bred of fear, prevents him from assimilating it into his life.

The journey to Mary's house/body on the sea near the *Baie des Trépassés*, the Bay of the Dead, has all the characteristics of a descent into the abyss. As soon as they set out at sunset, the narrator and his driver of the rented wagon are enveloped in disorienting dense fog, "a wet blackness impenetrable to the glimmer of our only lamp" (6). As in all Gothic and uncanny experiences, the ordinary appears threatening; when the pall occasionally lifts, the feeble light "would drag out of the night some perfectly commonplace object—a white gate, a cow's staring face, a heap of roadside stones—made portentous and incredible by being thus detached from its setting, capriciously thrust at us, and as suddenly withdrawn" (7). Afterward the darkness grows "three times as thick," and the narrator's sense of descending a gradual slope becomes "that of scrambling down a precipice" (7).

A hint of the narrator's sensitivity to the eroticism of the experience in which he is involved is his description of the sea. He speaks of its "hungry voice I heard asking and asking, close below us. . . . The sea whined down there as if it were feeding time, and the Furies, its keepers, had forgotten it" (9, ellipsis mine).[22] His allusion to the Furies, symbols of female rage and the erotic feminine/maternal, should prepare him for his encounter with Mary Pask, but instead he resists the connection by persisting in his past view of her, "But what could have induced the rosy benevolent Mary Pask to come and bury herself there?" (9).

The unconscious irony of the image "bury" becomes conscious when the narrator enters Mary's house. An old woman carrying a candle, presumably a servant, greets him and then leaves, plunging him into "total darkness" and "complete silence," which "closed in again like the fog" (11). These death sensations no doubt trigger the narrator's memory that Mary Pask had died the previous autumn and that he had even read a cable to Grace concerning her sister's wish to be buried in her garden. Lest such a major memory lapse seem incredible, Wharton has the narrator confess his own dismay that this is the second instance of such forgetfulness and that it is perhaps a symptom of a previous illness. With this setting and context—a weak, frightened man entering a dead woman's dark house on a precipice above the sea—the reader of Wharton's Gothic is prepared, even if the narrator isn't, for his confrontation with his deepest fears about the forbidding female body.

When Mary appears, the encounter is both hilarious and pathetic. The narrator is groping around for a match, feeling an increased sense of "irritated helplessness," when he sees on the stairs "a figure in white shading a candle with one hand and looking down," bearing "a strange resemblance" to the

Mary Pask he used to know (13). Mary Pask will continue to "look down" on the narrator by toying with his alarm that he is conversing with a ghost, and in significant ways she does only resemble the woman she was.

As the narrator superstitiously blows out one of the three candles she lights, Mary chuckles when she says, "I've got beyond all that, you know . . . Such a comfort . . . such a sense of freedom" (17).[23] Like Ellen Olenska, Mary Pask has gone "beyond" by "dying"; she has faced the threat of oblivion, so nothing, including social ridicule, superstition, or social restraint, can now frighten her.[24] As a result Mary lives as she wishes and speaks freely about her needs and desires. She sleeps during the day, in a shady corner of the garden. When the narrator tries to leave, Mary frankly and plaintively expresses her loneliness: " 'At times I'm really lonely . . . ' Her voice cracked in a last effort at laughter, and she swayed toward me, one hand still on the latch. 'Lonely, lonely! If you *knew* how lonely! It was a lie when I told you I wasn't! And now you come, and your face looks friendly . . . and you say you're going to leave me! No-no-no-you shan't! Or else, why did you come? It's cruel' " (21–22). This last year, she tells the narrator, has been even lonelier than the years after the marriage of her sister Grace when only Grace's hypocritical "concern" remained of their relationship. She has fantasized, she tells him, that a man will come and love her. Flinging herself at the narrator, she pleads, "Oh, stay with me . . . just tonight . . . It's so sweet and quiet here . . . No one need know . . . no one will ever come and trouble us" (22).

At that moment a fierce gust slams open the lattice and fills the room with "the noise of the sea and with wet swirls of fog" (23). The two stood there, the narrator recollects, "lost to each other in the roaring coiling darkness" while he tries to breathe "with great heaves that covered me with sweat" (23). The erotic, primal quality of this scene captures both Mary's sexual longing and the narrator's intense fear of it. Granted, he presumably believes she is a ghost, but the fear and loathing come as well from her physicality. Her hand becomes a trope of her and the disgust he feels: "round, puffy, pink, yet prematurely old and useless. And there, unmistakably, it lay on my sleeve: but changed and shriveled—somehow like one of those pale freckled toadstools that the least touch resolves to dust" (15). When he looks at "the soft wrinkled fingers, with their foolish little oval finger tips that used to be so innocently and naturally pink, and now were blue under the yellowing nails," his flesh rises "in ridges of fear" (15). Given his revulsion, Mary's sexual gestures repel him: "The horrible thing was that she still practiced the same arts, all the childish wiles of a clumsy capering coquetry" (16). When Mary eventually expresses her sexual needs, the narrator bolts away, slamming the door on her now collapsed body and a "pitiful low whimper" (23).

The experience plunges him into "nervous collapse" that yields a significant insight about women's lives: "Supposing something survived of Mary

Pask—enough to cry out to me the unuttered loneliness of a lifetime, to express at last what the living woman had always had to keep dumb and hidden? The thought moved me curiously—in my weakness I lay and wept over it. No end of women were like that, I supposed, and perhaps, after death, if they got their chance they tried to use it" (24–25). His weeping over Mary Pask suggests that he is weeping as well for his own "unuttered loneliness of a lifetime." Certainly his frightened assertion that he could not have spoken of the affair to Grace "or to anyone else . . . I could not even have written to her—not to save my life" tells us that he isn't able to reveal his emotional vulnerability to anyone (1–2). Shouldn't I bury it, he asks himself, "in those deepest depths where the inexplicable and the unforgettable sleep together?" (26).

No doubt this fear exists because of his sense that if he were to tell Grace, she would "just set me down as 'queer'—and enough people had done that already" (26). No less than Mary Pask, the narrator has clearly had to keep much of himself "dumb and hidden" because he is somehow "queer" and "Other." In fearing and loathing Mary Pask, as he does in his encounter with her, he is fearing and loathing his vulnerable, suppressed, feminine self, but the experience temporarily allows him to weep for both her and himself.

Being male and being part of society means that such "weakness" has to be purged from his consciousness, however, so he goes to the Swiss sanatorium to bury the encounter and the realizations he has gained from it. His first object, when he returns to New York, is to "convince everybody of my complete return to mental and physical soundness; and into this scheme of evidence my experience with Mary Pask did not seem to fit. All things considered, I would hold my tongue" (26). Like Alice Hartley in "The Lady's Maid's Bell," who also determines to hold her tongue about her supernatural experiences, the narrator senses that being socially accepted demands repression of one's vulnerability and uncanny realizations.

When the narrator finally feels restored enough to visit Grace and talk to her about Mary, no doubt it is because she says to him "But tell me—tell me everything," that he gets a knot in his throat and thinks that he "felt almost as uncomfortable as I had in Mary Pask's own presence" (28). Grace has asked him to talk, to share himself with her, and the invitation to speak makes him feel as uncomfortable with his vulnerable inner self as he had been with Mary's.

Eventually the narrator learns from Grace, after a conversation riddled with misunderstanding, that Mary hasn't died at all but instead suffered a cataleptic trance. Later, as Grace continues talking about Mary, he states flatly, "I felt I should never again be interested in Mary Pask, or in anything concerning her" (31). Like the narrator in "The Young Gentlemen," who never visits Cranch's dwarf sons again and dismisses them from his life, this narrator ultimately can't accept the femaleness he has encountered in Mary Pask's house, especially if it is "real" rather than ghostly. The "weakness" it engenders has to be purged from his identity rather than integrated. We know, however, since the narrator is telling us the tale in retrospect, that rather than being "overlaid with layer upon layer of time and forgetfulness," this encounter still lives in him, rejected but alive.

"Bewitched," written three years after "Miss Mary Pask," in 1925, is an amalgam of characters and settings from earlier Gothic texts, but it contains a significant breakthrough in the creation of the male character through whose consciousness the story is told. The "weakness" that allows the narrator in "Miss Mary Pask" partially to understand his feminine self becomes a strength in Orrin Bosworth, who acknowledges, respects, and accepts feminine power.

Orrin is an imaginative man, the youngest and most communicative of the three who arrive at the Rutledge home to investigate Mrs. Rutledge's charge that her husband has been bewitched into having an affair with a ghost. An entrepreneurial farmer, he has won community status as a selectman of the town. But, as we are told, he had been born "under the icy shadow of Lonetop," the local mountain, and "the roots of the old life were still in him," a heritage and characteristic reminiscent of Charity's affinity, in *Summer*, with life beyond social boundaries on the Mountain (*HB* 103, 104). For Orrin, possessing "the roots of the old life" means believing in "things below the surface of his thoughts, things which stole up anew, making him feel that all the old people he had known, and who 'believed in these things,' might after all be right" (105–106). "These things" include the power of witches and witchcraft, which intrigues Orrin.

His open-mindedness has come, at least in part, the story suggests, from his twice yearly visits as a child to his great-aunt Cressidora Cheney, "shut up for years in a cold clean room with iron bars in the windows" on a bleak hill farm (104). During one memorable visit to his relative, who is kept imprisoned "like a canary bird," he tells his mother, he brings a canary in a wooden cage to make her happy (104). "The old woman's motionless face lit up when she saw the bird," we are told, but the shadow of the woman's bony hand startles the bird into frantic fluttering, precipitating an act which the young Orrin remembers afterward with its "deep fringe of mystery, secrecy and rumor" (104–105). At the sight of the frightened bird, "Aunt Cressidora's calm face suddenly became a coil of twitching features. 'You she-devil, you!' she cried in a high squealing voice; and thrusting her hand into the cage she dragged out the terrified bird and wrung its neck. She was plucking the hot body, and squealing 'she-devil, she-devil' as they drew little Orrin from the room. On the way down the mountain his mother wept a great deal, and said: 'You must never tell anybody that poor Auntie's crazy, or the men would come and take her down to the asylum at Starkfield, and the shame of it would kill us all. Now promise.' The child promised" (105).

Much is suggested by this interpolated tale: a woman "shut up for years" in cold isolation, imprisoned, the "iron bars in the windows" tell us, because she is "crazy." In killing the lively bird Aunt Cressidora kills the "witch," the natural being, as her own nature has been killed. Her life is a secret kept from men, because, were they to know about her madness, they would imprison her more cruelly.

The setting and the woman's killing of the bird echo Susan Glaspell's "A Jury of Her Peers," published in 1917, eight years before "Bewitched." In Glaspell's short story Minnie Foster Wright is in jail, accused of strangling her husband with a rope. When the isolated, lonely Wright house is visited by the Sheriff, the county attorney, and their wives, the primary evidence that could indict Mrs. Wright, a strangled bird, is found by the two women. The women continue to piece together Minnie's story: a lively young woman who loves to sing becoming the lonely wife of the taciturn John Wright; Mr. Wright's probable killing of the bird, and by extension his wife's life spirit; and Minnie's agitated reaction, reflected in her uneven quilting stitches and her unkempt kitchen. All are clues that the women's husbands ignore as trivial. But the women know they suggest a motive, so they don't share their observations with their husbands, just as Aunt Cressidora's story is kept from "the men."

Reading "Bewitched" in the context of "A Jury of Her Peers" encourages the reader to wonder whether Aunt Cressidora has been *made* crazy by the isolation of the "bleak hill farm" in which she is now kept. Just as the clues to Minnie Foster's story in "A Jury of Her Peers" are trivialized by the men but interpreted by their wives, Aunt Cressidora's story is one that only those like Orrin Bosworth, open to mysterious "things below the surface of his thoughts," can understand.

In contrast to Orrin are the other men called to the Rutledge home. Deacon Hibben periodically intones "These are forbidden things" while he is being told the story of Saul Rutledge having the life sucked out of him by his ghostly lover Ora Brand. Sylvester Brand is the father of the dead Ora and another daughter, Venny, who, Orrin recalls, "ran wild on the slopes of Lonetop" while her sister is away at school and is "too wild and ignorant" to tend Ora's grave when she dies (*HB* 107, 108). Sylvester Brand is a Gothic villain figure, with a "heavily-hewn countenance," a "bull neck," and a "rough bullying power" (80, 117, 92). There is "something animal and primitive about him," Orrin notices, as he stands "lowering and dumb, a little foam beading the corners of that heavy purplish underlip" while he sullenly agrees to an exploration of the charges against his dead daughter (93). This animal quality makes the reader suspect that Brand's brutality is as much to blame as anything else for his wife's having "pined away and died," Ora's having "sickened and died" when she returned home from school, and Venny's running "wild on the slopes of Lonetop" and then, by the story's end, dying suddenly of pneumonia (107). Indeed, the three women's deaths recall the deaths by suicide and madness of the mother and two daughters haunted by incest in the "Beatrice Palmato" fragment.[25]

Just as the "Beatrice Palmato" fragment reveals Mr. Palmato's dominance over the women in his family and his control of their sexuality, Wharton uses the Gothic elements in "Bewitched" to tell a story of dread and destruction of female sexuality, which takes the form of an accused witch. Because, like traditional religion, the Gothic imagination "reverently acknowledges awesome and terrible spiritual forces operative in the world," Gothic literature draws on both religious symbols and witchcraft (Bayer-Berenbaum 34). At the same time, "the religious censorship of forbidden thoughts and behavior is most repugnant to the Gothic endeavor," as is the Christian separation between the natural and the supernatural, the "real" and the spiritual (34). So the Gothic often deliberately distorts traditional religious images and personages. Such a satirical distortion is at work in the portrayal of Deacon Hibben, with his "long face, queerly blotched and mouldy-looking, with blinking peering eyes," whose repetitive, authoritative response to the story of ghostly intercourse that the Rutledges tell is, "these are forbidden things." (*HB* 80, 101, 102).[26]

Even more distorted is the rigidly sanctimonious Prudence Rutledge, who adamantly believes that her husband Saul is bewitched and that, according to Exodus 22:18, Ora Brand must be destroyed with "a stake through the breast" because *"Thou shalt not suffer a witch to live"* (102, 103). Like Hawthorne's Richard Digby in "The Man of Adamant," whose religious intolerance and bigotry become part of his outward demeanor, making him look "less like a living man than a marble statue, wrought by some dark-imagined sculptor to express the most repulsive mood that human features could assume," Prudence Rutledge has eyes like "the sightless orbs of a marble statue" (Waggoner 232; *HB* 86). Her white face is "limited" and "fixed," and her "small narrow head," with hair "passed tight and flat over the tips of her ears into a small braided coil at the nape," is "perched on a long hollow neck with cord-like throat muscles" (83). Like Richard Digby's "marble frown," Prudence Rutledge's constricted, phallic features also reflect sexual fear, dread, and anger, evident in her barely contained rage at her husband and his spectral partner in infidelity (Waggoner 233). "Ain't I seen 'em?" she almost screams. Her solution to her anger is phallic as well, "A stake through the breast! That's the old way; and it's the only way" (*HB* 102). [27]

True to Wharton's Gothic, the coldly rigid Prudence and her "haggard wretch" of a husband, who looks like "a drowned man fished out from under the ice," live in a house that is desolate, neglected, and bitterly cold, like both of them (92, 91). The snow, falling in a "steady unwavering sheet against the window" while the men hear the Rutledge story is another Gothic indicator of psychic isolation. It seems to Orrin Bosworth as if "a winding sheet were descending from the sky to envelop them all in a common grave" (96).

Orrin's awareness of death in this situation parallels his sense, as he looks at the wan, hollow-faced Saul, "sucked inward and consumed by some hidden fever," that "they were all at that moment really standing on the edge of some forbidden mystery" (94). That the "forbidden mystery" is the mystery of the feminine becomes clear as Orrin listens to Saul's story of love for Ora, blocked by her father and continued after her death in the abandoned house by the pond. In a stream of consciousness he remembers his mad Aunt Cressidora, the burning of one of Sylvester Brand's ancestors as a witch, the death of the "savage" Sylvester Brand's wife and daughter, and the wildness of his remaining daughter (107). These connections suggest his awareness, albeit unacknowledged, that the "forbidden mystery" involves the story of women's lives and the male power that keeps their female power restrained.

When Orrin drives by the abandoned house in the hollow by the pond, where the air was "as soundless and empty as an unswung bell," he again thinks of the "dark mystery, too deep for thought" being enacted in it (113, 114). The phrase "dark mystery" recalls Wharton's reference, in her unpublished autobiography "Life and I," to the "whole dark mystery" of sexuality about which she felt "such a dread" before her marriage and yet was "expressly forbidden to ask about, or even think of!" (34–35). Indeed, the female iconography of the hollow, the body of water, the deserted hut, the bell, all suggest the female sexuality embodied in the site, much like the deserted house in *Summer* where Charity plunges into sexual passion. At the same time the "stinging wind barbed with ice flakes" prepares us for the phallic destruction of the female spirit contained in "the crazy house" (*HB* 113, 117).

Eventually all the men are gathered in the hollow, noticing a woman's footprints in the snow. Not surprisingly, the villain Brand is the one who, "moving on as if to an assault, his head bowed forward on his bull neck," pushes inward on the door of the house (117). When he meets "an unexpected resistance," he thrusts his shoulder against the door, collapsing it and stumbling into the hut's darkness (117). As Orrin plunges into the darkness after him, he sees "something white and wraithlike surge up out of the darkest corner of the hut" and hears what he soon learns is Brand's revolver going off and a cry (118).[28] The language echoes and revises that in "Miss Mary Pask," where the narrator senses that "something white and wraithlike seemed to melt and crumple up before me in the night" (23). This female wraith doesn't melt and crumple, it surges, but its power is countered by the powerful phallic revolver.

When we learn the next day that Vanessa Brand is dying of pneumonia, we are led to surmise that she was the one who has been having the affair with Saul Rutledge, left the footprints in the snow, and was shot in the dark hut by her father. As her coffin is lowered into her sister's grave, however, we understand that it doesn't really matter which woman was Saul Rutledge's lover, a live woman or a ghost, nor does it matter how either died, since both girls, "the handsomest girls anywhere round," meet the same fate, their sexuality feared and their lives controlled and ultimately ended by patriarchal power.

Prudence Rutledge, who, with her religious dogmatism and frozen emotions, has internalized a "patriarchal presence," is satisfied that Ora is quieted now that "she don't lay there alone any longer" (Daly 50; *HB* 123). Orrin notes at the funeral, as Prudence's lids again remind him of marble eyeballs, that she "looks as if the stone-mason had carved her to put atop of Venny's grave" (*HB* 121). But her bony bloodless hands also remind him of Aunt Cressidora's as she strangled the canary bird "because it fluttered" (121). The comparison emphasizes that Prudence, like Cressidora, has sought to kill liveliness and naturalness in another that has since died in herself. In this she is reminiscent of Zeena in *Ethan Frome* as well, who, like Prudence, is a "stony image of resentment," with a "sallow face," narrow lips, and "pale opaque eyes which revealed nothing and reflected nothing" (*EF* 138, 136, 187).[29] Prudence's bonnet, a "monumental structure" with its "perpendicular pile," like Zeena's "hard perpendicular bonnet," is a visual image of rigid phallic strength that denies the feminine (*HB* 121; *EF* 67). Cressidora's story is a reminder, however, that such rigidity has roots in suppression, shame, and unhealthy isolation.[30]

Orrin Bosworth, the consciousness through which the story is filtered, suggests the merging of gender selves that has been evolving in Wharton's Gothic texts. Successful in the outside world, he also accepts and respects the mysterious inner world, below the surface of the rational mind. The etymology of his name connects him with the ghost Ora, since both derive from the root *orare*, to speak, pray, beseech, and are echoes of "oral," "oracle," and "oracular." The similarity of their names suggests that Ora and Orrin are the joint means by which the mysterious is revealed and woman's story, if not fully told, is at least acknowledged and respected.

"Dieu d'Amour," like "Bewitched" and the later "Mr. Jones," also portrays the reviving of woman's story from patriarchal control. Wharton wrote "Dieu d'Amour" the day after viewing a twelfth-century castle on a two-thousand-foot rocky peak in Cyprus, called Dieu d'Amour by the Crusaders for the god Eros. Though Wharton apparently didn't make the arduous climb to the site herself, her traveling companion Margaret Chanler, who did, called it "the most fantastic fairy castle imaginable" (Lewis, *CSS* 2:551). Wharton later referred to the ten-week Aegean trip during which she saw this castle as "a state of euphoria" and "unbroken bliss" (*BG* 372, 373). The experience belonged, she recalled, to "a quite other-dimensional world" (Lewis, *Biography* 469). The escape from practical reality and into an altered state expressed in these comments is reflected in the Gothic quality of "Dieu d'Amour." Setting, action, and characters all carry the symbolic weight of a Gothic journey into the self. As in the other Gothic stories of this period, "Dieu d'Amour" reflects Wharton's retrieval from restraint of the spiritual and physical feminine self.

The castle in the story is typically Gothic, set on a dangerously steep pinnacle reached by tunnel-like passage ways in which bats hang, "nuzzling creatures dangling and swinging" over one's head, suggesting that the castle "was not a wholesome place for the soul" (*CP* 103). Much of the castle is in ruin, and the ominousness of it reflects the lives within: the king of Cyprus, who kept "an obstinate and mournful state in the upper apartments"; his queen, who "counted her pearls, and sat in a window staring northward, dark and sumptuous among her slaves," whom she torments; and their disaffected young daughter, Princess Medea (104). The place seems the most evil at dusk. At midday, "turreted, balconied, galleried to catch the sun," and surrounded by an "abyss of light and sea," it seems made for "delicate enchantments," a reminder of the "old stories" that the place was built by Venus, Queen of Cyprus, for herself and her son Cupid (103). This reference to the castle's matriarchal past, called "an old wives' tale" by "the learned," prepares us for the story's revival of this past and its repudiation of scholarly disdain.

The omniscient narrator uses Godfrey, an orphaned young page to a knight, as the story's consciousness, and plays ironically on his youth and naivete, the way "The Triumph of Night," "The Young Gentlemen," and "Miss Mary Pask" played on the male limited-omniscient narrators' physical and moral weaknesses. As Godfrey makes the tunnellike ascent to see Princess Medea, he plunges into another "tunnel-like passage" at the top, ending at a low cedar door (105). He must stoop his tall shoulders in order to creep in and be dragged "through obscurity and out into a vaulted room" by Medea's servant girl (106). This vaginal ascent at the beginning of the story leading to an *Alice in Wonderland*-like reentry into the womb figures the story's revisiting and reclaiming of the female self.

The sight in the room Godfrey enters, of the last sunlight "as bright as a new day," and the Princess Medea standing "penciled against this resurrection light like a little dark saint on a gold ground" serves as both predictor and corrective, for Medea will seize the chance for a new life and new self but not necessarily as a saint (106). The narrator emphasizes this corrective by adding, "But in reality she was not dark: under her coif and veil her hair spiralled out like the gold wire of the old heathen ornaments which the labourers dug out of the vineyards in the valleys" (106).

Godfrey is secretly teaching Medea to write, an act as subversive in her life as it was in Wharton's own: "Her royal parents would have been scandalized at her wishing to acquire so unprincely an art; or the queen might have been jealous and suspicious; one could never tell. She seldom visited her poor ailing son, and gave little thought to her daughter. The Princess Medea, it was whispered, might have done as she pleased in graver matters; but this clerkly business would have needed explaining. It savoured too much of necromancy. So she and her ladies kept the matter to themselves, and thus added the requisite touch of peril to a task which might otherwise have grown dull. For the princess was royal enough to show no clerkly aptitude. She could embroider like Queen Penelope if she chose—but write!" (107). Wharton might well be describing her own parents' response to her writing as "something between a black art and a form of manual labor" (*BG* 69). Familiar too is the suggestion of a jealous, suspicious, and emotionally neglectful mother.

"Life and I" makes clear that Wharton saw her youthful self as a Gothic heroine, caught in a frighteningly repressive system, hounded by a disapproving mother, and denied essential knowledge about her own sexuality. However distorted such a view might have been, Wharton's perpetuation of it years later demonstrates its emotional validity for her and reinforces the biographical parallels in this story about a young captive writer who escapes to a life that validates and is validated by her female heritage.

Godfrey's visit brings Medea's petulant responses "I don't want to write," and "Everything displeases me," the latter reminiscent of Charity's "Oh how I hate everything" at the beginning of *Summer* (*CP* 108, 109). Significantly, Medea is experiencing similar pressure to marry an older man, for she reports to Godfrey that "they are marrying me to my uncle, the Prince of Antioch," who, she adds, "grunts and storms, and breaks out all over in sweat. But what can you or I do to prevent it, my poor Godfrey?" (110). Medea's answer rests in her musings about Queen Venus, goddess of love and former princess of the house, "Queen Venus . . . who was my great-great-grandmother" (111). Her matriarchal heritage no doubt gives Medea the courage to escape the typical Gothic fate of marrying male power. Godfrey's admonition that the stories of Venus "are sorcerers' tales, and forbidden, as your Highness knows," is reminiscent both of the patriarchal warnings against talk of the sexy ghost Ora from the Deacon in "Bewitched" and of the implicit warnings Wharton got from her mother that she is "expressly forbidden" to talk or think about sex or herself as a sexual woman (109).

Godfrey senses that, in spite of Medea's talk about taking lovers after her marriage, a path her mother has followed, "her mockery was the mockery of despair, and that a new soul in her, helpless and inarticulate as a newborn infant, was stirring and crying to him for help" (113). He is half right. Although Medea is at the vulnerable stage of searching for an alternative to her mother's comatose existence as a decorated sex object, "staring northward, hour by hour," saying and seeing nothing, and she talks of escaping with him, his boast that "of course he would save her, his little saint," is ironically misplaced (104,113).

Medea escapes instead with an androgynous-looking female pilgrim, dressed in goatskin and "with eyes gleaming through wisps of unkempt straw-coloured hair," who appears one day to deride the social and religious corruption of the town and its castle (115). More strident about her religious beliefs than the Wild Woman in "The Hermit and the Wild Woman," she nonetheless also has the spiritual calming effect on Godfrey that the Wild Woman has on the Hermit. Unlike that earlier woman of moral principle, this pilgrim stays alive and helps another woman write a new text for her life. Nor does Medea live out the fate of her namesake, struck dumb by love and using her magical powers to save Jason and his Argonauts, betraying her father and killing her brother for him, only to be rebuked and abandoned in the end. This Medea rejects the myth of giving everything for the man she loves. She recalls instead Medea, the Mother Goddess of the Medes, known as "Wise One," whose name, like Medusa's, derives from the Sanscrit concept of *medha*, "female wisdom" (B. Walker 628).

Godfrey responds viscerally to the sensory renewal the pilgrim brings to the desecrated chapel of Saint Hilarion, a cavern off the dark stairs to the castle. A richly dyed carpet, lighted candles, and herb twigs have restored this female space. Considered "entrances to the underworld" as late as the fifteenth century, caves were associated with "the Great Mother's yonic gate" (B. Walker 156).[31] While in the cave Godfrey is "wrapped in an atmosphere of prayer. Words of devotion rose, forming themselves unbidden on his lips. His soul seemed lifted on another's rapture, as the body floats on a summer sea" (*CP* 124). The metaphor is a reminder that the castle is surrounded by the sea, symbol of female power.

Although Godfrey has the feeling that Dieu d'Amour, like the chapel, "had been cleansed of old evils" and that "he sees with his inner sight the beating of the wings of dawn," he doesn't realize that it is the pilgrim who has the power to "purify and transform" the castle of "lust and terror and misery" (127, 128, 129). His response now, as earlier when he first saw the chapel and felt "lifted on another's rapture, as the body floats on a summer sea," recalls Otto's " 'numinous' state of mind" in religious experience and also common to the Gothic. Otto describes this sense of "mystical awe" as "the feeling of personal nothingness and submergence before the awe-inspiring object directly experienced" (7, 17). Wharton's suggestion in "Dieu d'Amour" of the religious awe to be found in female power takes this Gothic story further than any before it and introduces a theme that Wharton will explore more thoroughly in *Hudson River Bracketed* and *The Gods Arrive*.

Once realizing that Medea has left without him by escaping with the pilgrim, "grown lad that he was, and a princess's champion, Godfrey burst into sobs. For he understood at last that God had stolen his lady from him" (*CP* 139). The ironic "grown lad" descriptor reveals that like his maturity, Godfrey's understanding is limited. Though he assumes that Medea has entered a convent, he never learns anything more about her or her life that might confirm his assumption. Having seen Medea's face "drawn inward, and distant," and her eyes looking as if they had traveled "from some far country," the reader suspects that Medea, like Ellen Olenska before her, has been "beyond," to the "ground of the soul" (125; Otto 36). Rather than having been stolen by God, Medea has, with the help of a female pilgrim who disrupts a system controlled by the patriarchy, retrieved her independence.

5 | Surviving the Abyss and Revising Gender Roles

Wharton's late years, from 1929 to her death in 1937, were a time of both fruition and sadness. "A First Word" and the epilogue of *A Backward Glance*, her autobiography published in 1934, reflect this antithesis. Wharton alternately projects the mature wisdom and happiness of a woman who has lived a full and successful life and the loneliness and sorrow of one who has lived through the deaths of many dear friends. As she writes in "A First Word," "There's no such thing as old age; there is only sorrow." Sorrow, she concludes, along with "the habit of having habits, of turning a trail into a rut," causes old age, but several sentences later she counters with the triumphant dictum that "in spite of illness, in spite even of the arch-enemy sorrow, one *can* remain alive long past the usual date of disintegration if one is unafraid of change, insatiable in intellectual curiosity, interested in big things, and happy in small ways" (vii).

The epilogue, as well, contains the same antitheses between joy and sadness: "In our individual lives, though the years are sad, the days have a way of being jubilant. Life is the saddest thing there is, next to death; yet there are always new countries to see, new books to read (and, I hope, to write), a thousand little daily wonders to marvel at and rejoice in. . . . The visible world is a daily miracle for those who have eyes and ears; and I still warm my hands thankfully at the old fire, though every year it is fed with the dry wood of more old memories" (379, ellipsis mine).

Given the many deaths of intimate friends Wharton had experienced up to and during this period—Henry James in 1916, Howard Sturgis and Edgerton Winthrop in 1920, Sara Norton in 1922, Walter Berry in 1927, Teddy Wharton in 1928, and her beloved housekeeper Gross and maid Elise in 1933—it isn't surprising that death is a unifying theme of the three Gothic stories of this period, "Mr. Jones," "Pomegranate Seed," and "All Souls'." "The disappearance of one dear friend after another must always be the chief sadness of a life bound up in a few close personal ties," she admits in *A Backward Glance* (375). Wharton's own aging and her tenuous health obviously also contributed to her preoccupation with death. The destruction of her gardens at Ste. Claire during the brutal winter of 1929 precipitated both intense emotional and intense physical distress, for Wharton's gardens were expressions, even representations, of herself. As she exclaimed to her old friend Gaillard Lapsley: "Oh, Gaillard, that my old fibres should have been so closely interwoven with all these roots and tendrils" (Lewis, *Biography* 487). An attack of grippe in 1934 was followed by a mild stroke in 1935. Death, like sexuality, was one of life's dark powers needing to be faced, understood, and assimilated.

Religious spirituality was one means of facing mortality and finding inner peace. Kenneth Clark, who inherited Wharton's library, noted the predominance of books on religion (Lewis, *Biography* 510). Nicky Mariano, a friend who traveled with Wharton to Rome in 1932, writes about their going to a Pontifical Mass together and how unusually meditative Wharton seemed during the ceremony: "I felt deeply moved and at the same time acutely aware of Edith's presence—the presence not, as I had feared, of an impatient and rather spoilt woman, easily bored and anxious to move on, but of someone quite close to me, carried away with me and like me into another sphere, with no stiffness or impatience left in her, no thought of the passing hour or of other plans" (Lubbock, *Portrait* 233–34).

Mariano adds that the experience left her with the belief that "Edith may have been perhaps much nearer to actual conversion to the church than any of her friends ever thought" (Lubbock, "Memoirs"). Other friends were more skeptical that Wharton would ever submit her strong will and intellect to church doctrine and discipline (Lewis, *Biography* 511). Nonetheless, a conversation that Wharton had near the end of her life with Elisina Tyler about the "limitless spaces" that religious thought helps one understand suggests her abiding interest in spirituality (510).[1]

Wharton's Gothic, which had, throughout her career, carried her "into another sphere," beyond the rational and realistic, continues to serve that function during this period, but with increasing emphasis on acknowledging and even reclaiming the powerful forces inherent in the feminine. The female protagonists in "Mr. Jones" and "Pomegranate Seed" are each forced to confront a ghostly presence in their house and through it their assumptions about themselves as women. The protagonist of "All Souls'," in a deathlike experience, also faces intensely disorienting awareness about herself and her life.

With this last story and the last two completed novels, *Hudson River Bracketed* and *The Gods Arrive*, Wharton also further evokes another preoccupation of her Gothic, the merging of feminine and masculine by creating characters who overtly conjoin these distinct ways of knowing and being as Wharton has defined them. Although the Gothic texts of this late period reveal how conflicted Wharton still was about what it meant to be a woman, they also reflect how far she has come in embracing the feminine rather than suppressing it. The last two novels even suggest that exploring the depths of oneself and thereby reclaiming one's feminine/maternal self is a spiritual act essential to one's completeness as a human being.

"Mr. Jones," published in 1928, is a stunning revision of the Gothic stories that have come before it. In it a middle-aged woman does nothing less than re-claim her female heritage from male control, both internal and external, by re-claiming her ancestral home and the women's stories and lives it embodies. By entering the house and crossing thresholds within it she claims her right to con-trol her own body. By confronting the older woman who, as the surrogate of male control over women's lives, tries to prevent her from entering the house and its rooms, the heroine confronts her fear of the mother and the sexuality and death she figures.

We are told in the story's first line that Lady Jane Lynke, the heroine, is "unlike other people" in acting on her impulses (*G* 281). In this case being im-pulsive involves visiting unannounced the estate she has inherited, Bells. The estate's name recalls the early Gothic story "The Lady's Maid's Bell," where the new maid Alice Hartley is frightened by bells rung by the dead former maid to alert her to her mistress's physical distress. This Bells is haunted as well, by the same suggestion of male violence against women, but Lady Jane is as assertive as Alice is timid about asking questions. Thirty-five years old, unmarried, and a writer of unsentimental travel books, Jane "has led an active, independent and decided life" ever since leaving home at an early age (282).

Her first response to Bells is decidedly emotional, however. " 'I shall never leave it!' she ejaculated, her heart swelling as if she had taken the vow to a lover" (283). The reaction recalls Wharton's own response to Ste. Claire, "I am thrilled to the spine . . . and I feel as if I were going to get married—to the right man at last!" (Lewis, *Biography* 421, ellipsis mine). Just as Ste. Claire and Pavillon Colombe immersed Wharton in a female heritage and in physical surroundings of her own making, so Jane, through this inheritance, considers this house a reconnection to her past. For it is the long tale of "the unchronicled lives of the great-aunts and great-grandmothers buried there so completely that they must hardly have known when they passed from their beds to their graves" to which Jane feels she is adding another chapter. " 'Piled up like dead leaves,' Jane thought, 'layers and layers of them, to preserve something forever budding un-derneath' " (*G* 289).

The metaphor of the women's lives as leaves extends the tree metaphor Jane uses for the house when she first sees it, overhanging a moat "deeply sunk about its roots" like "an aged cedar spreading immemorial red branches" (281–82). The tree metaphor, along with the description of the house "lying there under a September sun that looked like moonlight," accentuates the scene's female ico-nography (282). The moon is "the favored spiritual symbol of the matriarchal sphere," and the moat suggests a "primordial" life source associated with woman (Neumann 55, 47). Wharton has used water in several earlier Gothic settings to suggest this connection between houses and female spirit and power. Lyng, the haunted house in "Afterward," which the narrator calls "a deep dim reservoir of life," sits "hidden under a shoulder of the downs" next to a fish pond (*G* 73);

Kerfol, the haunted mansion in the story of the same name, is surrounded by a moat (albeit now filled with shrubs and brambles); the haunted hut in "Bewitched" sits at the bottom of a slope next to a pond; Mary Pask's house sits on a cliff above the sea; and the castle Dieu d'Amour sits on an island surrounded by the sea.

The red cedar tree metaphor is a reminder that the tree is a primary symbol of the Great Earth Mother, source of all vegetation: "It bears, transforms, nourishes; its leaves, branches, twigs are 'contained' in it and dependent on it" (Neumann 49). Bachofen, in *Myth, Religion, and Mother Right,* carries the symbol further by referring to Glaucous's phrase in the *Iliad,* "The generations of men are like the leaves of the forest," and adding, "The leaves of the tree do not rise from one another but all alike from the branch. So also the generations of man in the matriarchal view. . . . The engendered belongs to the maternal matter, which has harbored it, brought it to light, and which now nurtures it. But this mother is always the same; she is ultimately the earth, represented by earthly women down through the endless generations of mothers and daughters" (Neumann 52–53). Wharton of course speaks of the leaves as generations not of men but of women, "The unchronicled lives of the great-aunts and great-grandmothers . . . piled up like dead leaves" (G 289).[2]

Jane's contemptuous assumption that her male heirs had accumulated their property wealth "mostly by clever marriages" foreshadows her discovery of just such use of a woman, an injustice that still haunts Bells (283). The men in "Kerfol" and "The Young Gentlemen" discover and then choose to ignore the story of a woman married for her money and subsequently imprisoned by her husband, but Jane can't ignore the story she uncovers because it continues to threaten women, including herself. Male dominance lives within her, and her own story, "Mr. Jones," shows her confronting it, but it also leaves ambiguous whether she overcomes it.

In finding the 1828 monument to her ancestor Peregrine Vincent Theobald Lynke and "Also His Wife," whom she eventually learns was named Juliana, in the chapel near the house, Jane is essentially finding her benefactors. For it is because the Count and Countess remained childless that she eventually is the one to inherit Bells. What they also leave Jane is a sordid legacy of a gambler and womanizer marrying a deaf and dumb young woman for her money and then leaving her at Bells for months at a time under the control of Mr. Jones, a servant who denies her access to the outside world. On learning this story we understand better why the narrator initially refers to Bells as "mute and solitary as the family vault," for it has kept its secret of a woman treated as a possession for several generations (282). Jane is thus discovering the Gothic story about women's objectification that Wharton has told throughout her career, in "The Duchess at Prayer," *The House of Mirth,* "The House of the Dead Hand," "Kerfol," "The Young Gentlemen," "Dieu d'Amour," *The Age of Innocence,* and the

Beatrice Palmato fragment. In discovering this story of female objectification and suppression, Jane (and one can't help but think Wharton as well) is acknowledging that, however "free" she may think she is, it is her own story she is uncovering, that her internalized patriarchal dominance has the power to keep her silent and constrained if she allows it to.[3]

Jane feels her relationship to the house's threatening male power immediately. Denied entrance to Bells by a frightened-looking woman who intones "Mr. Jones says that no one is allowed to visit the house," Jane admits later to friends that she was afraid of Mr. Jones. Though Bells is her "new home," she tells the young servant that she wants to come in because she is "interested in old houses" and knows "some of the family" (285). Perhaps it is the "spectral vista of a long room with shrouded furniture" or the sense that someone is watching her that causes this assertive "blunt tweed figure in heavy mud-stained shoes" to prevaricate (284–85). In any case, instinctual fear prevents her from claiming entrance into the past and the self that are rightfully hers.

When Jane does finally inhabit the house, her movements in it are hampered by the housekeeper, Mrs. Clemm. As a "rosy-cheeked old person" who had "curtsied" Jane across the threshold, Mrs. Clemm initially seems to represent bucolic servility and welcome (290). But her appearance and actions just as quickly peg her as a repressive and repressed maternal keeper of the house/female body, preventing Jane from exploring it and discovering its secrets. The "glossy false front" of Mrs. Clemm's black silk dress immediately suggests her untrustworthiness (290). Suggestive, too, of constraint and secretiveness is that "her small round face rested on the collar like a red apple on a white plate: neat, smooth, circular, with a pursed-up mouth, eyes like black seeds, and round ruddy cheeks with the skin so taut that one had to look close to see that it was as wrinkled as a piece of old crackly" (290).[4] The apple is a potent female symbol of knowledge, of immorality, of love and sexuality, of death (B. Walker 49–50).[5] Mrs. Clemm's intensely red, wrinkled cheeks and "pursed-up mouth" portend her role as one who possesses woman's fundamental knowledge but defiantly refuses to reveal it.

Her actions confirm this. The biggest secret she keeps concerns the ghostly existence of Mr. Jones, who ostensibly was the one refusing Jane entrance into the house. He is, Mrs. Clemm says ambiguously, "more dead than living" and "between life and death, as it were," and so "in no state for you to see him" (G 292, 293, 294). Mrs. Clemm also tries to prevent Jane from learning about other secrets by "losing" the key to the house's record room and trying to keep Jane out of the house's "blue room." In this latter room the persistent Jane first feels the presence of and then sees the ghost of Mr. Jones, sitting at the desk in which she finds the letters revealing his cruel, repressive treatment of the mute Juliana. In the blue room as well the portrait of Juliana, now in the salon, had obviously been painted. In it, leaning against the desk with a window in the background "framing snow-laden paths and hedges in icy perspective," the young woman looks out "dumbly, inexpressively, in a stare of frozen beauty" (303, 302). The blue room, with its color suggesting both depression and privilege, can tell a story that Mrs. Clemm doesn't want Jane to hear.

As keeper of the keys to rooms, Mrs. Clemm potentially controls Jane's access to knowledge about herself as a woman, but Jane persistently, in spite of her nagging fear, crosses the thresholds into these female spaces. Repetitively we are told that Jane "stood on the threshold" of the blue room, then "crossed the threshold" only to recall later "the uneasy feeling which had come over her as she stood on the threshold" (296, 297, 298). When Mrs. Clemm stands "on the threshold, cheeks shining, skirt rustling, her eyes like drills," to tell Jane that the muniment room cannot be opened, even by the locksmith Jane has called, Jane threatens to "break in that door myself, if I have to" (306, 307). "As symbol of a woman's sexuality, the threshold motif vividly condenses the traditional patriarchal control of woman's sexuality," their interior controlled and entered by men (Rabuzzi 89). But if a woman is fully to know herself she must claim the mysterious inner world of the mother, woman's interior space beyond the threshold.[6] Jane assertively, even aggressively, counters Mrs. Clemm's attempts to prevent her from learning about herself.

When Jane insists that she is going to look through the drawers of the desk in the blue room (with its Freudian connotations of the female body) and then admits that she has seen Mr. Jones sitting at it, Mrs. Clemm stretches her arms in front of her face, "as if to fend off a blaze of intolerable light, or some forbidden sight she had long since disciplined herself not to see" (G 311). This attempt to hide from the light of awareness recalls Lily Bart's last tormented hours, when "her mind shrank from the glare of thought as instinctively as eyes contract in a blaze of light—darkness, darkness was what she must have at any cost" (HM 512). The "forbidden" sight, used in "Bewitched," "Dieu d'Amour," and "Life and I" as a descriptor of female sexuality, carries the same weight in this story. Mrs. Clemm has tried to ignore the violence against women that Mr. Jones represents in having kept Juliana and generations of women after her, including herself, oppressed and silent about their oppression.

The threat Mrs. Clemm and Jane sense in claiming knowledge and control from the patriarchal Mr. Jones is real, as Jane learns when she finds Mrs. Clemm in her room, strangled. Called to the scene by Georgiana, the interchange between the servant and Jane, "She just lies there" and "Where is it your aunt's lying?" reminds us that even in death Mrs. Clemm can't be trusted to reveal the truth (G 316). Significantly, as Jane "crossed the threshold" into Mrs. Clemm's "neat, glossy and extremely cold" room, she remembers "the housekeeper's attempt to prevent her touching the contents of the desk" (317). If only unconsciously Jane is making the connection between Mrs. Clemm's restriction of knowledge about her female heritage and selfhood and the housekeeper's own repressed femininity.

Georgiana, "her face buried in her lifted arms," finally looks at Jane "with eyes as fixed as the dead woman's" and sobs out that the ghost of Mr. Jones has punished her aunt for disobeying him and having "meddled with his papers" (318–19). That she hides from the sight of truth as Mrs. Clemm had, stares "with Mrs. Clemm's awful eyes," and then falls to the floor in a deathlike swoon suggests that Georgiana too will become a victim of Mr. Jones's violence (319). Georgiana's eyes, "as fixed as the dead woman's," and the dead Mrs. Clemm's "stony face and fast-glazing pupils" link them metaphorically to the many female victims before them in Wharton's Gothic fiction: Juliana, with her "stare of frozen beauty" (302); the queen in "Dieu d'Amour" who "sat staring northward, hour by hour, and said nothing, and saw nothing" (*CP* 104); Prudence Rutledge in "Bewitched," who looks "as if the stone-mason had carved her" as a grave figure (*G* 275); the Duchess in "The Duchess at Prayer," who is replaced by a stone replica after her husband poisons her.

Jane's fate is less clear but potentially more secure. The pathological, patriarchal control Mr. Jones represents is within her house, within herself. But because he isn't part of her family the way he is for Mrs. Clemm and her niece, he doesn't have the full weight of traditional power in Jane's life he has had in those of his ancestors. Also, Jane has *seen* Mr. Jones, which Mrs. Clemm has never done. That is, Jane has understood what the housekeeper hasn't about this dangerous male dominance and so is less apt to become a victim of it. Jane is also a writer and so has control over "letters" that counters Mr. Jones's control. Unlike Juliana, who, like women before her in Wharton's Gothic fiction (Sybilla in "The House of the Dead Hand," the Duchess in "The Duchess at Prayer," Anne in "Kerfol"), is a mute victim of male power manifested by nobility or intellect or both, Jane is not a mute writer of letters that she is unable to send. Rather, she is a published writer of books who thereby communicates with the outside world. As a reader as well, of Juliana's history, she illustrates that Mr. Jones can no longer claim those records as "his papers."

Last, Jane has a "male" part to her life, an alternative to the role played by Mr. Jones, which encourages her to pursue assertively what she wants to know and possess without victimizing another. This male element is suggested by the obvious parallels drawn between Jane's friend Edward Stramer and Jane in "Mr. Jones," which make them seem like two sides of one person. As such the two characters are a significant contribution to Wharton's evolving portrayal, in her Gothic fiction, of the gender-integrated individual. That Edward Stramer is called by his last name in the story, while Lady Jane Lynke is called by her first, the way Alice Hartley and Emma Saxon were called Hartley and Emma in "The Lady's Maid's Bell," accentuates the sense that Edward and Jane are two parts of one individual. Like Jane, Stramer is a writer, and like her too he visited Bells as a child, with a friend's mother, where they were refused entrance into the house with exactly the reason given Jane. When Jane asks, "And you didn't try to force your way in either?" Stramer's response concurs with Jane's actions: "Oh no: it was not possible" (288).

When Jane feels that "the house was too old, too mysterious, too much withdrawn into its own secret past, for her poor little present to fit into it without uneasiness," she asks Stramer, the fellow writer, to come stay with her and work on his novel (298). It is Stramer who notices that Juliana's picture was painted in the blue room and asks whether Jane has read her archives. His insistent detective work—noticing that Mrs. Clemm "positively glows with life whenever she announces a death" and trying to find Mr. Jones's room in the house—encourages Jane to take action (306). Stramer points out the big dusty footprints on the floor of the muniment room as Jane and he search for information about Juliana and her husband, and he reads through the letters with Jane when she finds them in the desk drawer in the blue room. Together they compile the "dirty record" of Juliana's enforced seclusion, her husband's gambling debts and philandering, and the orders he gives to Mr. Jones to keep Juliana confined despite her despair at such a lonely existence. Stramer articulates Jane's unspoken sense that Mr. Jones is a ghost, and together they question Georgiana about Mr. Jones after finding Mrs. Clemm strangled. Stramer assists but never overpowers Jane. Instead, his presence in her house provides her with additional strength to do what she wants to do. Stramer is Jane's masculinity, meshing with her femininity to her best advantage.

"Pomegranate Seed," written two years after "Mr. Jones," in 1930, significantly revises the earlier story as well as Wharton's treatment of gender in her Gothic fiction. The powerful controller of letters is now a woman rather than a man, and the one controlled is a man rather than a woman. Most significantly, the writer wields her control from the Gothic abyss, the dark source of sexuality, birth, and death figured by the Mother. But "Pomegranate Seed" is essentially the story of another woman, Charlotte Ashby, who tries to understand this female power by trying to interpret the letters issuing from it that so disturb her sense of herself.

Just as Jane is initially afraid to enter her home in "Mr. Jones," so Charlotte is afraid to enter hers in "Pomegranate Seed." In the early days of her marriage to the widower Kenneth Ashby, she had happily entered their house just as she had felt secure about her relationship with her husband, but now "she always wavered on the doorstep and had to force herself to enter" (G 323). She pauses on the doorstep and hesitates before inserting her key in the lock. Charlotte's "premonition of something inexplicable, intolerable, to be faced on the other side of the curtained panes," her fearful hesitancy as she approaches the house, the threshold, the lock suggests her fear of her own body and her feminine self

(331). Indeed, her persistent search to understand the source of her fear involves peeling off layer after layer of assumptions about herself as a woman.[7]

When she married Kenneth Ashby, Charlotte accepted that they would live in the house he shared with the first Mrs. Ashby, Elsie Corder, and that they could not afford to replace the furnishing or hangings selected by her. Wharton's meticulous attention to the renovation and decoration of her own homes and her writing about the reflection of one's self in the decoration of houses make a reader of her fiction flinch at Charlotte's seeming lack of awareness. In concurring with her husband, Charlotte is essentially agreeing to appropriate the identity of the wife before her.[8] Initially she does so comfortably. In fact, when she had visited Elsie the first and only time, she looked at her drawing room with "innocent envy, feeling it to be exactly the drawing room she would have liked for herself" (324). It is only after Kenneth has moved Elsie's picture from the library to the nursery and the face in the portrait "no longer followed her with guarded eyes" that Charlotte admits to being "more at home in her house, more at ease and in confidence with her husband" (330).

Despite her appropriation of Elsie's furniture the good-humored but passive Charlotte is clearly unlike the "distant, self-centred woman" whose portrait reveals a "long coldly beautiful face" (324, 330). When Kenneth's friends comment that "Elsie Ashby absolutely dominated him," Charlotte responds jokingly with "he may be glad of a little liberty for a change" (327). When her husband begins receiving letters that clearly make him uncomfortable, Charlotte hesitates to question him directly about them the way, the clues suggest, Elsie probably would have. Instead she chooses a more underhanded way to find out what she wants to know, spying on Kenneth from behind the door in his library as he enters the house and sees the most recent letter. She wants, she reasons, to "see what happened between him and the letter when they thought themselves unobserved," phrasing that reveals the human potency she grants this written communication (333).

Charlotte has loved Kenneth's "long shabby library, full of books and pipes and worn armchairs inviting to meditation," but true to Wharton's Gothic, this library will be the source of unsettling discovery for Charlotte (323–24). From her secret vantage point in the library she sees her husband pale, then stare at and kiss the letter's pages. The sight gives her the incentive to press him with questions about the writer and his relationship to her, questions that her husband just as persistently resists. Rather than gaining insight from Kenneth in a reasoned way, Charlotte ends up immersed in the uncanny, "as if the strange talk she had just had with her husband must have taken place in another world, between two beings who were not Charlotte Gorse and Kenneth Ashby, but phantoms projected by her fevered imagination" (342).

Throughout her attempt to understand the powerful control her husband seems the victim of, Charlotte herself senses that within her house is something she can't explain, can't relate to the twentieth century world outside her house, "Something as old as the world, as mysterious as life" (331). She feels unable to "penetrate the mystery," "completely in the dark," and "groping in the fog," as fearful and confused as heroines in traditional Gothic novels wandering in dark castle hallways or the young Edith Wharton questioning her mother about "the whole dark mystery" of sexuality, which fills her with dread (335, 350, 352). Charlotte too is groping with fears about sexuality, struggling to understand what she senses is another woman's power over her husband.

When Charlotte feels that she had "faced the phantom and dispelled it" by persuading her husband to escape the power of the letters he has been receiving and take a vacation with her, the self-congratulation she indulges in is quickly and painfully overshadowed by her husband's disappearance (352). "Courage—that's the secret! If only people who are in love weren't always so afraid of risking their happiness by looking it in the eyes" she boasts to herself, presuming incorrectly that she has triumphed over the risk (352). This misplaced hubris is matched by that of an earlier revelation, when Kenneth moves Elsie's portrait from his library to the nursery: "Kenneth's love had penetrated to the secret she hardly acknowledged to her own heart—her passionate need to feel herself the sovereign even of his past" (330). Implicit in this admission is that Charlotte feels that now she *is* "the sovereign even of his past."

Quickly Charlotte learns that she hasn't triumphed, isn't a sovereign over Kenneth, doesn't fully understand what she's dealing with. Although she tells her mother-in-law that she had known "for a long time now that everything was possible," even Kenneth being taken from her by the dead Elsie, Charlotte can't read Elsie's letters as Kenneth can, can't fully understand the mystery that Elsie represents (365). Charlotte is perhaps the most brave of those in Wharton's Gothic who face the dark abyss of the feminine, but her fate, like Jane's before her, is left uncertain.

Read in the context of Wharton's previous Gothic fiction, where the feminine is repressed and oppressed by the masculine, this story's most significant achievement is the deconstruction of these earlier gender distinctions in the portrayal of Elsie and Kenneth. The most notable detail about the letters Kenneth receives from Elsie is that the handwriting is both female and male, "so visibly feminine" in spite of its "masculine curves" (325). "For all its strength and assurance" the writing is "without a doubt a woman's," according to Charlotte's analysis, even though Kenneth counters that "the writing is generally supposed to look more like a man's" (325, 336).

Elsie Corder's name, echoing both Eleusinian and Kore, marks her connection to woman-centered myth.[9] At the same time Elsie's ability to dominate Kenneth after her death, as she has done while alive, by disorienting him and eventually drawing him to her with her letters, emphasizes her "male" power of control and intellect. Even her portrait, which Charlotte feels is following her with "guarded eyes" and Kenneth believes will be "looking down on" (and ostensibly guiding) his and Elsie's children while they grow, wields affective power rather than representing her as a possessed piece of art, as portraits of women do in "The Young Gentlemen" and "Mr. Jones."

Elsie's amalgamated powers of fe/maleness are a reminder that the myth of the Kore-Persephone abduction by Pluto was preceded by an earlier religious belief according to which Persephone was the "Death-goddess" and a "Queen of She-Demons" (B. Walker 786). Indeed, she was "Queen of the Underworld long before there was a masculinized Pluto" (786). Known as "Destroyer," Persephone was "the Crone form of the Triple Goddess Demeter, whose other *personae* were Kore the Virgin and Demeter-Pluto the Mother (or Preserver)" (786).

Elsie is a reminder, too, of the defiant Persephone created by Wharton in her 1912 poem, "Pomegranate Seed." Unlike the Hellenic Persephone, Wharton's resists Demeter's reclaiming her as if she were the person who had not lived in the underworld. She also contradicts Demeter's assumption that her new knowledge is of "some dreadful thing" (289). Instead she proudly claims her new life and rejects her mother's plea to return to earth:

I, that have eaten of the seed of death,
And with my dead die daily, am become
Of their undying kindred, and no more
Can sit within the doorway of the gods
And laughing spin new souls along the years.
. . . .
The kingdom of the dead is wider still,
And there I heal the wounds that thou hast made. [290–91, ellipsis mine]

At this Demeter concedes, "Stand off from me. Thou knowest more than I, / Who am but the servant of some lonely will" (291). Like this Persephone, Elsie is clearly a powerful female force rather than a victim of male violence as Hellenic myth portrays Persephone/Kore.[10]

Kenneth too is other than the controlling male character typical in Wharton's Gothic. As Elsie's husband, "he was more like an unhappy lover than a comfortably contented husband," let alone a dominating one (G 329). Kenneth doesn't dominate Charlotte either, but has instead exhibited a "persistent, almost too insistent tenderness" and given her the feeling that he is "too eagerly dependent on her, too searchingly close to her, as if there were not air enough between her soul and his" (343). A lawyer, he submits to Charlotte's cross-examining about the letter writer's identity "with a sort of contemptuous composure, as though he were humoring an unreasonable child," but this intellectual superiority dissolves into terror and distress when Charlotte points out that she saw him kissing the latest letter (347). When pressured by Charlotte to explain why they can't go away together, Kenneth covers his face with his hands and weeps. When she guesses that the writer of the letters won't let them go away, Kenneth clutches her hand convulsively, as if he were "slipping over a precipice" (350). Kenneth isn't strong enough to acknowledge to Charlotte, or perhaps even to himself, Elsie's terrible female power. The repression weakens him and his relationship to Charlotte.

As a result of Kenneth's secrecy about Elsie, Charlotte feels "excluded, ignored, blotted out of his life" (340). Kenneth's mother, too, excludes Charlotte from her knowledge of Elsie's power over her son. The senior Mrs. Ashby has been kind to Charlotte, but Charlotte's belief that her "almost uncanny directness might pierce to the core of this new mystery" and then explain it to her is only half right (344). Indeed, Mrs. Ashby's resistance to admitting that she recognizes Elsie's handwriting and understands her power recalls the secretive Mrs. Clemm in "Mr. Jones." When Charlotte threatens to open the latest letter, it sounds like Jane's threat to break into the muniment room. The description of Mrs. Ashby's reaction—her "glossy bloom was effaced by a quick pallor; her firm cheeks seemed to shrink and wither"—at once echoes and comments on the language used to describe Mrs. Clemm when she hears Jane's threat: "bathed in that odd pallor which enclosed but seemed unable to penetrate the solid crimson of her cheeks" (360–61; 307–308). While Mrs. Clemm's face doesn't fully register what she knows (the pallor doesn't penetrate her crimson cheeks), Mrs. Ashby's facial transformation reveals her awareness.[11] She scolds Charlotte about opening Kenneth's mail behind his back, however, rather than supporting Charlotte's need to understand what has happened to him.

The mother figure's propensity for keeping knowledge from a younger woman in these stories encourages us to read Charlotte's agonized request, "Mother! What do you know? Tell me! You must!" as a rephrasing of Wharton's agonized request of her mother, recalled in "Life and I," to tell her what she knows about sexuality, "I'm afraid Mamma—I want to know what will happen to me" (*G* 361; "Life" 34). Mrs. Ashby's ability to "pierce to the core of this new mystery," with the play in this phrase on core/Kore, emphasizes her role as a source of knowledge fundamental to a woman. Core calls to mind an apple—figure of love and sexuality, knowledge and death—and Kore, the pomegranate seed, female-genital symbol of "love and death, rebirth and fertility" (B. Walker, 806); Friedrich 177). Then too, there is Charlotte's sense, when she looks at Mrs. Ashby's face, of "what depths of the unknown may lurk under the clearest and most candid lineaments" (*G* 364). The "unknown" has been synonymous in Wharton's Gothic with the abyss, the dark source of knowledge about the feminine/maternal that most characters flee from in fear.

By the story's end, when Charlotte realizes that Kenneth has joined Elsie, despite her mother-in-law's resolute declaration that he will return, she stands up "slowly and stiffly" because "her joints felt as cramped as an old woman's" (367). Given that the senior Mrs. Ashby is also "slightly lame" the detail encourages us to see Charlotte becoming the older Mrs. Ashby (359). Charlotte's new-found understanding of Elsie's power links her not only with the senior Mrs. Ashby but with Elsie as well, the second Mrs. Ashby, as her realizations increase. The three Mrs. Ashbys recall again the Triple Goddess Demeter, embodiment of women's stages of life—innocent youth, middle-aged maturity, and old age—and women's different ways of knowing throughout their life.

In spite of the limited-omniscient narrator's assertion that Charlotte Ashby is a "sophisticated woman," possessing "few illusions about the intricacies of the human heart," the story plays on her innocence, on the limitations of her sophistication (328). Though she acknowledges "old entanglements," she has no idea that her husband's extend beyond death. Newly married and baffled by the cause of her husband's emotional upheaval, Charlotte is, in comparison to Elsie and her mother-in-law, innocent about the powers of passion, will, and death that Elsie wields.

As mother, lover, and influential writer, Elsie is the most dominant of the three Mrs. Ashbys. She represents a maturity, a fullness of power that Charlotte cannot match and that the senior Mrs. Ashby is overwhelmed by despite herself. Though deemed "a distant, self-centered woman," Elsie is known to us only through Charlotte's perspective, so we have reason to think more generously of her strength than Charlotte does. Her writing, so indistinct, so difficult for Charlotte to decipher, exemplifies Mary Jacobus's description of women's writing that deconstructs male discourse and writes "what cannot be written" ("The Difference" 13). The "mine" and "come" that Charlotte detects in Elsie's letter are words of desire. These are not Juliana's plaintive letters, in "Mr. Jones," questioning her unwanted seclusion and her oppression, but rather letters that, by encoding desire, challenge boundaries of time, of distance, of gender. In Elsie, Wharton inscribes a femininity that is neither mute nor constrained.[12]

When Mrs. Ashby senior looks at Elsie's writing, her face wears "a look of fear and hatred, of incredulous dismay and almost cringing defiance" (G 364). But she denies what she sees. "There's nothing in this letter," she tells Charlotte, nothing, that is, that she is willing to talk about, to share with Charlotte (366). Her paleness, her shrunken and withered cheeks, her fear, all indicate how much, in her old age, she is still denying about female desire.

"Pomegranate Seed" takes its readers into the mystery of passion and death and gives us a glimpse into the abyss. It defiantly removes a woman from the restraints under which the women in other Gothic stories have suffered, and provides, in its tripartite portrayal of the three Mrs. Ashbys, an overview of women's response to their own power.

Each of Wharton's last two completed companion novels, *Hudson River Bracketed* and *The Gods Arrive*, published in 1929 and 1932, respectively, contains echoes and significant revisions of the story preceding it, "Mr. Jones" in 1928 and "Pomegranate Seed" in 1930, as well as of the Gothic elements in earlier novels, *The House of Mirth, Ethan Frome, Summer,* and *The Age of Innocence.* Wharton's most significant achievement in her last two novels is her male protagonist's response to the abyss, the mysterious feminine that so threatens earlier male characters. Rather than being terrified by the maternal depths and the loss of rational control and well-defined ego they signify, Vance Weston embraces the experience of falling into this mysterious altered state because he recognizes that what he calls "The Mothers" is a source of his creativity. Crucial to Vance's openness to the feminine/maternal is his willingness to face and assimilate what he calls "the Past," which is both his literary, intellectual heritage and his personal, primal past.

Wharton's recasting of this primary element in the Gothic experience as she has developed it in her fiction alters how she handles other elements as well. Realizations in libraries, ascents up mountains, and mysterious houses common to Wharton's Gothic take on decidedly different significance in these last novels than they have earlier. These revisions in turn help Wharton complicate and enrich gender roles in the novels, such that Vance Weston and Halo Spear enact the stereotypes of the villainous man and victimized woman while also refuting those roles and embracing one another's characteristics. Wharton now sees the conflict *between* the masculine and feminine spheres, so apparent in the short stories, as a conflict *within* both a woman and a man, evident in Vance's and Halo's parallel realizations and experiences in their respective development processes. Wharton thus moves closer toward the evolution of characters who accept their femininity as well as their masculinity.

The ironic comment, at the beginning of *Hudson River Bracketed,* that Advance Weston had "soared to these heights, and plumbed these depths" because of several superficial accomplishments by the time he is nineteen prepares the reader for his intense experience of the heights and depths during the course of the novel (*HRB* 3). Initially a smug young man who believes, like his parents, that "the real business of life was to keep going, to get there—and 'There' was where money was, always and exclusively," he also has traits that portend his embrace of an identity that conflicts with the traditional male money-making identity that he expects to have (15).

Like Charity Royall at the beginning of *Summer,* Vance, at the beginning of *Hudson River Bracketed,* feels "a passionate desire to embrace the budding earth and everything that stirred and swelled in it" (12). Though he longs to know the names of the natural things around him, he also "wasn't in the mood for books, with this spring air caressing him" (13). It is while in this "fog of formless yearnings" that he sees his grandfather on his way to a tryst with the young woman he himself had once been involved with (20). The sight plunges Vance into a nervous breakdown, complicated by an unidentified medical condition. That he should feel such revulsion and have such a calamitous reaction to what, on the face of it, appears to be just a bit of sexual dalliance, albeit by two people he knows intimately, suggests his precariously tentative sense of himself and his sexuality.

Upon coming out of weeks of unconsciousness, he listens to his family "as though he were dead, and the family chatter came to him through his mound in the Cedarcrest cemetery," with his mind in "an airless limbo between life and death" (28). The intolerable oppression makes him feel "like a captive walled into a dark airless cell, and the walls of that cell were Reality, were the life he would in future be doomed to" (30). His depression leads him to consider suicide with his father's revolver, but when he feels "the arms of Life, the ancient mother, reaching out to him, winding about him, crushing him fast again to her great careless bosom," he commits himself instead to living and to writing as a way of "reconciling his soul to its experiences" (31, 32).

Vance's near-death experience recalls Lily Bart's depressive spiral into self-destruction; Charity Royall's deathlike marriage to her guardian in *Summer*; the narrator's plunge into his paralyzing vision in *Ethan Frome*; Ellen Olenska's going "beyond," returning as if from the dead to her childhood home, and creating a new life for herself in *The Age of Innocence*; and Wharton's own near-death experience with typhoid as well as her several nervous breakdowns. Wharton has Vance extend Ellen's creativity and imitate her own by becoming a writer as a result of having plunged to the depths of his soul and defying death. Out of Vance's experience comes an ever-increasing respect for the state of being beyond the rational and controllable, in the spiritual depths that, because of the vulnerability and overwhelmingness they engender, can terrify if one resists their pull.

Henceforth Vance will welcome his lapses into the dreamlike state of creativity that at first he understands little about: "He could not imagine putting down on paper anything that had not risen slowly to the verge of his consciousness, that had not to be fished for and hauled up with infinite precautions from some secret pool of being as to which he knew nothing as yet but the occasional leap, deep down in it, of something alive but invisible" (176–77). Eventually, when comparing his work with that of other contemporary writers, he is better able to clarify that to get to "the real stuff" one must fall into "the depths ruled by The Mothers," the mysterious Mothers of *Faust*, "moving in subterranean depths among the primal forms of life," the depths "which held the source of things" (336, 391, 444). Like the "warm darkness of the pre-natal fluid far below our conscious reason" from which derives, Wharton believes, the ability to be aware of ghosts (and by extension all fictional characters), "The Mothers" are, for Vance, the source within him of his creativity (G vii).

In acknowledging the feminine/maternal as an integral part of his being, Vance acknowledges a spiritual source of power as well as a creative one. A conversation with his grandmother about God leads him to realize that, "Perhaps what she called 'God' was the same as what he called 'The Mothers'—that mysterious Sea of Being of which the dark reaches swayed and rumoured in his soul . . . perhaps one symbol was as good as another to figure the imperceptible point where the fleeting human consciousness touches Infinity" (*HRB* 449).

The depths as Wharton has defined them are thus the source of one's spiritual power, a self-empowerment possible because of the acknowledgment of one's feminine/maternal self. This shift in control from external, patriarchal God to internal "Sea of Being" may well mirror Wharton's own transition from a lifetime of suspicion about Christianity as she experienced it as a child to the spirituality in which she found peace later in life. In "Life and I" she recounts being horrified as a child "by the sanguinary conception of the Atonement" and yet not questioning the reality of "this dreadful Being," whom she accepted "as one of the dark fatalities that seemed to weigh on the lives of mortals" (40).

Vance's rejection of his grandmother's God suggests a similar distrust of giving an external patriarchal being the power one might find in oneself. As he says to his grandmother early in the novel, "what I want is to get way out beyond Him, out somewhere where He won't look any bigger than a speck; and the god in *me* can sort of walk all round Him" (*HRB* 17). While at first he thinks of his soul as "a stranger inside of him, a stranger speaking a language he had never learned, or had forgotten" he evolves into an understanding and acceptance of the creative life source preceding language, much like Kristeva's *sémiotique*, the surge and pulsing of "archaic processes" feeding one's creativity (47; Van Buren 19).

Wharton further recasts her Gothic text by having Vance first experience the "dark Unknown," which he comes to call "The Mothers" and "that mysterious Sea of Being," in a mysterious old house, the Willows (*HRB* 61).[13] The connection between feminine life force and house suggested in Wharton's earlier Gothic fiction now becomes overt. In discussing the house as a dream image of the human body, Freud distinguishes houses with smooth facades as male and those with balconies and projections as female (Chandler 12). In this interpretation the Willows, which Vance first sees as if in a dream, is distinctively "female": "The shuttered windows were very tall and narrow, and narrow too the balconies, which projected at odd angles, supported by ornate wooden brackets" (*HRB* 58). The Willows once belonged to Elinor Lorburn, in whose "gentleman's library" Vance learns about "the incomprehensible past to which she and the house belonged, a past so remote, so full of elusive mystery, that Vance's first thought was: 'Why wasn't I ever told about the Past before?' " (68, 61–62).

The capitalization of "the Past," a device of which Wharton makes liberal use in *Hudson River Bracketed*, encourages a symbolic reading of the word as meaning not only the intellectual heritage found in Elinor Lorburn's books but also the archaic, primal origins of all life. Both meanings conjoin in Vance's comparison of the house to the "haunting sonority" of a church bell he once heard tolling the hour one night during his youth and his reaction to the poetry he reads in the house's library, as if "the bell was swinging and clanging all about him now, enveloping him in great undulations of sound like the undulations of a summer sea" (59, 63).

Vance's reference to the house as a bell with "a past so remote, so full of elusive mystery," that "its age, its mystery, its reserve laid a weight on his heart," recalls Lady Jane Lynke's more tentative, even frightened reaction to Bells, her ancestral home, in "Mr. Jones," as "too old, too mysterious, too much withdrawn into its own secret past, for her own poor little present to fit into it without uneasiness" (*HRB* 62, 58; *G* 298). Vance's immediate enthrallment with the Willows and the ease with which he claims it as a source of creative sustenance contrasts vividly with Jane's hesitancy about claiming her feminine self embodied in Bells. Of course there is no misogynist Mr. Jones terrorizing the Willows. Instead there is Elinor Lorburn, whose presence emanates from her portrait in the library and her glasses on a copy of Coleridge's "Kubla Khan" lying open on her reading table next to her Gothic armchair, as if she had just gotten up from it and "ascended to her frame" (*HRB* 61). An unmarried woman, she seems sad to Vance but not "shrunken," a woman who has "ripened" rather than "withering," because both "her books, and some inner source of life, had kept her warm" (333).

Vance's response to Elinor Lorburn recalls Newland Archer's response to Ellen Olenska, in *The Age of Innocence*. Ellen too possesses an inner vitality and strength and the "mysterious faculty of suggesting tragic and moving possibilities outside the daily run of experience" that Vance senses from Miss Lorburn's portrait (*AI* 113). Ellen's "peeling stucco house with a giant wisteria throttling its feeble cast-iron balcony," whose mysterious atmosphere so unsettles yet enthralls Newland, is elaborated on and extended in the Willows (65). Yearly "losing more of its paint," the facade of the Willows suggests "vastness, fantasy and secrecy," a sense communicated by the veil of ancient weeping willows in front of it and by a huge ancient wisteria climbing from balcony to balcony (*HRB* 498, 57). Halo Spear's reference to Elinor Lorburn's "funny library" echoes Ellen's fond reference to her "funny house" that is "like heaven" because it provides her with a nourishing maternal realm where she can freely live the life she pleases (67; *AI* 70). Likewise, the Willows provides Vance with the "great nutritive element" of continuity, that "underlying deep," that feeds his creative life (*HRB* 498). The house's "revelation of an unknown world" to Vance is an intensification of Newland's bewilderment with Ellen's paintings and books in her house, his sense that the atmosphere of her drawing room "was so different from any he had ever breathed that self-consciousness vanished in the sense of adventure" (68; *AI* 68).

The parallels between Ellen and Elinor, their houses, and the responses of the two male characters to them show Wharton's persistent interest in this dynamic but also her revision of it. Ellen's impact on Newland's life is most pronounced during the 1870s when she tries to escape her past by returning to her childhood home; her maturity triumphs over her own fears and gives Newland an experience of womanhood he would never know again. By the end of *The Age of Innocence,* however, she exists only in Newland's imagination when he visits Paris, living what appears in his daydreams as a life filled with "the incessant stir of ideas, curiosities, images and associations" in culturally rich France (362). Elinor, living in the 1830s, is, in Vance's mind, "a creature apt for love, but somehow caught in the cruel taboos and inhibitions of her day, and breaking through them too late to find compensation except under another guise: the guise of poetry, dreams, visions" (*HRB* 359). Her life becomes not only an inspiration for his writing but also the subject of it in his first novel, *Instead.*

Significantly, he shares his vision of Elinor with Halo Spear, with whom he consults while writing the book and who becomes increasingly associated in his mind with Elinor and her house. This primary Gothic element, the encounter in a mysterious house with an alternative way of being, takes on, in *Hudson River Bracketed,* a significance well beyond that in *The Age of Innocence,* especially because Vance fully accepts the house's power to take him into an alternative consciousness and because Halo as well is drawn by the house into her own reconsideration of her identity. In Halo, the intelligent, independent woman Elinor Lorburn was lives on to flout the "taboos and inhibitions of her day." Vance's and Halo's common respect for and immersion in the spirit of the Willows is the most fundamental of the many parallels between them in both *Hudson River Bracketed* and *The Gods Arrive.*

Vance and Halo have each been called Wharton's alter ego, but in fact, like her characterizations of Newland and Ellen, both are elements of Wharton's "self" (Fryer 102; Kellogg 276). Vance and Halo, the masculine and feminine, "belong to each other," as Halo says at the end of *The Gods Arrive,* are together a whole personality (*GA* 432). Recognizing that Halo Spear is as much a central character as Vance Weston, that their stories are parallel, is essential to understanding Wharton's key point in these last two novels: that woman and man must each accommodate the logical and the unreasoned, control and lack of it, sociability and solitude, culture and the depth of feeling from which it emerges.[14] Both must accept the fear and pain of facing the dark sides of themselves and their lives together if they are to be mature individuals, rather than perpetuating the Gothic stereotypes that paralyze both women and men. In the novels Vance plays the egocentric, destructive Gothic villain and Halo the passive, self-destructive Gothic victim, but each goes through an individual yet similar process of resisting these stereotypical roles and becoming a person who is autonomous yet connected to others, both "masculine" and "feminine."

The characteristic Vance most shares with Gothic villains before him is his penchant for treating his frail wife Laura Lou like a possession and trying to do the same to Halo. From the moment when he first angrily claims his, rather than Bunty Hayes's, ownership of Laura Lou—"How dare you, after this after-noon—how dare you speak to me as if you belonged to that fellow and not to me?"—until her death at the end of *Hudson River Bracketed*, Vance assumes his wife to be whatever he wants her to be (*HRB* 214). Laura Lou is in the process of gaining a modicum of education, paid for by her fiancee Bunty Hayes, when she meets Vance again after three years, but she loses that small opportunity for self-advancement when she marries him rather than Bunty.

Because of his physical attraction to Laura Lou, Vance convinces himself he loves her, but his arrogant, intellectually condescending disregard of her as an individual makes him as cruel as earlier Gothic villains. "What's the use of trying to write poetry, when she *is?*" Vance rhapsodizes about Laura Lou, do-ing her the dangerous disservice of seeing her as art rather than as a person (212). In his analysis of her appearance, as well, he compares her to "those mar-ble heads of Greek priestesses with the smile under their lids" and later, on their wedding night, he refers to her "little marble image" (205, 248). Though meant admiringly, the images menacingly remind the reader of the Duke in "The Duchess at Prayer," whose creation of a marble statue of his wife is a prelude to killing her. More metaphorical but no less destructive spirit-killing takes place in "The House of the Dead Hand" and *The House of Mirth* because Sybilla and Lily allow themselves to be confused with images in paintings and treated as objects of collectable, admirable art.

Vance's proprietary response to Laura Lou also resembles Newland Arch-er's to May Welland. Before their engagement Newland watches May watch *Faust* and "contemplated her absorbed young face with a thrill of possessorship in which pride in his own masculine initiation was mingled with a tender rev-erence for her abysmal purity" (*AI* 4–5). He is "proud of the glances turned on her," and her "vacant serenity of a young marble athlete" initially enhances her appeal for him (79, 141). Likewise, Vance notices that "every masculine eye was turned to them" when he takes Laura Lou to dinner, and he "noticed how peo-ple turned their heads" when Laura Lou enters an art gallery they've gone to together (*HRB* 251, 421). "Masculine pride flushed through him, and he slipped his arm possessively in hers" (421–22). But just as May's art object beauty means that "not a thought seemed to have passed behind her eyes" and makes her "in-capable of growth," an obliviousness that later dismays Newland, Vance is in-creasingly disheartened by his wife's "little unchangeable self," her inability to share his intellectual life (*AI* 211, 351; *HRB* 386). While knowing Ellen helps Newland understand a woman's power when her intellectual and spiritual life make her more than an art object to be admired, so Vance, in knowing Halo Spear, eventually understands what Laura Lou's life isn't.

When he marries her, though, Laura Lou is "as much of a luxury as an exotic bird or flower: that she might help him in wage-earning or housekeeping had never entered his mind. He had simply wanted her past endurance, and now he had her; and exquisite as the possession was, he was abruptly faced with the cost of it" (*HRB* 250). Never able to handle the cost or understand the consequences of his wife's lack of a life of her own, he leaves her daily in their one-room, dilapidated apartments as one might an inanimate object, while he pursues an intellectual life apart from her. Since from the moment of her marriage to Vance, "everything she was, or wanted, was immersed in himself," Laura Lou quickly loses whatever identity she had and then fades away into death (239). Her end is reminiscent of Lily Bart's who, "since she had been brought up to be ornamental," like "some rare flower grown for exhibition," and so is "very expensive" to keep, dies penniless and physically wasted in a dreary boarding-house room (*HM* 480, 512, 14).

Lily Bart has spirit and individuality enough to know instinctually that she doesn't want to marry someone in order to be kept as a beautiful object, and it is her inability to create an alternative life script that dooms her. Laura Lou seems to have none of Lily's spunk or native intelligence, but in any case the readers learning of her plight are given slight detail about her upon which to build the admiration we feel for Lily. Laura Lou serves mainly as the possessed object but also as a female component of Vance's nascent individuality as it develops in the novel, a vulnerable, sexual part of himself that he alternately prizes and mistreats through neglect. This parallel is most apparent in their common description as children. *"Little Children, Love One Another,"* the tattered calendar over their bed reads in the shanty in which they spend their first night after their marriage (*HRB* 245). "He had bound himself fast to this child," Vance realizes that night, "he, hardly more than a child himself in knowledge of men and in the mysterious art of getting on" (247).

Beyond their shared passion, Vance and Laura Lou know little about one another. Vance shares almost none of his intellectual life with Laura Lou, and she becomes "mysterious" to him after they marry, the "closest part of himself henceforth, yet utterly remote and inexplicable; a woman with a sealed soul, but with a body that clung to his" (248). The description of her place in his life echoes his early description of his own soul as a "mysterious stranger within one's self, closer than one's bones and yet with a face and speech forever unknown to one" (47). Although he has opened himself to the sexual vulnerability that Laura Lou embodies, he doesn't understand it and makes no attempt to. His agonized questions "What do I know about her? What does she know about me?" terrify him (248). When he imagines Laura Lou dead and himself free of the responsibility he has incurred by marrying her, he is horrified, because, like lightning, the vision "lit up whole tracts of himself that he had never seen" (249). Again, as with Laura Lou's death, Lily Bart's last night comes to mind, when, trying to lose herself in chloral-induced unconsciousness, she is suddenly awakened, "as though a great blaze of electric light had been turned on in her head, and her poor little anguished self shrank and cowered in it, without knowing where to take refuge" (*HM* 520). Lily dies suppressing her inner life, never facing the terror of self-scrutiny and self-acceptance.

Vance doesn't understand himself either at this point, but he finds the sustenance that Lily never does from nature. Once outside he is possessed by "a sense of unifying power" with the world around him (*HRB* 249). Facing the sea he has "a mystic vision" that gives him "the meaning of beauty, the secret of poetry, the sense of the forces struggling in him for expression" (249). Laura Lou, he realizes, is "the vessel from which he had drunk this divine reassurance, this moment of union with the universe" (249). Vance's transcendental experience provides spiritual support not available to Lily, but his relegation of Laura Lou to "vessel" reveals how much he still needs to understand about human beings before this mystic vision can be truly incorporated into his life. His cruel objectification is also evident when, after Laura Lou's death, he acknowledges the pathos of her "thwarted destiny" while referring to her as "that larval image among the white roses" (552, 551). We might read this cruelty as simply Wharton's satirical thrust at immature male artists were it not so reminiscent of her earlier Gothic men, whose objectification of women kills them.[15] In this context, Vance is not only immature but dangerous.

Halo Spear, the other woman in Vance Weston's life, is, from the start, a female parallel to him rather than being submerged in him like Laura Lou. With these parallels, Wharton further evolves the theme of gender mutuality that she has been developing throughout her career in the Gothic subtexts of her realistic novels (in contrast to the conflict played out in the Gothic short stories). As a reminder of the destructiveness of those conflicting roles, Halo's personality has elements of the Gothic victim just as Vance's has elements of the Gothic villain.

First, the parallels between Halo and Vance. Like Vance, Halo gains spiritual strength from nature. Only she, of all her family and close friends, is attuned to the "enveloping harmony" of the view from Eaglewood, the family home, overlooking the Hudson and the cliffs beyond (75). For her, the beauty is "so ever-varying, so soul-sufficing, so complete," providing a sense of "inner communion" her acquisitive family doesn't have (77, 80). She is a lover of learning as well, just as Vance is. The books in the library of her cousin Elinor are "treasures," and her knowledge of them is wide ranging (88). She quotes *Faust* in German and enthuses to Vance about the beautiful music of poetry. Both feel the mystery of the Willows and respect Elinor Lorburn's spiritual presence in it.

Like Vance, Halo is impulsive and scorns pretension. "And what a wonderful thing life would be without idle preliminaries—" she muses, and she believes that "getting at once to the heart of things: that was the secret. But how many people know it, or had any idea where the heart of things really was?"

(91). Halo has "a way of dashing straight at the essentials," Vance says of her, just as she says that he has "that way of going straight to his object, dashing through all the customary preliminaries" (356, 224).

Like Vance, Halo knows financial difficulty firsthand; while living with her family she lives with "pecuniary makeshifts, with the evasions and plausibilities of people muddling along on insufficient means, bluffing, borrowing, dodging their creditors," a financial state Vance lives in once he leaves his family (499). Financial debt plays a role in both their marriages, though with crucial differences. When Vance marries Laura Lou, he is strapped with the obligation to repay Bunty Hayes the thousand dollars Hayes loaned her for her education, while Halo feels obligated to marry Lewis Tarrant because of the loans he has made to her family.

Both Halo and Vance suffer from intense loneliness in unhappy marriages. Her marriage is described as the "dull backwater," his as the "blank enigma" (501, 428). Though "it was a word she did not admit in her vocabulary," Halo is lonely and finally confesses it to her family friend, George Frenside (220). Vance, too, is lonely in his marriage, and "his inner solitude was deeper than ever" as time passes (310). Because the financial favors Lewis has done Halo's family are "the links of her chain," her "common sense warned her to make the best of her fate" (353). Vance too feels "handcuffed and chained" to his life with his wife and "imprisoned by fate," just as Halo describes herself as "chained to" Lewis Tarrant "for life" (442, 297, 352). Although Vance realizes that it *isn't* fate but rather "his own headlong folly" that has gotten him into his marriage, he wishes to be "free, free, free, in body as well as mind, yes, and in heart as well as soul" (297, 296). Halo echoes these words and sentiments when she explains to Vance that she has inherited money and the Willows, has decided to leave her husband, and is now "free, free, free!" (557).

While Halo's life parallels Vance's in ways that indicate Wharton's deliberate pairing of them, as feminine and masculine counterparts, Halo also has the traits and experiences of Gothic victims before her, suggesting that she, like Vance, must undergo a transformative revision of her sense of herself. As a young woman she is as devoid of an independent life script as Lily Bart is twenty-four years earlier in *The House of Mirth*. Halo's musings about herself reveal a sense similar to Lily's that, as hateful as the thought is, marriage is her only way to a financially independent life, that she is devoid of any talent except as a marriage partner, that only "luck" will save her from being bought by a man:

> Ah, how she envied the girls of her age who had their own cars, who led their own lives, sometimes even had their own bachelor flats in New York! Except as a means to independence riches were nothing to her; and to acquire them by marriage, and then coldly make use of them for her own purposes, was as distasteful to her as anything in her present life. And yet she longed for freedom, and saw no other way to it. If only her eager interest in life had been

matched by some creative talent! She could half-paint, she could half-write—but her real gift (and she knew it) was for appreciating the gifts of others. Even had discipline and industry fostered her slender talents they would hardly have brought her a living. She had measured herself and knew it—and what else was there for her but marriage? "Oh, well," she thought, for the thousandth time, "something may turn up." [109]

Because she summarily dismisses her own talents and devotes no imaginative energy to finding an alternative to marrying a man as payment for the debts incurred by her family, Halo puts herself in the position of sacrificial victim. She knows intellectually that even for a comfortable amount of money, "there was a price not worth paying. That price was herself; her personality, as the people about her would have called it; the something which made Halo Spear and no other. Of that something, she often told herself, she would never surrender the least jot" (183). Yet she does just that, surrenders her freedom to be herself by marrying Lewis Tarrant when her brother's theft of antique books from the Willows causes her disinheritance. Even after becoming aware of her husband's cruelty and her own unhappiness she believes herself "chained to him for life" because it is "her business" to suit him (352, 353). Not to is to cause her family's collapse. Her intellectual belief in herself isn't yet matched by the inner courage or self-understanding and self-acceptance such belief demands, the kind of depth and courage Ellen Olenska displays when she refuses to return to her husband despite financial and familial pressures to do so.

Wharton's persistent reference, in *Hudson River Bracketed*, to Halo's "shortsighted eyes" also emphasizes her shortsightedness about her possibilities, a deficiency that allows her to be "bought" by her husband but which she eventually corrects in *The Gods Arrive* by going through the kind of spiritual journey into herself that Vance goes through (69, 90, 103, 106, 279, 340, 353). Although Halo's moral sensitivity in deciding to "cover" for her family through marriage is acknowledged, her solution isn't condoned (501). "Why had she not washed her hands" of her family and "gone her own way in the modern manner?" the narrator asks rhetorically (501). Because, we are told, she felt a sort of "grateful tenderness" to her parents for their affection and their cultivation of her mind and spirit. She loved their "romantic responsiveness as much as she raged against their incurable dishonesty" (501). What she considers Tarrant's financial generosity to her family causes her to mistake tender gratitude for love, and "on this tidal wave of delusion," along with the knowledge that she has been disinherited and the belief that she has no other choice, she is "swept into" her marriage (501). Her seeming lack of control over this life choice resembles Vance's being swept by physical passion into marriage with Laura Lou, giving us feminine and masculine reasons for becoming enmeshed in inauthentic selves.

Halo's husband, Lewis Tarrant, has the attributes of the cruel would-be intellectuals in earlier Gothic stories: the Duke in "The Duchess at Prayer," Lombard in "The House of the Dead Hand," Culwin in "The Eyes." His "thin lips," "cold eyes," "nervous transparent hands," "thin sensitive nose," "dissatisfied mouth," "ivory-like sallowness" and "ironically-lifted eyebrows" are the outward attributes of a cold, thin-spirited man who takes pleasure in bullying and humiliating others when he can (274, 350, 192, 185, 480). We know more about the psychology of Lewis Tarrant than we do about earlier tyrants; we know, for example, that his penchant for demeaning others comes from insecurity. Halo realizes that beneath her husband's controlled exterior lurks "an exaggerated craving for recognition," that "the myth of his intellectual isolation was necessary to Tarrant's pride," and that "the satisfaction of asserting his superiority by depreciating what she had praised would outweigh any advantage he might miss by doing so" (216, 219, 220). She knows too, however, that whatever its underlying cause, her husband practices a refined cruelty, that he has a "deadly patience" for retaliation and a "faculty for provoking violent scenes—his cool incisiveness cutting into the soul like a white-hot blade into flesh. The pound of flesh nearest the heart—that was what he always exacted" (487, 488).

Besides the financial reasons, Halo stays in this self-destructive relationship with Lewis Tarrant and enters another just as self-destructive with Vance because of her sense that "her real gift" is "appreciating the gifts of others," that is, being their muse (109). Such a role defines her as other than a human being, a dangerous position that women before her in Wharton's Gothic have been in when they become objects of art. At the Willows Halo avidly takes on the role of "monitress and muse" to Vance (231). Later as her marriage unravels and she becomes increasingly lonely, she struggles with the conflict between being muse and lover. She is "passionately in love with his mind" she says of Vance, yet "would it not have mortified her to be treated forever like a disembodied intelligence?" (484). No sooner does she realize this than she is extolling just such a role: "To be his Muse, his inspiration—then there really was some meaning in the stale old image!" (485).

Vance obliges Halo's view of herself as Muse by seeing her as a woman he wants to kiss and hold but also as the "disembodied intelligence" she is afraid of becoming, "the goddess, the miracle, the unattainable being who haunted the peaks of his imagination" (362, 439). Just as he considers Laura Lou to be a vessel from which he drinks divine "reassurance," he feels Halo to be "the mysterious vehicle of all the new sensations pouring into his soul" (249, 101). He tries to make both women into means to his end, as containers of inspiration he controls.

It is harder to restrain Halo in this limited role than it is Laura Lou, however, because of her wariness about it. When Vance has Halo read draft chapters of *Instead* and she tells him the novel needs more work, he theatrically declares that he should burn it, since her opinion, her very being is his. You are "the whole earth to me!" he asserts, to which she wisely responds, "That's too much to be to any one" (437). Nonetheless he persists in his usurpation of her identity by assuming that "he and his art and this woman were one, indissolubly one in a passionate mutual understanding" (438). While Vance is being enveloped by a sensational vision of soul clasping soul and body clasping body in a "hallucinating fusion of sight and touch," Halo resolutely insists that as long as they are both married, friendship is what joins them (441). Before she can say "You see we belong to each other after all," as she eventually does, Halo needs to create an independent life by claiming her power and putting it to work for herself as well as for another (*GA* 432).

In *Hudson River Bracketed* Halo is the custodian but not the owner of her female power as it is embodied in the Willows. Her relation to the house is defined by Vance, a definition she must and will eventually revise by reclaiming the Willows and thereby her female heritage. Vance realizes that Elinor Lorburn and her house belong to the mysterious "dark Unknown," the past that encompasses not only the books he hasn't read and the history he doesn't know about, but also, he eventually understands, the maternal origins he acknowledges as the source of his creativity. It is, after all, in the Willows library that Vance first reads *Faust* and learns about "the mysterious Mothers, moving in subterranean depths among the primal forms of life" (*HRB* 336). While Laura Lou is a "painted veil over the unknown," Halo is "the mysterious custodian of the unknown" (300, 357). As such, she too understands that the house symbolizes "that great nutritive element" of "continuity," the "underlying deep" (498). Halo's reference to Vance as a "groping embryo" plunging into this deep recapitulates the intrauterine language of "nutritive element" and the house as maternal embodiment (498).[16]

In seeing Halo as "old Miss Lorburn's reincarnation" in appearance as well as in her understanding of her ancestor's "inner source of life," Vance equates Halo with the mysterious house that incorporates female power (94, 333).[17] "The magic threshold" of the Willows becomes analogous to the threshold of Halo's "welcoming mind" (154, 411). Later, however, in seeing Halo's face as "almost as ghostly" as Miss Lorburn's, Vance also suspects that Halo has had to sacrifice her "vision of life" just as her ancestor, the "thwarted lady above the mantel," had to do (358). The insight frees Halo from being an unblemished, static emblem, with no possibility for change.

Halo's strength in *Hudson River Bracketed* derives not only from her intelligence but also from her dominant role in introducing Vance to experiences that the reader of Wharton's Gothic recognizes as consciousness-expanding. Halo takes Vance to Thundertop, for instance, the "steep overhanging rock" from which they view "the outspread earth" and the sunrise (98). Vance's sense of disembodiment on Thundertop resembles a mystical experience, recalling for the reader the "intensity of sensation and expansion of vision" provided by peaks, precipices, and mountain summits in traditional Gothic fiction (Bayer-

Berenbaum 140). The height and the misty panorama recall, as well, Lily's and Selden's climb, in *The House of Mirth*, to "an open ledge of rock" above an outspread landscape (*HM* 101). In that scene, Lily learns that she can "never even get [her] foot across the threshold" of Selden's republic of the spirit, and we readers learn, from the characters' mutual flirtation with and denial of commitment, how paralyzed both are by their fear of intimacy (113). By contrast, Halo's sharing this special place with Vance (as well as the rocky pool where they have breakfast together afterward) is an act of intimacy that she initiates and in which he participates. This mutuality is clear from their response to the sunrise: "Vance drew a deep breath. His lips parted, but no word came. He met Miss Spear's smiling eyes with a vague stare. 'Kubla Khan?' she said. He nodded" (*HRB* 99).

Coleridge's "Kubla Khan" has already become a code word for the two even though at this point they barely know one another. This is the poem lying open in a book on the table next to Elinor Lorburn's Gothic chair in her library at the Willows, the poem she was reading the night she died. When Vance reads it "passionately, absorbedly" during his first visit to the Willows, "his whole being swept away on that mighty current" of the poem's music (63). When Halo, whom he hasn't met yet, coincidentally visits the library and finds Vance there, she responds to his breathless "who wrote this?" by identifying the poet and the poem and chanting it line by line (64). Halo's obvious feeling for the poem and her allusion to it during the mystical sunrise she shares on Thundertop with Vance suggest that she understands the power of the creative act even though she is not the one who becomes a writer.

The poem serves Wharton well as a controlling metaphor for the "unknown world" Vance finds in the Willows library and the depths of creativity he later associates with the Mothers. It serves equally well as an emblem of the union of gender-identified characteristics that Wharton has been evolving in her Gothic texts. Coleridge's theory of imagination called for the conciliation of active and passive powers, of the conscious, intellectual control of ideas and the unconscious reservoir of images and associations (J. Baker 191, 151). In his introduction to "Kubla Khan" Coleridge describes the poem as a dream vision, and though its dream origin has been contested, the poem is significant nonetheless because of its "unconscious revelations of the hidden depths" from which Coleridge's poems derived (178). Called "a poem about poetry" and "an outstanding example of the secondary imagination at work," "Kubla Khan" is both an example of an inspired act of creation and a comment on poetic inspiration (G. Watson 122; McFarland 202).

The poem has also been read as being about natural, uncontrollable life forces like sexuality, with its "sacred river" running through "caverns measureless to man / Down to a sunless sea," and its "deep romantic chasm" from which "with ceaseless turmoil seething, / As if this earth, in fast thick pants were breathing, / A mighty fountain momently was forced" (C. Baker 64). In G. Wilson Knight's reading of the poem, the paradoxical nature of the pleasure dome suggests the sexual union between the masculine and the feminine as well as "some vast intelligence enjoying that union of opposites" (95). What has been called the "conventional Gothic-oriental tale matter" in the poem accentuates by allusion the mysterious, erotic quality of the poem and its natural fe/male iconography (Schneider 282).[18]

Connecting "Kubla Khan" with Vance and Halo and the two of them with Elinor Lorburn enmeshes all three in a generative matrix. Their affiliation with the poem is also an affiliation with the depths, of which Coleridge wrote "few in any age have courage or inclination to descend," yet which he realized fuels creativity (J. Baker 178). The poet often acknowledged the otherworldliness of creative awareness, "that state of nascent existence in the twilight of imagination and just on the vestibule of consciousness where ideas and imagination exist" (Lowes 55).

Wharton's language of creativity is much like Coleridge's. In her 1925 book *The Writing of Fiction* she writes about the "gist" of art, the "elusive bright-winged thing," nesting "in that mysterious fourth-dimensional world which is the artist's inmost sanctuary and on the threshold of which enquiry perforce must halt" (*WF* 119). A comment about the process of creativity in *A Backward Glance* is similar yet with a significant difference. There she writes that the creation of art, "though it takes place in some secret region on the sheer edge of consciousness, is always illuminated by the full light of my critical attention" (205). Aptly, at this later stage in her life, Wharton acknowledges the passive sense of altered consciousness while maintaining her active "critical attention." It is this coalescence of passive immersion and active attention, vulnerability and strength, yielding and leading that Wharton eventually has Vance and Halo each exhibit within himself and herself by the end of *The Gods Arrive.*

Until this point Vance in particular has much to learn about understanding and protecting one's vulnerable, yielding self. This is dramatically revealed when he takes Laura Lou, the embodiment of vulnerability in his life, on a climb up the mountain to Thundertop in the snow. He is enamored by her appearance, her hair like "golden filigree," her lips like "jewels," but this pleasurable enjoyment of Laura Lou as valuable possession is clouded by his realization that "behind that low round forehead with its straying curls there lurked a whole hidden world" about which he knows almost nothing (*HRB* 300). He chooses to stay silent about their marriage or about her feelings for Bunty Hayes, communication that might strengthen the marriage and their understanding of one another, and instead he decides to repress it all. Such denial plays out in Vance's urging the frail Laura Lou up the mountain toward Thundertop, an effort that results in pneumonia for her and near death.

Vance later returns to the ledge on Thundertop and there has the valuable realization, while looking down "into the nocturnal depths," that his marriage to Laura Lou had become "a habit, an acquiescence, nothing more," and that Laura Lou might want release from her confined and diminished existence as much as he does (376). He decides to ignore the truth of this realization, however. When he returns home to find that Laura Lou has left him because he has "unwittingly" wounded her, the thought opens "an abyss at his feet" (385). Instead of looking into that abyss and facing his complicated relationship with his fears and vulnerability, he "win(s) back" Laura Lou (385). A week later Vance is bemoaning her "little unchangeable self" but not his own little frightened self (386).

Halo Spear is the one who gives Vance the key to the world of "beauty, poetry, knowledge" and thereby to self-awareness (300). Fittingly she is custodian of Elinor Lorburn's library in the Willows, a setting, like a mountain peak, that the reader of Wharton's Gothic texts recognizes as consciousness-expanding. "The Angel at the Grave," "The Eyes," "Afterward," "Pomegranate Seed," *Summer*, and *The Age of Innocence* all have characters who make self-revising discoveries in libraries. In the Willows library Halo introduces Vance to "Kubla Khan" and the "unknown world" of the Past, to knowledge that he realizes is now vital to his existence (68). "I must find out—I must find out" he chants to himself about the world "of which he must somehow acquire the freedom" (123). The library, he comes to feel, has "lifted him to other pinnacles, higher even than Thundertop" (152). Vance's desire for the "freedom" from smallness, from smugness, from fear that knowledge promises, as well as his elation with the expansive view he gets as a result of this knowledge, suggests that his intellectual growth will help him, unlike other male characters in Wharton's Gothic texts, embrace rather than imprison his "feminine self."

Halo will need to embrace her "masculine self," her independence and personal worth, but she already has a broad intellectual background when she meets Vance. She lives comfortably and unassumingly with the intellectual power that has been the sole and usually abused purview of male characters in Wharton's earlier Gothic. Her library, in her apartment with Tarrant, which has the appeal of "some calm natural object, tree or field," overlooks "the sweep of the East River glittering far below" (185). The view from the library resembles the view from Eaglewood, Halo's childhood home, and from Thundertop, her inspirational ledge overlooking the Hudson.

Halo already is, it is clear in *Hudson River Bracketed*, a learned, aware woman. Yet a library is still the setting for new realizations. In her library Halo admits to her old family friend George Frenside that she isn't happy in her marriage. She has made the admission to no one else, and it takes her, at least initially, "out of a world of suffocating dissimulations into a freer air" (184). In her library, too, Vance declares "we're so close . . . leaning over into the gulfs of each other . . . Don't you see there's no difference any more between you and me?" a declaration that, Halo admits, frightens her but that will precipitate her leaving her husband (438). She, like Vance, has had the experience of opening her eyes "on the edge of a sheer drop" when a quarrel with Lewis makes her question the viability of her marriage (349). Like Vance returning to Laura Lou, Halo returns to Lewis; in spite of the emptiness of her relationship with her husband, she believes she is "chained to him for life" because he has financed her family (352). Unlike Vance, however, who doesn't have to act on his unhappiness in his marriage because Laura Lou dies, Halo finds the courage to leave her husband despite the ramifications of that act.

It is Halo who understands Vance's special relationship with the Willows, one that mirrors Wharton's passionate belief in having a spiritual home reflected in an appropriate physical one. When Halo reads Vance's novel based on the life of Elinor Lorburn at the Willows, she realizes that "suddenly lifted out of a boundless contiguity of Euphorias, his mind struck root deep down in accumulated layers of experience, in centuries of struggle, passion and aspiration" embodied in "this absurd house" (354). The Willows was to him, she realizes, "the very emblem of man's long effort," his "Chartres, the Parthenon, the Pyramids" (354).

With Halo's help, Vance achieves inner strength from learning about the Willows that Lily Bart's rootlessness in *The House of Mirth* denies her. Vance has realized that his earlier homes have been just houses, "shells shed annually, almost, like a crab's" with no "traces of accumulated living and dying" (201). Wharton conveys in *The House of Mirth,* in much the same way Halo does in *Hudson River Bracketed,* the essential continuity a house can embody: "In whatever form a slowly-accumulated past lives in the blood—whether in the concrete image of the old house stored with visual memories, or in the conception of the house not built with hands, but made up of inherited passions and loyalties—it has the same power of broadening and deepening the individual existence, of attaching it by mysterious links of kinship to all the mighty sum of human striving" (*HM* 516).

Halo has shared the Willows' past with Vance, and he in turn has revitalized and enriched the familiar family home that had been considered "the joke of her childhood," the home that will eventually be hers (*HRB* 354). Clearly, in *Hudson River Bracketed,* Halo and Vance possess traits that both reinforce and counter the Gothic gender stereotypes. Central to Wharton's vision in *Hudson River Bracketed* and *The Gods Arrive* is that both Halo and Vance face realizations about themselves that help them achieve more authentic selves, ones less bound by gender constraints.

The Gods Arrive culminates in a realization of gender integration only suggested in previous Gothic texts. Halo and Vance both play traditional Gothic roles of victim and villain but eventually unlearn them. In this process of "unlearning," Lewis Tarrant, Halo's husband, and Floss Delaney, Vance's former lover, serve as anachronistic reminders of destructive kinds of masculinity and femininity that need to be acknowledged, understood, and then rejected.

At the outset of *The Gods Arrive* Halo has left Lewis and is sailing away to Europe with Vance. She has escaped, thereby, Gothic victimization, a life of entrapment with a man whose "uneasy vanity . . . would not be put off with anything less than her whole self, her complete belief, the uncritical surrender of her will and judgment" (*GA* 8, ellipsis mine). Yet she has to admit that her husband "still frightened her," that the satisfaction he gets from "hurting and humiliating her" still has power over her (5). She has been able to escape because she has received what Virginia Woolf had realized, four years earlier, was crucial to a woman's independent life, a legacy. Just as the narrator of Woolf's *A Room of One's Own* can say that because of the legacy from her aunt, Mary Beton, "I need not hate any man; he cannot hurt me. I need not flatter any man; he has nothing to give me," so Halo is "a free woman" because of the death of her old cousin, Miss Lorburn of Stuyvesant Square, free to live unencumbered by male authority (38; *GA* 10). "This was her first chance to be her real self," Halo says of her choice to live unmarried with Vance (33).

Yet though Halo believes her life "had struck root in the soul-depths . . . and that put her beyond all reach of malice," she still exhibits a victim's mentality (5, ellipsis mine). "If she were not Vance Weston's for always the future was already a handful of splinters," she thinks as she sails away with her lover (4). When Vance tells her to drop a telegram she has received just before sailing unopened into the ocean, she thinks, "with a little thrill of feminine submission: 'How strong and decided he seems! He tells me what to do—he takes everything for granted. I'm the weak inexperienced one, after all' " (6). We don't need the narrator's reminder of Halo's "short-sighted gaze" to help us realize how dangerously limited and inaccurate this view of herself and Vance is (3).

Once in Europe, Halo is the one who takes charge as guide, interpreter, and home finder and designer. Yet her persistent willingness to value her strengths only as a service to her lover encourages Vance eventually to demean and dismiss her. Halo's power is her ability to introduce Vance to experiences that emulate the mysteriousness and dislocation of the creative act. When she and Vance arrive in Spain, Halo guides him through a cathedral in which he feels "as if he had dropped over the brim of things into the mysterious world where straight lines loop themselves into curves," a description of the locus of creativity akin to Wharton's description of it as "that mysterious fourth-dimensional world" (21; *WF* 119). Vance struggles to describe the experience as "the feel of poetry, just as it's beginning to be born in you" (*GA* 22).

When he and Halo become disoriented and can't find the way out, Vance recalls the descent to the Mothers in *Faust*, which had been his metaphor in *Hudson River Bracketed* for the plunge into the source of creativity, as well as all the other "subterranean mysteries" that take one into "the dark heart of things"

(23). We have only Vance's response to the place, not Halo's, his wish to "let the immensity and the mystery sweep over him like the sea," but her silence as she slips her hand into his suggests her empathic response to this experience that is at once spiritual and uncanny (23).

Halo takes the lead for Vance not only in these other-dimensional experiences but in the daily experiences as well, where her actions promote physical and spiritual well-being. She speaks fluent Spanish, making Vance feel that "it was strange and delicious to be sitting there at ease with this young woman who knew what everybody was saying, could talk to them, laugh with them, ask the way, bandy jokes, and give him the sense of being at home in it all" (25). Indeed, Halo is the literal home creator as well as the figurative one. That she finds them rooms "so high above the town that they commanded the jumble of roofs and towers descending to the bridge, and a glimpse of the brown hills beyond" reminds us of her significance as the one who knows how to find the ways to expanded consciousness. Yet she also has skill in "driving nails and mending broken furniture" (29).

Halo's Achilles Heel, however, is her propensity for self-abasement, her belief that no happiness can equal that of "a woman *permitted to serve* the genius while she adored the man" (italics mine, 29). In explaining to her mother why she has chosen to live unmarried with Vance she mentions only his needs, his wishes, and nothing about her own: "I went to him because he was lonely and unhappy and needed me, and I mean to stay with him as long as he wants me" (61). Although she feels herself "sinking into the character of the blindly admiring wife," she is as yet unable to garner the inner strength needed to shed the victim's persona, much like Wharton's early Gothic women, Sybilla in "The House of the Dead Hand" or Paulina in "Angel at the Grave" (40).

Halo's weak sense of identity is also manifested in her need to possess Vance, as Gothic men need to possess women, and to live her intellectual life through him. The crucial question for her is, "would he weary of her, or would she be able to hold him?" (83). She dreams of having a "lasting hold over him" in intellectual and creative matters and finds instead that "it was in this region that she found herself least wanted" (85). Halo knows her learning and cultural experience exceed Vance's, and she feels justifiably angry that "this clever young man thought that her affections blinded her, or that her literary standards were less exacting than his" (85). But rather than expressing this anger she silences herself by suppressing her reactions and feelings. The more she tries to be "careless and buoyant" when she is feeling angry and lonely, the more Vance dismisses her (60, 28, 42, 46, 65). When Vance disappears for days without telling her where he's gone, she blames herself: "She had always been too critical, had made her likes and dislikes too evident" (102). All that matters, she concludes in an orgy of self-denial, is that "she should go on serving and inspiring this child of genius with whom a whim of the gods had entrusted her" (103).

Halo thus encourages Vance's egocentric demeaning of her as Other, but she doesn't cause it. During much of the novel Vance plays a role reminiscent of Wharton's earlier Gothic bullies. His observation that Halo has "just the shape of the head of one of those statues of the Virgin they carry in the processions," for instance, is an ominous allusion to the dangerous objectification of women perpetuated by male Gothic characters, in which the women they bully collude (35). Halo's sense that Vance "ascribed her own lukewarm share in their talks to feminine inferiority" is confirmed by his thought that "you could never cure a woman" of giving advice to "fellows who were trying to do things!" (45, 181). Vance's impression that Halo is an "obstacle" that arrests his thoughts accords with his cruel propensity for leaving her for days and even weeks at a time without communicating his whereabouts, as if she were, like Laura Lou, an inanimate possession waiting at home (76). His "masculine longing to be left alone" signals a disavowal of his femininity that, by the end of the novel, he understands to be self-limiting (79). Escaping Gothic gender limitations means that he and Halo as well must learn to incorporate strength and vulnerability, independence and dependence, intellect and spirituality within themselves, traits that have characterized each at various points in their lives.

In Lewis Tarrant and Floss Delaney, Halo's husband and Vance's former lover, the novel provides retrospectives of the unrevised masculine and feminine that have haunted the Gothic texts of the past and still haunt Vance and Halo. Like Halo, Vance, and Laura Lou, Lewis Tarrant has gray eyes, a subtle but insistent reminder that all these characters are aspects of a single being, the many selves that Vance recognizes one has (*HRB* 65, 88, 205; *GA* 141, 260). Lewis is the part of the self whose instinct is "to retreat from the unknown, the unexpected, to place the first available buffer between himself and any incident likely to unsettle his nerves or alter his plans" (*GA* 139). He is the rigid, the repressed, the cruelly unyielding self. Vance recognizes the attribute, "this curious human inability, in moments of the deepest stress, to shake off the conventional attitude and the accepted phrase" (145). Recalling Lawrence Selden and Lily Bart at the end of *The House of Mirth*, when "an immediate outrush of feeling," of which both are incapable, is the called-for response, Lewis Tarrant had "disciplined himself out of all impulsiveness" and so "stood powerless on the brink of the deeper feelings" (*HM* 496; *GA* 145). "In my opinion she ought to suffer," he tells Vance in response to Vance's urging him to divorce Halo (*GA* 146).

Floss Delaney is the unrevised feminine self, the objectified woman who commodifies human feeling and human beings because she sees herself as a commodity. Despite his passionate response to Floss, Vance repeatedly refers to her as an art object: "her arms and shoulders looked like sun-warmed marble," "Her face was as smooth as marble" (235, 249). She sits in "one of her quiet sculptural attitudes" and her eyes shine "like jewels" (295, 297). As she explains her latest real estate deal she exhibits a "statue-like calm" in contrast to Vance's "inward turmoil," and he finally comes to realize that "he could no more influence or shape her than he could bend or shape a marble statue" (371, 383). Despite the fact that she makes herself and her attention so dear, or perhaps because of it, Vance is obsessed with owning her, "She's mine—I must keep her!" he thinks during one of their several unconsummated encounters (296).

Unlike Halo, who, when Vance and Lewis confront one another over her divorce, is mortified to find herself "gazing at herself stripped and exposed, between these two men who were disputing for her possession," Floss encourages men to consider her an expensive commodity available for the right price (153). At one point Vance notices that Floss, surrounded by men, "spoke little, smiled even more rarely, but sat there, composed, almost indifferent, while the faces about her shone with curiosity and admiration" (237). It is entirely in character for Floss to have extorted a young lover's "socially ambitious" family into buying her land at inflated prices by revealing his love letters and threatening to marry him, though Vance is horrified when he learns about the story (398). The feat of getting their land at her price without having to marry to do so gives Floss the satisfaction of good sex; Vance notices a "veiled radiance in her face which he had seen in it only once or twice, in moments of passionate surrender" (396). Floss the blackmailer is brilliantly soulless in the role Lily Bart shrinks from assuming in *The House of Mirth*.

Floss's sleepy repetition of "I'm dead tired, dead," and "I'm dead tired" after she describes her deal to Vance reiterates the immersion in deathlike loss of self she represents for him (397, 399). Her "polished exterior" is the "vehicle" for a primal passion that recalls the "sacred river" with its "ceaseless turmoil seething" in "Kubla Khan" (207, 205; C. Baker, 63, 64): "to hold Floss Delaney was to plunge into a dark night, a hurrying river. It was as if her blood and his were the tide sweeping them away. Everything else was drowned in that wild current" (*GA* 296). This "old mysterious bond of blood" to which Vance refers in talking about his feelings for Floss might as well be an umbilical embryo/maternal connection, for, with Floss, Vance loses himself as if he were returning to prenatal existence (383). He himself suggests this connection when he muses that "certain obscure fibres in both their natures seemed inextricably entangled. There was a dumb subterranean power in her that corresponded with his own sense of the forces by which his inventive faculty was fed," a power not unlike the one he has already identified as "The Mothers" (378).

While Halo takes Vance to the heights both literally, as in their trip to Thundertop, and figuratively, by helping him expand his awareness, Floss is a woman of the depths. When she and Vance are driving together one night he suggests that it would be lovely to see the sunrise from the top of a big hill. Eventually the road "breasted a wide stretch of open heath, soaring, soaring" (290). When they reach the summit Floss is fast asleep. Vance realizes that "she had seen nothing, felt nothing, of the beauty and mystery of the dawn" (290).

The plunge into the maternal abyss that Floss provides for Vance is intensely pleasurable, even addictive. But Floss herself, the inspiration of it, is incapable of an authentic relationship. Vance's belief that he and Floss "belonged to each other, that they were necessary to each other," the belief Halo will later express to Vance, is true in the figurative sense that such a primal force is an integral part of oneself (383). Vance's belief is wildly inaccurate in the literal sense, however, given that Floss is "an apparition" in a "swaying dream," an object, a force, but not an authentic person (293, 216).

Another reminder, in addition to the characterizations of Lewis Tarrant and Floss Delaney, of the Gothic text Wharton is revising in *The Gods Arrive* is the Churley house and family that Vance and Halo become acquainted with during their stay in England. The "melancholy Churley family," Colonel and Mrs. Churley, and their son Chris Churley, as well as their house Les Mimosas, constitutes an interpolated Gothic tale within the revisionary novel (166). Like the Duke in "The Duchess at Prayer," Lombard the scholar in "The House of the Dead Hand," or the rich industrialist John Lavington in "The Triumph of Night," the Colonel, a retired Indian cavalry officer, is a representative of the male power structure who intimidates and oppresses his wife, "crippled with rheumatism and half blind" (164). While he goes off for long rambles each day he is "rather opposed" to Mrs. Churley receiving visitors, a repressive scenario not unlike that between the Duke and the Duchess in "The Duchess at Prayer," Mr. and Mrs. Brympton in "The Lady's Maid's Bell," and Yves de Cornault and his wife Anne in "Kerfol" (193). So Mrs. Churley, with her "small muffled-up body, and a hollow-cheeked face with tossed white hair," lies alone on her sofa all day (194).

Les Mimosas, like houses in the earlier Gothic stories, is a "dismal-looking house up the hill" with a "barricaded house-front," an "untended garden," shuttered windows, and "the heavy smell" of a place long unaired (164, 193). When Halo ventures in to see Mrs. Churley to talk with her about her son Chris, a neighbor offers to "slip down and mount guard in case he [Mr. Churley] should come back," while his wife "gazed with a sort of spectral timidity at her visitor; . . . as though she were a ghost who feared to look at the living" (194, ellipsis mine). Colonel and Mrs. Churley portray gender division at its most Gothic, a system that Halo and Vance struggle to refashion.

The son, Chris Churley, though not a character type common to Wharton's Gothic, functions in the novel as an exaggerated, even grotesque, version of Vance. A garrulous, eager, slightly infirm young man with "literary" pretensions and a taste for dissipation, Chris Churley visits Vance to interview him for a publication. The article, as with every writing project the young man has talked or thought about, is never written. Halo's advice that Chris should force himself to write whether he wants to or not is dismissed by Vance as "inconceivably stupid" (181). Vance continues by blustering to himself, "If only outsiders wouldn't give advice to fellows who were trying to do things! But probably you could never cure a woman of that" (181).

As anyone who writes knows, and as Vance comes to realize, Halo's advice is correct. Eventually Vance does tell Chris, "nobody can write who doesn't set his teeth and dig himself in. Your first mistake was ever imagining it was fun" (243). Despite Vance's attempts to help this young man who reminds him of himself, Chris eventually commits suicide. "I was meant to be a moment's ornament," he tells Vance at one point, the words Wharton once used to describe Lily Bart (243). Chris, like his parents, functions in the novel as a fun house mirror might, as an exaggerated distortion of traits that have the potential to destroy, either oneself or another. This is what Halo and Vance could have been, Wharton tells us through the Churleys.

Instead, Halo and Vance have parallel experiences of self-examination and renewal, mystic journeys into the depths of themselves that result in their eventually coming together at the same point of self-knowledge. Both go through a period of self-imposed solitude when they feel themselves losing their internal balance, and both experience physical and spiritual illness that yields new understanding of their feminine and masculine selves.

One of the key things that distinguishes both Halo and Vance from the "trivial, over-dressed, and over-fed" socialites and pseudointellectuals they encounter during their sojourn in Europe is their need for order (215). Halo realizes that "beauty, order and reasonableness" become more dear to her when she is in "the noisy anarchy" of her brother Lorry's circle, and she becomes increasingly aware of "how deeply rooted in her were the old instincts of order and continuity" (83, 306). "In Vance too they existed," she knows, and indeed we hear about Vance's "craving for order and harmony" (306, 169, 201). This "order" accrues meaning as an alternative to the aimless superficiality of "Bohemia" at which Wharton directs her satirical vituperativeness in *The Gods Arrive*. The need for order provides her protagonists with a moral edge over the other characters in the novel and signals their common respect for continuity over historical amnesia. The latter is favored by Halo's brother Lorry, who blusters: "Who ever consulted you and me when the Pyramids were built—or Versailles? Why should we be saddled with all that old dead masonry? Ruins are what we want—more ruins!" (128).

That this view comes from the mouth of Lorry, who proved his moral and intellectual bankruptcy in *Hudson River Bracketed* when he stole and sold Emily Lorburn's books for extra spending money, ridicules not only his idea but traditional Gothic as well. One finds a spiritual center not in ruins, not in the destruction of the past, but rather in a renewed understanding and acceptance of one's cultural and personal history, especially as it is embodied in old houses like the Willows.

Both Halo and Vance go through processes of reconceiving themselves and finding a spiritual center, processes that involve acts of regression. During the longest of Vance's disappearances, Halo loses herself in flower gardening to the point where "thanks to hard work and stupefying sun, she no longer remembered whether it was days or weeks since she had heard from him" (304). Her engrossment in this natural environment contrasts starkly with a comment Floss Delaney makes about a hot English day, that "you felt it must have cost a lot of money to make" (295). Halo's garden and its failings become symbolic for her; the writhing green caterpillars eating leaves, the seeds that don't sprout, and the young shoots devoured by slugs are "the mean cares, the gnawing anxieties, that crawl over the fair face of life," the failures and disenchantments (305). "I suppose I've been too long alone," Halo muses (305). This "self-imposed" solitude, however, will yield substantial growth.

The appearance at her door of George Frenside, an old family friend who has known her since childhood, makes Halo realize that "she had not put her spiritual house in order" and that "she hardly knew what she was feeling or whither she was drifting. Solitude had woven its magic passes about her, pouring a blessed numbness into her veins. And now, at this sudden contact with the past, every nerve awoke" (307–308). Frenside's intense questioning about her motives in refusing a divorce that her husband is now apparently willing to grant her makes Halo aware of her intense loneliness, her belief that loving is pretending, and her unfruitfully static relationship with Vance.

When Halo goes through Vance's mail and finds newspaper articles from clipping services about his activities in London, including his dalliances with Floss, Halo is enraged that Vance should be confiding in trivial people and "this vile creature," while she, "who had given him her life, sat alone, forgotten, as utterly cut off from him as if she had never had any share in his existence" (321, 322). This recognition scene resembles an earlier one when Vance has gone off for days and Halo is tempted to search his desk for the manuscript of his latest work in progress, since he no longer shares his writing with her; she imagines she will find not a manuscript but love letters from another woman. But at this earlier point she doesn't open the "hidden drawers," can't "bear the sight of the truth" about her sexual fears, her sexual identity as it relates to her lover (106). Halo's isolation and lonely despair resemble the condition of previous Gothic women—Juliana in "Mr. Jones," the Duchess in "The Duchess at Prayer," Anne in "Kerfol." Unlike them, however, Halo has the wherewithal to change her situation, to pack her bags and leave.

Instead Vance returns, and Halo adopts her familiar, submissive, self-silencing persona. She asks no questions about his weeks away and tries to ignore her suspicions. "The thing to do, she told herself again and again, was just to be natural, to behave as if nothing were changed" (331). Of course things have changed, whatever Halo tries to pretend. To Vance she seems "remote and ghostly," the more so because "she was so patient with him, didn't nag, didn't question, didn't taunt" (325, 326). Vance wonders whether "that curious tolerance made her less woman, less warm to the touch," and he observes that her "quiet unquestioning tenderness was like a barrier" (326–27). His reactions confirm Halo's transformation into an object—silent, smiling, remote.

Only when Vance asks her to listen to his latest novel in progress, "Colossus," does Halo find the courage to speak her mind. Despite Vance's defensive sneering about her "amateur judgments" and her inability to understand what he's trying to do, Halo decides she must be truthful, a decision that begins her return to herself (335). She knows that her comments that the book lacks a focus and is too filled with the influence and echoes of others will wound Vance's vanity, but she also now knows that "if she spoke at all she must speak as truth dictated; she could not tamper with her intellectual integrity, or with his" (336). Typically, his angry retort that a writer asks others for their opinion to please them rather than himself leaves Halo feeling frightened by "her over-scrupulous sincerity" (337).

Vance's silence thereafter about the novel and his admission of unrequited lust for Floss Delaney brings Halo to the suggestion that they should part. Aptly, the discussion takes place while "the palms were wrestling in dishevelled fury with the first autumn gale" (339). As in the Gothic short stories, the furious weather mirrors human emotions. In listening to Vance's admissions about Floss, Halo feels that his words "cut like a blade sharpened to wound her" (343). That the cruelty resembles her husband's "cool incisiveness cutting into the soul like a white-hot blade into flesh" signals that Halo finally understands the threat she faces in staying with this man (*HRB* 488).

Halo's critical acumen is proved correct once again, when the consensus about *Colossus* after it is published is that "it was much too long, nothing particular happened in it, and few people even pretended to know what it was about" (*GA* 349). By this time, however, Halo is entering a spiritual dormancy period much like one that Vance will later enter, and she is putting her life with him behind her. There is now "something slow and hesitating in her slightest decisions, in her movements even," a "stealing inertia" that makes her feel incapable of decision-making, "as though her central spring were broken" (349, 350). The state resembles Lily Bart's at the end of her life and Charity Royall's when she is brought down from the Mountain by Lawyer Royall.

Unlike Lily and Charity, Halo seizes control of her life. When she visits her husband to accept his offer of a divorce, his determined self-control over his emotions contrasted with her straightforward honesty recalls the tortured scene between Lawrence Selden and Lily Bart at the end of *The House of Mirth* when she comes to tell him what she now understands about herself. While Lily realizes that she can't reject the woman she was, Halo realizes that "this cold embarrassed man, having once been a part of her life, could never quite cease to be so" (353). She and Lewis "had the same emotional reactions"; he is part of the self that Halo is slowly revising.

Halo is now capable of declaring, "I want my freedom" (354). The irony of Lewis's patriarchal response, "Freedom? Freedom to live without a name, or any one to look after you?" is blatantly apparent when Halo insists "I want to be alone; to go my own way, without depending on anybody. I want to be Halo Spear again—that's all" (355, 362). Her revelation that she is expecting a baby makes the contrast with Lily and Charity the bolder. Lily fears the birth of her aware self. Charity faces herself in bearing a child but doesn't have the maturity or the strength to live free of patriarchal control. Halo has both the maturity and the internal strength to reconceive her independent self in the process of bearing a child. As she declares passionately to Lewis, "Can't you understand that a woman should want to be free, and alone with her child?" (360).

Having parted from Lewis and Vance, Halo experiences a "dark blur of pain" followed by a time when "blackness closed in on her" and "she thought the dead in their graves must be as she was" (422). She has fallen into the maternal abyss, the overwhelming awareness of her essential aloneness and potential loss of self that terrifies Lily Bart, tests Charity Royall, and strengthens Ellen Olenska. Out of "that annihilation" comes a new feminine self: "a new life had emerged, her own interwoven with her child's. The numbness gradually became quietude, the quietude a kind of sober joy, till she could now look back on that first phase of anguish as mystics do on the dark passages of their spiritual initiation" (422).

Emphasizing this rebirth of her feminine self is Halo's decision to reclaim the Willows, the house that embodies her female heritage and identity: "The thought of the old place drew her back with a thousand threads of association; and the mere fact that the house was her own, the only place on earth that she could dispose of as she chose, made her wish that her child should be born there" (422–23). Significantly, when her mother remonstrates that at the Willows Halo won't be able to keep the birth a secret, that she "can't possibly keep people from talking—," Halo responds that she wants people she cares about to talk about her baby (423). Halo's renewed trust in verbal honesty is another indication that she has saved herself from Gothic oblivion.

Halo's time of "ruminating calm," her time of "rest and renewal" after her descent into the abyss mirrors Vance's journey into himself (424, 422). He too, during his obsession with Floss, feels as if "some spring in him was broken," as if, he tells Halo eventually, "my mainspring was broken" (259, 431). *Colossus*, he now understands, is "a kind of hybrid monster," with all the faults Halo had noticed (386). Vance also eventually becomes aware of Floss's unremitting vacuity, after trying to "dominate her with the full strength of his will" (383–84). This is the last gasp in the novel of Vance's controlling, villainous persona.

When he returns home to Euphoria to see his dying grandmother, her last words to him are "Maybe we haven't made enough of pain—been too afraid of it. Don't be afraid of it" (402). With her "great billowing expanse of flesh," Mrs. Scrimser has been the kind of "Great Mother" to Vance that the equally large Catherine Spicer is for Ellen Olenska in *The Age of Innocence* (401). Despite Vance's periodic disdain for his grandmother's eccentricities, her belief in him, along with her spirituality and emotional generosity, have made her seem "nearer to him than any one else" (402). Thus he is willing to hear her admonition about the need to confront the disorienting, frightening, and uncontrollable in oneself.

His grandmother's insight makes Vance feel "a boundless need to deal with himself," to do the kind of self-searching we know Halo has had to do (404). He decides to stay at the isolated Camp of Hope in the northern woods of Wisconsin with a "short-sighted" ex-teacher, Aaron Brail, to whose house he glides off in a sleigh as if "into the unknown" (406, 405). This blatantly symbolic language gives an allegorical quality to Vance's sojourn. Aaron Brail, whose name suggests both blindness and an alternative way of "seeing" knowledge, helps Vance learn about the unknown within him. Just as Halo would stagger into the house stupefied by heat and labor in her garden to sleep as if in a "fit of drunkenness," so Vance comes home from tramping in the woods "so drunk with sunlight and cold that sleep struck him down in the doorway" (303, 407).

His dreams are haunted by Floss and Halo. When insomnia strikes, he broods that "the whole question of woman was the age-long obstacle to peace of spirit and fruitfulness of mind; to get altogether away from it, contrive a sane and productive life without it, became the obsession of his sleepless midnights" (407). While he wants to believe that escaping "woman" is the answer to a complete and happy life, he learns during his retreat that he must instead accept and assimilate the feminine into his sense of himself. "All he wanted was to be himself, solely and totally himself, not tangled up in the old deadly nets of passion and emotion," he insists (407). Yet a solely "masculine" life without passion and emotion is not a complete life, as he ascertains from observing Brail.

His sense that his host has come to the woods to escape something leads Vance to the realization that he himself "would never be able to rest long in evasion or refusal" (408). Reading one of the classics of Christian mysticism, *The Confessions of Saint Augustine*, brings Vance all the closer to an understanding of the self-confrontation that being spiritually "full-grown" entails. This awareness is intensified when he becomes ill with pneumonia and experiences "physical suffering and helplessness"; afterward, his legs weak "like a baby's," he begins to understand how realization and acceptance of one's vulnerability paradoxically make one stronger and more mature (412).

Brail's confession that he had come to the woods to escape his love for a woman lion-tamer is so preposterous that it is hard to read it in other than the metaphorical way Vance does. He knows it is now time to "fly from his shielded solitude and go down again among the lion-tamers," that is, accommodate himself to womanhood that counters ferocious male power with its own strength, will, and calm (414). Seeing a vision in his mind of Brail, "spectrally followed by the limping figure of Chris Churley . . . the two deniers, the two fugitives," strengthens Vance's resolve to accept rather than hide from the awareness that his journey into himself has given him (415, ellipsis mine).

That Vance craves, "with a sort of tremulous convalescent hunger," a sight of the Willows, "where his real life had begun," just as Halo's decision to live there "had been her final step toward recovery," conjoins them in a common respect for the archetypal feminine that the house embodies (416, 422). The thought of the Willows draws Halo back "with a thousand threads of association," while "every fibre" of Vance's past is "interwoven" with the "strange old dwelling" (422, 417). This fibrous image used for both of their responses carries associations of the house as the source of nourishment, a point Wharton makes in *Hudson River Bracketed* when she tells us that Vance's mind "struck root deep down in accumulated layers of experience, in centuries of struggle, passion and aspiration" embodied in "this absurd house" (354). That, as Wharton emphasizes, it is a woman's house, first Emily Lorburn's and now Halo Spear's, reiterates that it is not only a cultural past Vance and Halo return to through their association with it but a feminine/maternal source. This interrelationship of memory, the maternal, and rootedness recalls Charity's memories of Harney at the end of *Summer,* that "they had passed into her blood, and become a part of her, they were building the child in her womb; it was impossible to tear asunder strands of life so interwoven" (*S* 231).

A "singular lassitude" possesses Vance after visiting the Willows, and he feels "self-contempt" for the sense of himself as a "frightened child" hiding in memories (*GA* 420). Like the "stealing inertia" Halo feels during her period of retrospection, a time when she is also physically pregnant, Vance's lassitude signals that he is still immersed in the process of fundamental change, pregnant with a new self. His admission to Halo, when he sees her again, that his only strength left is "the strength not to pretend" and that he is "only just learning how to walk" reflects his acceptance, finally, of his dependency and vulnerability (431, 432).

By contrast, when she sees Vance powerless, Halo feels "strong, confident, sure of herself" (429). Her solicitude and her explanation that she now owns the Willows make the reunion scene with Vance reminiscent of the one at the end of *Jane Eyre,* when Jane tells the blinded Rochester, "I am independent, sir, as well as rich; I am my own mistress" (438). Halo's pregnancy and her emblematic gesture to Vance of lifting up her arms in "the ancient attitude of prayer" have led readers of this final scene to conclude that Wharton has retreated to a conservative, essentialist view of women as mothers and of men as the children they care for (*HRB* 432). Halo's assumption, without benefit of advanced reproductive technology, that her unborn baby is a boy further implicates her as a Virgin Mary figure, holy and inviolate bearer of a male savior, "the Incarnate Word."[19]

Read in the context of Wharton's career-long experiment with gender in her Gothic, this scene represents a crucial turning point in her perception and portrayal of the nature of women and men. The child motif can be read as paving the way for "a future change of personality" and as a "symbol which unites the opposites; a mediator, bringer of healing, that is, one who makes whole" (Jung 9[1]:164). In this sense Halo is in the process of bearing her masculine self—confident, assertive, articulate, independent—while at the same time her response to Vance indicates that she also possesses a nurturant, receptive, feminine self.[20] Vance's experiences in the woods, on the other hand, have led him to reject the detached, emotionally frozen masculine self, the one who sees the feminine as something to escape in order to be "solely and totally himself, not tangled up in the old deadly nets of passion and emotion" (407). In returning to the Willows, with which "every fibre of his past was interwoven," and to Halo, emotionally and spiritually receptive to and accepting of his dependence, Vance is in the process of bearing his feminine self and accepting the feminine as part of life (417).[21]

Thus Halo's assertion, "You see we belong to each other after all," can be read as Wharton's declaration that femininity and masculinity belong together, that being a complete human being, "full-grown" as Vance observes, quoting from Saint Augustine, means synthesizing these elements in oneself and living a life that allows for the expression of feminine and masculine ways of knowing and being.[22] Both Halo and Vance now understand what it means to be both autonomous and helpless, a person of reason and emotion, "masculine" and "feminine." Both have known the dark depths of the feminine/maternal self and have been nourished and enhanced by immersion in it rather than terrified or destroyed.

"All Souls'," Wharton's last completed piece of fiction, written in 1937, the year of her death, takes us *into* the dark depths of the self as they are experienced by the female protagonist Sara Clayburn. The story is, on one level, about awareness of one's essential aloneness in life and the terrified, empty self one discovers one is alone with. At the same time, by using a narrator of unidentified gender who possesses characteristics of both genders, Wharton provides a fitting culmination to her evolving development of the fe/male self who acknowledges the frightened self within yet is able to comfort and accept that self.

As in *Ethan Frome*, the narrator in "All Souls' " frames Sara's story by telling her/his vision/version of what must have happened to Sara. Most significant to readers of Wharton's Gothic is that the narrator relies on both scholarly knowledge and intuition, "masculine" and "feminine" ways of knowing and being in telling Sara's story and interpreting and responding to her needs. Though beginning with a lawyerlike explanation, peppered with parenthetical comments, of why s/he is the one telling the story of Sara's "mysterious week-end," the narrator then reveals a predilection for the supernatural by explaining that ghosts are most apt to haunt suburban houses and "calm matter-of-fact people" like cousin Sara (G 3, 4).

Also significant, given the resonant suggestion that the threshold is the entrance to woman's interior space, is the narrator's scornful comment that a "fashionable essayist . . . hasn't even reached the threshold of his subject" because he believes that "ghosts went out when electric light came in" (3–4, ellipsis mine). The controlled voice returns in the closing frame, but in it the narrator explains the theory that Agnes, Sara's maid, is a channel for supernatural communications and the irresistible power of Covens.

In telling the story, not in Sara's words, but "as I built it up gradually out of her half-avowals and nervous reticences," the nameless narrator is in essence claiming the story as her/his own, speaking, creating, writing, rather than maintaining Sara's silence (6). Part of this story tells of the ancient female tradition of witchcraft, a femaleness that doesn't fear death, indeed communicates with those who inhabit "the other side of the veil" (33). Perhaps because of that fearlessness, such women can engage in uninhibited sexuality, immersed in a "primitive joy of the body" that Sara can barely allow herself to imagine (Dinnerstein 122).

Much in the setting of "All Souls' " is familiar to the reader of Wharton's Gothic. Like Brympton Place in "The Lady's Maid's Bell," the Cranch house in "The Young Gentlemen," and Bells in "Mr. Jones," Whitegates is an old family house whose isolated location "would certainly have seemed remote and lonely to modern servants" (5). Set "on a height," like the equally remote and lonely houses in "The Triumph of Night" and "Bewitched," Whitegates is enveloped in a symbolic snowstorm just as the houses in those earlier stories are. Even without the narrator's preparatory remarks about the "queer and inexplicable" business that took place at Whitegates and the need to understand that ghosts haunt ordinary houses and "calm matter-of-fact people," we would expect a story of heightened psychological, emotional, and spiritual awareness in the house/self known as Whitegates. Even its name resonates. Gates, particularly narrow ones, frequently appear in "initiatory and funerary rituals and mythologies," suggesting a passage from one mode of being to another, a rite of passage (Eliade 181). "Gates make possible the underworld perspective" (Hillman 181). White "reverberates . . . with Melvillian abyss" (Zilversmit, "All Souls' " 317, ellipsis mine).

"It must be lonesome, winters, living all alone up there atop of that hill," townspeople remark of Sara Clayburn's decision to remain at Whitegates after her husband's death (61). When Sara falls and breaks her ankle, her doctor, too, remarks, "This is a pretty lonely place when the snow begins" (9). But Sara scoffingly denies such a possibility, given that she has her old servants to keep her company. Her apparent unwillingness to acknowledge the loneliness of Whitegates portends her lack of awareness about living life alone, without servants, without the outward fulfillers of life's needs who substitute for self-nurturing.[23] The narrator's comments that Sara had "inherited from her mother-in-law two or three old stand-bys who seemed as much a part of the family tradition as the roof they lived under" and that Agnes was "the dour old Scottish maid whom Sara had inherited from her mother-in-law" also prepare us for Sara's inevitably unsettling realization that her servants are animate individuals, not inherited pieces of property whose only purpose is to service her every need (5, 8).

Outwardly Sara Clayburn appears more than capable of taking care of herself. A "muscular, resolute figure of a woman," she is, the narrator comments, "very much like her house," sturdy, open, equipped with modern appurtenances, and, above all, orderly and dignified (5, 4). Like Lady Jane Lynke, in "Mr. Jones," a "blunt tweed figure" who is "unlike other people," Sara Clayburn "seldom did what other people expected" and so stays at the family house after her husband dies (4). To Sara, who considers Whitegates the source of the "family roots," leaving is out of the question, and besides, "She had always been regarded as a plucky woman; and had so regarded herself" (14). She is clearly used to being authoritative and in control, even, the suggestion is, of her own mortality. She intends to keep "that stupid fat Presley boy" who is to inherit her home "out of here as long as I can" and does so by attending his funeral with "a faint smile under her veil" (5).

When the brisk and plucky Sara falls on a frozen puddle near her house and is rendered helpless from a broken ankle, her forced immobility, which she describes as her "imprisonment," suggests the domestic imprisonment of women in earlier Gothic stories—the Duchess in "The Duchess at Prayer," Sybilla in "The House of the Dead Hand," Anne in "Kerfol," Juliana in "Mr. Jones." Rather than projecting the source of the imprisonment onto a male figure, however, as she did in the earlier Gothic stories, Wharton places Sara's sense of imprisonment in her own body. The drive with which Sara explores the basic fears within her self/house, engendered by this immobility, is like that of Lady Jane in "Mr. Jones" and Charlotte in "Pomegranate Seed," who also face disturbing truths about themselves in their houses. While in the early Gothic stories a detached, usually male, narrator would learn the story of a constrained woman and then easily, or with some effort, dismiss the story, the women in these late stories—Jane, Charlotte, and especially Sara—are facing their own inner darkness, the feminine/maternal self who terrifies as she draws one to her.

When Sara awakens the next morning after her fall and none of the servants come to her room, even after she rings, she is forced to admit that "something uncommonly strange must have happened in the house" (2). Indeed, something strange has happened inside her. In becoming intensely aware of her body because of its impairment, Sara is forced to face her essential nature as a woman. Hobbling around her silent house, she is beset by elemental fears. Despite the dawn, her shuttered room is still "in deep darkness," and "mysterious things— dreadful things—were associated with darkness" (11, 13). Sexuality, death, loss of control, all that the dark Gothic abyss signifies threatens the strong and orderly Sara.

Even when she sees daylight, she is discomforted by the "deep nocturnal silence in that day-lit house" (13). It is the silence that most distresses and overwhelms Sara: "Silence—more silence! It seemed to be piling itself up like the snow on the roof and in the gutters. Silence. How many people that she knew had any idea what silence was—and how loud it sounded when you really listened to it?" (13–14).

Soon the silence becomes "cold" and "unanswering," "inexorable and hostile," "an impenetrable substance made out of the world-wide cessation of all life and all movement" (17, 18). This threatening, deathlike silence recalls Lily Bart's last hours in *The House of Mirth*, when, "in the mysterious nocturnal separation from all outward signs of life, she felt herself more strangely confronted with her fate . . . the terrible silence and emptiness seemed to symbolize her future—she felt as though the house, the street, the world, were all empty, and she alone left sentient in a lifeless universe" (*HM* 519, ellipsis mine). For Sara too, "that was what laid a chill on her: the feeling that there was no limit to this silence, no outer margin, nothing beyond it" (*G* 18). She, like Lily, is feeling what death must be like.

Stronger and more determined than Lily, however, Sara pushes into the depths of her fears, searching for clues to the "mysterious and dreadful Something" haunting her house and trying to discover whether she is alone in it (16). "I must find that out, I must find that out," she chants to herself "in a sort of meaningless singsong," exhibiting the commingling of fear and curiosity of Gothic heroines before her (18). Her chant echoes Vance Weston's "I must find out—I must find out," words he repeated "chantingly, unmeaningly, as if they had been an incantation" in Elinor Lorburn's library (*HRB* 123). As he feels "a great tidal pressure" of "rhythm and movement" in the English prose he reads, "The walls of dark musty books seemed to sway and dissolve, letting him into that new world of theirs—a world of which he must somehow acquire the freedom" (123). Like Vance, Sara is entering a new world that she can "feel only, and not define," an inner world of her essential self (123).

After finding the room of her maid Agnes dark, cold, empty, and immaculately neat, Sara suspects that her normally attentive, home-bound servant is engaged in a "mysterious nocturnal escape" (*G* 16). Her conclusions that the whole house is "cold, orderly—and empty" and that she is "utterly alone" in it constitute fundamental realizations not just about her present state but about her existential situation, that in life, as in death, one is essentially alone (19).[24] Such a visceral awareness of mortality recalls the pain of "our earliest discovery of helplessness, vulnerability, isolation," the "terrified sorrow" of "the first, and worst, separation," that is, separation from oneness with the mother (Dinnerstein 121).

It is appropriate, then, that Sara instinctually seeks for the "clue to the mystery" in the kitchen (21). But that traditionally warm, welcoming, maternal space is cold, orderly, and empty like the rest of the house. Sara has no nurturance, no accepted feminine/maternal spirit within to substitute for that usually provided by her servants/mother surrogates. What she finds in the kitchen instead is a low, emphatic male voice, "passionately earnest, almost threatening," speaking in "a foreign language, a language unknown to her" (22). Just as she had earlier envisioned a "homicidal maniac" "waiting for her behind the heavy curtains of the room she was about to enter," Sara is again terrified by the thought of male sexual violence, the thought that "whoever was beyond the kitchen door would be upon her in a second" (18, 21).

When her terror is once more "surmounted by the urgent desire to know what was going on," she discovers that the voice is just that, a bodiless voice, emanating from a radio (22). Rather than a nurturing feminine/maternal voice within, at Sara's center is a frightening male voice. But its language is "foreign" to her. She doesn't recognize the power, the sexuality, the threatening potential for violence within her that the male voice communicates, just as unincorporated masculinity has been at the center of imprisoned women's lives throughout Wharton's Gothic fiction. Fittingly yet ironically, on hearing the voice, Sara yearns for her husband's revolver, the embodiment of aggressive, lethal male power. The response is fitting because it answers the threat in kind, yet ironic because Sara longs for aggressive power to destroy the unintelligible masculine self within her.

At the same time, Sara Clayburn only partially understands her feminine self. Just before falling and having her unnerving experience of her own mortality, Sara meets a pale middle-aged woman, a stranger to her, coming up her driveway "to see one of the girls" she tells Sara in a foreign voice (7). "What struck me as queer," Sara tells her cousin, the unnamed narrator of the story, "was that I didn't know her" (7). The next year, also on All Souls' Eve, Sara again sees "the strange woman" coming up her driveway, but this time Sara recalls, "I knew her and she knew me" and she describes her voice as "half-foreign" (30, 31). At Sara's angry order that the woman should leave, the sky darkens and she disappears behind some hemlocks.

The woman is, the narrator hypothesizes, either a ghost or a witch, come to summon Agnes and the other servants to a witch's coven. Sara herself believes that Agnes is a channel "through which communications from the other side of the veil" reach "the submissive household at Whitegates" (33). That the "unknown forces" with which Agnes is in contact, represented by the "half-foreign" woman, are overpowering becomes clear when the narrator explains that "anyone who has once felt the faintest curiosity to assist at a Coven apparently soon finds the curiosity increase to desire, the desire to an uncontrollable longing, which, when the opportunity presents itself, breaks down all inhibitions; for those who have once taken part in a Coven will move heaven and earth to take part again" (34).

The language—"desire" and "uncontrollable longing"—suggests sexuality, but it more broadly describes any overwhelming urge that would be especially frightening to one as controlled as Sara. Indeed, it might be simply the autonomous female power of witches that frightens the patriarchal Sara, who is accustomed to a "submissive" female household.[25]

When Agnes denies Sara's story, that she had been left alone the night of her fall, Sara initially decides to speak no more of it. Her reaction echoes that of the young Alice Hartley in the early story "The Lady's Maid's Bell" when she sees a pale thin maid in the dark hallway of Brympton Place. Alice decides to hold her tongue and ask no more questions after the housemaid, also named Agnes, invalidates her experience by telling her that she had seen no one and that she must have been dreaming. Like the male characters, as well, in the later Gothic stories "The Triumph of Night," "The Young Gentlemen," and "Miss Mary Pask," Sara prefers to "put the whole matter out of her mind, as far as she could," to repress it (28).

Although believing that "something strange had happened in her house," Sara's lack of communication with her servants about her experience amounts to a denial of it (28). She needs to maintain the status quo of dependency on her servants, but more than that, she wants to ignore what she has learned about her own empty life and her intense fear of death and sexuality. In denying her awareness of her own vulnerability, isolation, fear, and loss, she also renounces awareness of "the fundamental, primitive joy of the body" that is suggested by the narrator's description of the coven in which the servants supposedly engage (Dinnerstein 122). But such denial of vulnerability usually allows one "to maintain an illusion of total control; the illusion that in exercising competence we can exert absolute power over everything that matters" (122).

Sara's illusion of total control fails her. She tells her cousin from whom she seeks solace in New York on All Souls' Eve, after seeing the "strange woman" again, that she is never returning to Whitegates because she doesn't want "ever to risk seeing that woman again" (G 35). Sara says she can't believe that such incidents could occur in modern, populated Connecticut, yet she feels fear. This indicates that Sara is using the faculty Wharton describes in her Preface to *Ghosts*, a faculty found "in the warm darkness of the pre-natal fluid far below our conscious reason" that allows us to "apprehend" the supernatural, to fear ghosts without believing in them (vii). While "warm darkness" connotes peacefulness and comfort, such apprehension arising from the maternal darkness is terrifying if one has denied one's own physicality, vulnerability, and separateness, as Sara has done. In this case to become aware is to feel the terror of "sinking back wholly into the helplessness of infancy," to be overwhelmed by rather than learn from the primal maternal power, because one has never completely separated from it (Dinnerstein 161). The narrator tells us that Sara "never went back" to the house/self that connected her to "all the family roots," the self that knows its mortality and the overwhelming power of the feminine/maternal (G 4–5).

In referring to the "timorous and superstitious" who succumb to the "irresistible fascination" of the covens and to the "immense body of literature dealing with these mysterious rites," the narrator of "All Souls' " maintains an intellectual distance from the story and the powerful femaleness to which it alludes (34). Yet in spite of this intellectual distancing, the narrator tells the emotionally and spiritually powerful story of a woman who can acknowledge neither her masculinity nor her femininity, who confronts her orderly, civilized, empty, lifeless life, who is terrified by her isolation when she discovers that the servant "mother" she has depended on has a life, indeed a sexual life, apart from her.

This fe/male narrator, who lives in a flat in an "old-fashioned building" where s/he is "on more human terms with the staff than is possible in one of the modern Babels," gently cares for Sara when she arrives unannounced at the door, putting a comforting arm around her, warming the bed with a hot water bottle, undressing Sara and putting her into bed "like a baby," and tucking her under the covers (29). Like a nurturing parent, s/he reassures Sara that "I'm not going to leave you for more than a minute," sits with her in silence, and listens to her when she is ready to speak (30).

The narrator's last line in the story, that Sara "never went back" to Whitegates and his/her use of the past tense in the explanation that "Jim Clayburn and his widow were both my cousins" suggest that the narrator maintains contact with Sara and perhaps even cared for her until she dies (3).[26] Indeed, it is because of the narrator's "intimacy" with both Clayburns that their families decide s/he is the one to "get at the facts" about Sara's experience (3).

That the narrator's gender remains unidentified yet s/he possesses traits of both genders as Wharton has defined them is a triumphant coda to Wharton's exploration of gender conflict in her Gothic fiction throughout her career. In telling a vision/version of Sara's story, this narrator is telling her/his own story of what "must have happened" in an encounter with one's inner life and overpowering fears (6). In taking in and caring for the frightened Sara the narrator is also accepting and caring for her/his vulnerable, frightened self. In creating the narrator and Sara, Wharton portrays both the fe/male self that understands and accepts the fearful feminine/maternal within and the one who experiences it in all its terror. "All Souls' " makes clear that, to the end, Wharton used her Gothic fiction to probe the dark mystery of the feminine she had been taught to fear but could at last also embrace.

Notes

Preface

1. Little has been published about Wharton's use of the Gothic. Three studies are: Murray, Singley, "Gothic Borrowings," and Wolstenholme. Although Singley's article emphasizes Wharton's rewriting of the male homoerotic Gothic to include the female Gothic, as my book does not, her approach most resembles my own. Singley argues that "the power of the mother is subversive, restorative, and even eventually revolutionary" (275). Several critics have seen Wharton's ghost stories as her vehicle for exploring otherwise taboo feelings and experiences. See, for example, Lewis, "Powers"; Joslin; Bendixen; and Gilbert and Gubar, *No Man's Land.*

2. Norman Holland and Leona Sherman discuss how the Gothic admits "the projection of universal psychological issues" and observe that it has a "gender-linked 'appeal' " (289, 293). In his joint reading of the form with Sherman, Holland demonstrates his discomfort with the vulnerability the Gothic makes him confront, a response much like that of Wharton's male characters in her Gothic short stories. Kate Ferguson Ellis argues that the Gothic novel critiques the ideology of separate spheres by portraying the "safe home" as dangerous and imprisoning to women, thereby saying "what in the polite world of middle-class culture cannot be spoken" (7).

3. I use "woman" and "man" and "male" and "female" as biological indicators and "feminine" and "masculine" and "femininity" and "masculinity" as indicators of the qualities that Wharton, as a result of the many influences in her life, associated with being a woman or a man.

4. These views are expressed, respectively, by Malcolm (11); Ammons (15); Donovan, *After* (48); and Erlich (15).

5. In arguing that Wharton believed American women were kept powerless by their patriarchal society and that her novels angrily protest the tragedy of women's situation, Elizabeth Ammons assumes that Wharton was totally secure in her own femaleness. I believe Wharton had her own "terror of the female" that Ammons has Wharton attribute only to men (190). Josephine Donovan, in *After the Fall,* sees Wharton as rejecting the restrictive, static, mute maternal realm for the masculine world of art and symbolic discourse. Candace Waid, though acknowledging Wharton's "deeply ambivalent preoccupation with women," nonetheless bases her discussion on what she sees as Wharton's dichotomizing between the male (under)world of letters and the erotic and the female (surface) world of decoration (3–4). I argue, by contrast, that Wharton associates the supernatural and the abyss with the maternal and feminine and that, in her Gothic texts, she enacts both gender conflict and potential resolution to the conflict.

6. Julie Olin-Ammentorp discusses Wharton's "unstated belief in the funda-

mental inferiority of women" in her article "Wharton's View of Women in *French Ways and Their Meaning*" (15).

7. David Punter discusses the Gothic preoccupation with the taboo, "areas of socio-psychological life which offend, which are generally swept under the carpet in the interests of social and psychological equilibrium" (405).

8. The term "Gothic-marked" is Susan Wolstenholme's, to which I apply my own criteria. For Wolstenholme the mark of the Gothic is the composed stage scene, site of "muted protest" by which women writers, of which Wharton is one, both write their writing acts into their texts and recognize literary mothers (126, xiv).

9. Whitmont comments that if we want to know the next step in the path to our internal reality, we can "look for the thing that attracts and frightens at the same time," an ambivalence that is key to the Gothic as well (62).

10. Both Demaris Wehr and Naomi R. Goldenberg discuss Jung's limitations for feminists. Goldenberg emphasizes Jung's unwillingness or inability to consider his own family history in conjunction with his theory and his "disembodied thought" (116–17).

11. See particularly Pratt, *Archetypal Patterns*, and Perera.

12. These two poles are represented by Fiedler (12) and Kahane, "Gothic Mirror" (336).

13. The phrase "coming-to-awareness" is Martha Banta's. In *Henry James and the Occult: The Great Extension*, Banta explains James's "new psychological gothicism," his deliberate interconnection of the supernatural with the everyday as a means of deepening his portrayal of realistic human life (60–61).

14. Josephine Donovan uses the term "feminine-maternal" realm in discussing Wharton's writing, but she believes that Wharton perceives the feminine/maternal only hostilely, as a "horrifying stasis, an engulfing petrification, silence and muteness" (*After* 47).

1. The Gothic Text: Life and Art

1. Cynthia Griffin Wolff posits that "Life and I" was written in 1920 or 1922 (417, n.3).

2. Wolff discusses the tension in Wharton between doing and being, between creating art and becoming a beautiful art object. See especially 40–43.

3. According to Wolff, Wharton's experiences taught her that "strong emotions of any kind were innately dangerous" (38). For the young Wharton nothing was worse than to be mute. "To be 'mute' . . . is to be vulnerable to pain," and words offered "the promise of an escape from loneliness and helplessness" (25–26, ellipsis mine). I argue that in the Gothic stories dangerous emotion is projected onto the dangerous man, preying upon the mute woman, whose imprisonment is partly a result of self-censorship. Although she doesn't mention the Gothic, Wolff discounts most of Wharton's ghost stories as inferior fiction.

4. Wolff also notes that the inclination "to fall into the formula of nasty mother and clever daughter" ignores the complexity of the relationship between Lucretia and Edith Jones (32). Erlich posits that Wharton's image of her mother may well have been "a projection of the child's need for punishment rather than an accurate description," but she acknowledges that whatever the "historical truth," Wharton's "internalized mother" was a "persecutory figure" (25, 26).

5. As Pablo Freire writes, "The oppressed suffer from the duality which has

established itself in their innermost being. They discover that without freedom they cannot exist authentically. Yet, although they desire authentic existence, they fear it. They are at one and the same time themselves and the oppressor whose conscious-ness they have internalized" (32).

6. Several critics have noted that Wharton's use of "secret garden" in connec-tion with her writing probably refers to Frances Hodgson Burnett's 1911 children's classic of the same name. What is important for my purposes are the similarities *The Secret Garden* bears both to Wharton's childhood and to her Gothic. At the beginning of the novel, two emotionally abandoned children, Mary and Colin, are angry, pale, and lonely, living together in what Mary calls a "queer house," where "everything is a kind of secret. Rooms are locked up and gardens are locked up" (159). Both think the other is a ghost when they first meet, both live in their own world of stories and dreams. Together they enter the secret, neglected garden, care for it, and are re-juvenated by the activity. This plot resembles Wharton's Gothic heroes/heroines en-tering the spirit of the mother in a mysterious enclosure and being shaken and changed by the encounter.

7. Erlich calls Frederick Jones's library Wharton's "emotional center" (32). She notes that Wharton even makes the connection in "Life and I" between the library and her self or body and that books and libraries are thereafter "libidinized" (34, 154). Carol J. Singley and Susan Elizabeth Sweeney discuss Wharton's anxiety about reading, in her father's library, books forbidden by her mother. They quote Paula Berggreen as even suggesting that in disobeying her mother Wharton is figuratively gazing on her "father's nakedness" in the library (185).

8. Gilbert and Gubar also identify the "anxiety of authorship" that a woman writer experiences because of "her culturally conditioned timidity about self-drama-tization, her dread of the patriarchal authority of art, her anxiety about the impro-priety of female invention" (*Madwoman* 50). Singley and Sweeney discuss how Wharton expresses her anxiety about reading and writing in the narrative of "Pome-granate Seed." My sense of Wharton's gender discomfort in relation to writing dif-fers slightly but significantly from both of these useful studies. I believe Wharton felt anxious about writing not only because she was a woman but because speech and writing *do* have the potential to be aggressive, harmful acts regardless of which gender engages in them. Lucretia Jones's power to wound with words was an early model for her daughter of this potential. Thus although the culturally constructed anxiety Wharton felt about writing influenced her projective creation of menacing intellectual men in her Gothic fiction, she is also responding to her discomfort with destructive verbal power.

9. Howells refers to readers of the Gothic as "literary voyeurs" (15–16), and Wolstenholme extensively discusses this quality of the Gothic experience.

10. Fryer discusses the haunted quality of Wharton's creative process (158–59).

11. Wolff talks about Wharton's realization that good art develops from the art-ist's courage to plunge into the primal depths and confront "his most secret self" (9). Wolff stresses Wharton's need to outgrow and reject her relationship with her mother, however, while I see Wharton attempting to assimilate and recreate her ma-ternal relationship and using the Gothic abyss as a locus of this interaction.

12. A key characteristic of ghost stories by American women, according to Lynette Carpenter and Wendy K. Kolmar, is that they not only expand "reason" to include the supernatural but more often replace reason with sympathy as the key interpretive faculty (13).

13. Fleenor notes that "this confrontation can be seen in a literary context as the confrontation of the female author with the problem of being an author, not the father of her work but the mother of it" (16).

14. Jung's tendency to ignore socially derived, sexist assumptions in the construction of his archetypes, which I discuss earlier, also colors his theory of individuation; this emphasizes the importance of feminist archetypal criticism of women's rebirth journeys as portrayed in their writing.

15. Kahane points out that the maternal body carries such "archaic fantasies of power and vulnerability" because society encourages it with its cultural divisions ("Gothic Mirror" 350).

16. Tzvetan Todorov discusses the fantastic as a means of combating social and internal censorship. The function of the supernatural in particular "is to exempt the text from the action of the law, and thereby to transgress that law" (159).

17. Susan Goodman looks closely at Wharton's relationship with Sara Norton in developing her thesis that Wharton's heroines struggle to define themselves "through connections with other women" (3). Katherine Joslin also points out that although Wharton's intellectual friendships with men are emphasized, her "awakening" to intellectual and literary life came in her contacts with women as well as men (17–18); see also 54–57. Joslin notes that few scholars have concentrated on Wharton's "kinship with women" (19).

18. Olin-Ammentorp also makes this point in "Wharton's View."

19. See White, *A Study,* and Erlich in particular.

20. Wolff discusses the Wolf as Wharton's symbol for her own strong emotions (see especially 38–39).

21. Joslin discusses the importance of Pavillon Colombe and Ste. Claire to Wharton's sense of self-possession. The latter, she notes, has "all the characteristics of a satisfying lover" for Wharton (27). Gilbert and Gubar discuss Wharton's houses as symbolic alternatives to the House of Mirth (*No Man's Land,* 157–58).

22. Wendy Gimbel writes convincingly about houses as symbolic possibilities for female selfhood in *The House of Mirth, Ethan Frome, Summer,* and *The Age of Innocence.* She overlooks the importance of the dilapidated houses in this fiction, however.

23. In her essay on "All Souls'," Annette Zilversmit calls for Wharton criticism to explore "the world of the female that both sexes fear," the "wildness within." It is time, she argues, to reclaim "these forbidden selves, their buried texts, these alienated, tabooed, even most disagreeable desires and feelings," in our critical responses to Wharton. I see my study of the Gothic in Wharton's fiction as a possible response to this call ("All Souls'" 326).

2. Fearing the Feminine

1. Erlich believes that Wharton's "pride in her analytic faculty, which she considered a masculine attribute distinguishable from her feminine gifts, was to remain with her throughout life" and that she "developed strategies for developing the 'male' side of her personality to defend and protect the terrified female self" (47, 46). I think Wharton's response to masculinity and its traits is more complicated. In the early Gothic stories, especially, the masculine self terrifies and tyrannizes rather than protects the feminine self.

2. White, in reading "The House of the Dead Hand" as an incest story, as-

sumes the hand to be the mother's or grandmother's, "too weak to protect the daughter," or the "third hand," the father's penis, announcing "This is the house of incest" (*A Study* 41). Erlich, who also reads this as an incest story, comments that the hand might signify paternal abuse as well as self-abuse, since Sybilla is depicted the way masturbators are in the nineteenth century (42). Neither of these readers considers Sybilla's passive submission to her entrapment.

3. Erlich and White both note these sexual connotations, though they read the father's control as literally incestuous, as I do not (42; *A Study* 40).

4. Wolstenholme's comment about George Eliot's Gwendolen, in *Daniel Deronda,* that "she is always divested of control over the art which she claims," is even more true of Sybilla, who colludes in her father's control over her access to herself as woman (123).

5. Wolstenholme points out that " 'Gothic suspense' results from the tension between the uncovering of the story and the repression that resists this uncovering" and that the story "unfolds a guilty secret" (29). The secret in "The Duchess at Prayer," as in traditional Gothic, involves crimes against a woman, though Wharton's story bears her individual marking, the gendered conflict between woman as art and man as intellectual art owner. Eve Kosofsky Sedgwick discusses the nested story convention as a structural application of the unspeakable in Gothic fiction (20).

6. The Duke's penchant for snapping at "verbal errors" recalls Wharton's memories in "Life and I" of her mother's similar propensity.

7. MacMillan discusses the connection between enclosure and chastity in Gothic fiction, 50–52.

8. Sedgwick notes that "it is sexual activity that literal live burial most often punishes" (5). Wharton makes repetitive use of the figurative live burial/sexuality convergence in her Gothic ("The House of the Dead Hand," "Angel at the Grave," "Kerfol," "Mr. Jones," *The Age of Innocence,* and *Hudson River Bracketed*), especially as the sense is enhanced by suffocating weather (e.g., snowstorms in "Bewitched," *Ethan Frome,* and "All Souls' " and dense fog in "Miss Mary Pask.")

9. MacAndrew sees bells as "perfect symbols of androgyny with their phallic clappers inside their great, round, cavernous bellies" (247). Wharton later uses The Bells as the name of the estate that Jane Lynke recaptures from patriarchal control in "Mr. Jones."

10. Ellen Powers Stengel makes this observation in "Edith Wharton Rings 'The Lady's Maid's Bell' " (6).

11. Stengel comments that the effete Mr. Ranford is "on the level of the discourse nothing but a pale reflection of Mrs. Brympton" (8).

12. In arguing that *The House of Mirth* is "primarily a novel of identity," Joan Lidoff discusses how the other characters are projections of parts of Lily's personality she can't integrate. Thus hostility is projected onto Bertha and sexuality onto Gus. Though my own discussion concurs with many of the points in Lidoff's ground-breaking essay, I see the novel's treatment of the other characters, and especially Selden, as part of Wharton's larger exploration of gender (520, 522, 532).

13. MacAndrew notes that in Gothic literature "the reflections thrown back at the viewer from mirrors and portraits reveal the inner self" (217).

14. Gimbel discusses how Mrs. Peniston "adulterates the maternal image" in her response to Lily and how her cold, dark house figures this response (37).

15. Francis Russell Hart has pointed out that "the experience of the enlightened person feeling haunted by some demonic self" is at the heart of Gothic fiction (94).

16. Perera comments that the splitting off of female passion has produced "frustrated furies" (148). See Waid (46) and Donovan (*After* 60) for other readings of this allusion.

17. Radway explains that the female foil's "passionate sexuality is always linked by juxtaposition with her distasteful ambition, greed, ruthlessness, and vanity" in contrast to the heroine's "virginity, romanticism and desire for love" (149–50).

18. Gilbert and Gubar discuss the "sexually voracious" Bertha Dorset as a revision of Bertha Rochester in *Jane Eyre* (*No Man's Land* 2:145). Wharton encourages the parallel by having Carry Fisher comment to Lily that "Bertha has been behaving more than ever like a madwoman" (*HM* 384).

19. Key to the Gothic is the internal battle between "immediate ego-preservation" and "the apprehension of larger, less personal values that first makes itself known as dread," Judith Wilt explains in her discussion of the Gothic in George Eliot's *Daniel Deronda* (177). Waid discusses Bertha's letters extensively as the way into the underworld of writing and erotic experience that Lily rejects when she burns them (44, 47). I consider Lily's act a moral one as well.

20. Joseph Wiesenfarth's concept of the "novel of Gothic manners" is useful to my discussion. Working from Robert Heilman's notion of "new Gothic" as an enactment of intense internal states rather than external terror, Wiesenfarth identifies an assimilation of new Gothic into the novel of manners in late nineteenth-century fiction such as *Middlemarch* and *The Portrait of a Lady*. In this fiction, "the manners become the horror." In denying the legitimacy of strong feeling, respectability and codes of conduct become deadly for characters like Dorothea Brooke and Isabel Archer, whose "affective sel(ves)" are imprisoned by overbearing men. Wiesenfarth doesn't discuss Wharton, and he stresses the social critique inherent in the novel of Gothic manners, which my study does only tangentially, but there is illuminating overlap in our approaches (ix, 114).

21. Lois Tyson discusses in detail Selden's aestheticization of Lily and the desire for self-abstraction that both share and encourage in one another. She posits that the motive of both Selden and Lily is to "escape existential inwardness," which she explains as an awareness of one's "vulnerability to existential contingency" that increases proportionally with one's poverty (6). I argue that Selden's and Lily's fears go far beyond "the uncertainties of life in the concrete world" (6).

22. I disagree with Elaine Showalter's reading that Lily's interaction with these working-class women after she leaves Mrs. Hatch's is an indication of her "growing awareness and finally her merger with a community of working women" ("The Death" 143).

23. Christ discusses women's acute sense of nothingness in male-centered culture that often precedes an "awakening" (13ff.).

24. Wharton may well have been an unwanted child, given the twelve years between her birth and her younger brother's, her mother's age at her birth (thirty-seven), and (more hypothetically) the absence of her mother's name on the original baptismal certificate (Lewis, *Biography* 5, 15). Thus she would have felt firsthand the effects of a woman's being the "unwilling victim" of her own body.

25. Gubar sees Lily's body as the word, a script for Selden ("Blank Page" 81). Wolff's point is similar, that Lily's "Beautiful Death" is a final, literal metamorphosis into art (132). Wolstenholme argues that inconclusiveness about the word's meaning invites us to "double read" the ending either "romantically" or "realistically" (e.g., ironically) (144). My reading of the ending concurs most with Joslin's, that we should

read "the word as it is not written, the message as a non-message," given that Lily and Selden remain, in the end, unable to understand one another (68), and with Waid's, that the word is far from clear and that Selden's "transcendence" is "hollow and tinged with irony" (43). Also helpful in understanding this dual experience of the unspoken word is Sedgwick's discussion of the "unspeakable" as a Gothic convention, a barrier imposed between people (19).

26. Wolff suggests a similar reading in her comment that "there is a sensuous fulfillment in yielding, finally, to the imperative to be nothing more than beautiful; and there is relief in the relinquishment of all those difficult pretenses to adulthood—relief in a retreat to the velvet embrace of infancy" (131). By contrast, Showalter's belief that this hallucination speaks for "Lily's awakening sense of loving solidarity and community" with working women ignores the ominous and debilitating lethargy to which Lily finally succumbs ("The Death" 145). Erlich, too, reads this scene positively, as Lily now able to reach "beyond narcissism into imagining an 'other' and nurturing it" (67). I see Lily as "unawakened" and fatally absorbed by the "other."

3. Confronting the Limits of Reason

1. Louise J. Kaplan views the kind of "physical and emotional comings and goings" that Fullerton engaged in, and that were so agonizing to Wharton, as tyrannical and sees Wharton's submissiveness to Fullerton as a perversion (223, 227). In this reading Wharton is like one of the female victims in her early Gothic short stories, tyrannized by male intellectuals who regularly abandon them. Kaplan points out that Wharton reassesses Fullerton's "radiant reasonableness" and regains her self-esteem and autonomy (227). Wharton's portrayal of women and femininity in her Gothic undergoes a similar transformation.

2. Jung also addressed the mind/body distinction and, like Wharton, rejected its efficacy. He called the separation "an intellectually necessary separation of one and the same fact into two aspects, to which we then illegitimately attribute an independent existence" (8:326). The kind of opposition between spheres that Wharton was experiencing, however, Jung extolled as essential to a healthy psyche. He writes that "there is no energy unless there is a tension of opposites; hence it is necessary to discover the opposite to the attitude of the conscious mind" (7:53). This "tension charged with energy" enables "a living birth that leads to a new level of being, a new situation. The transcendent function manifests itself as a quality of conjoined opposites" (8:90). This energetic tension is at work in Wharton's Gothic, enabling her to envision, in her late fiction, a fe/male self.

3. White writes that the Hermit and the Wild Woman represent two sides of Wharton, but then she goes on to say that the Hermit most represents Wharton (*A Study* 72). It is worth noting that like the Wild Woman, who had been an unhealthy "cloistered woman," Wharton once described herself as "a dim woman cloistered in ill health (myself! E. W.)" (Donnée Book).

4. Jung writes that "the maternal significance of water . . . is one of the clearest interpretations of symbols in the whole field of mythology" and that "the maternal aspect of water coincides with the nature of the unconscious" (5:218, 219, ellipsis mine).

5. Just before hearing Grace laugh, Jane has had a conversation with Mrs. Fairfax about whether there are any ghosts at Thornfield.

6. Eino Railo discusses the "weird conception of eyes as a source of irresistible terror" in conjunction with Bulwer-Lytton's horror story "Dweller of the Threshold." In it a young student of the occult inhales an elixir that first brings blissful images. Then they are transformed into a larvalike human head covered with a dark veil through which glare "livid and demoniac fire eyes." Their "deadly malignancy" and almost human "hate and mockery" overpower the young man, and the hypnotic eyes follow him everywhere (265, 264). Wharton's story seems to play on Bulwer-Lytton's, for in "Dweller of the Threshold," the eyes retreat only when the man commits an immoral deed and reappear when he tries to rise morally, while Culwin's eyes appear when he deceives himself into thinking he is being moral and disappear when he resumes his typically immoral behavior. Although I have no evidence that Wharton read Bulwer-Lytton's story, biographical material about her often mentions that she was an avid reader of mystery and ghost stories. Hélène Cixous's reading of Freud's *Das Unheimliche* ("The Uncanny") discusses the substitutive relationship between the penis and the eye. The connection suggests that the grotesque supernatural eyes Culwin sees are figures of his debased sexuality (536). MacAndrew notes that eyes in Gothic literature "reveal the soul" (217).

7. Day discusses dream as the narrative model of Gothic fiction, which gives it a "familiar strangeness" (43). He also discusses the use of the "retrospective first person," memory made into narrative, which emphasizes that the Gothic fantasy is taking place within an individual imagination (46). Wolff is one of the few critics to emphasize that the narrator's reaction to Ethan Frome is the real subject of the novel (164). We are given, she writes, "a brief glimpse into the most appalling recesses of the narrator's mind" as he faces his inner world in the form of Ethan Frome, and she discusses parallels between Frome and the narrator (165). Wolff emphasizes the "abysmal horror" of the narrator's vision as he (and through him Wharton) faces the desire to regress (191). I see Wharton portraying this vision into the depths as salutary even if terrifying. This helps explain what Wolff calls the "surprising" fact that Wharton was "extraordinarily happy" when she was writing the novel (191).

8. In *The Great Mother* Neumann discusses the tree as the center of the vegetative symbolism of the Great Earth Mother (48).

9. MacAndrew talks about the old house as being "a lasting representation of the torments of the subconscious pressing upon the conscious mind and making a prison of the self" (49). Waid emphasizes the novel's "unrelenting infertility" and Ethan as "the figure of a barren woman" who has removed his nurturing center (75, 74). Gimbel connects Ethan's act with his mother's sickness and her withdrawal of love, which he experiences as exile from "the original home" (71–72).

10. The fact that all the characters are blood relations provides a context for their interrelatedness in other ways. Waid points out the interchangeable images of Mattie and Zeena, and she connects all three characters with the novel's infertility (73). Ammons also discusses Mattie as Zeena's double, but she believes the narrator's tale specifically reveals a male fear of female betrayal (67, 75). Goodman notes that "Ethan and Mattie are two parts of one whole, representing maleness and femaleness," but she doesn't pursue the parallels (74). None of these readers sees parallels among all the characters.

11. See Gimbel for a detailed discussion of Mattie's nonself and the parallels between her and Ethan's desire to remain children, immersed in the maternal. Although my discussion parallels Gimbel's in many respects, a crucial difference is Gimbel's slight emphasis on the narrator, whom I see as key to a reading of the novel.

12. By contrast, Gimbel reads Zeena as the Terrible Mother, embodying the black, regressive impulse of the psyche (70).

13. Waid notes that Ethan Frome is Wharton's "personal meditation on what it means to write books as bridges across the abyss of her greatest fears," in this case her fear of muteness and inarticulateness (62). I argue that what distinguishes Wharton's Gothic-marked novels is that they enter the abyss rather than bridge it.

14. Helen Killoran extensively documents the narrator's unreliability, though toward a different end, in her discussion of historical allusions in "Kerfol."

4. Reclaiming the Feminine

1. Monika M. Elbert argues that the war's destruction and the "excessively masculinized civilization" of which it was a result are reflected in the "matriphobic atmosphere" of *Summer*. Though Elbert's essay is convincing, I see hints in the novel's ending that Charity has not given up "her bond to the primeval mother within her" (4, 7).

2. Rudolf Otto discusses the numinous in religion experience as a feeling of dread, a feeling of something "uncanny," "eerie," "weird" (14). S. L. Varnado argues that the numinous is central to Gothic literature (6).

3. Neumann explains that the German *Berg*, or mountain, is symbolically related to phrases like *sich bergen*, "taking refuge," and *sich verbergen*, "hiding" (45). He continues that "the Great Mother is often represented sitting on the earth. . . . Her very unwieldiness and bulk compel the Great Mother to take a sedentary attitude, in which she belongs like a hill or mountain to the earth of which she is a part and which she embodies" (98, ellipsis mine). The mountain, "the immobile, sedentary symbol that visibly rules over the land," symbolizes the "female godhead" (99).

4. My reading of Charity's journey to her mother concurs with that of Susan Goodman, who writes that on making the trip to the Mountain, Charity is now free to accept herself rather than being ashamed of "the part of her that is her mother" (82).

5. The value of memory as "empathic introspection with one's past self" and its particular value to women as a way of keeping their identity intact is discussed by Judith Kegan Gardiner in "On Female Identity and Writing by Women" (189). My reading of the ending mediates between Wolff's assumption that Charity chooses to marry Royall and is beginning to love him and Gimbel's, that Charity shows no signs of being other than a victimized child (124). Generally readers of *Summer*'s ending see it as totally depressing (Ammons 137–41; Walton 92; McDowell, *Edith Wharton* 78). Both Nancy A. Walker and Barbara A. White explain dichotomous responses to the ending by reading *Summer* in the context of typical sentimental fiction.

6. Waid's discussion of the blue brooch as Charity's link to "mothers" is worth noting (116–18).

7. I am convinced by Wolff's argument that the fragment was written in 1918–19 rather than in 1935 as Lewis suggests (407–15; *Biography* 544).

8. Day explains that "the characteristic narrative form of the Gothic fantasy is designed to create a sense of formlessness and refuses to obey our assumptions about narrative as a meaningful sequence of action or to serve as an analogue to the world outside the text" (49).

9. Judith Herman and Lisa Hirschman, in "Father-Daughter Incest," describe

the typical incest victim as a girl estranged from her mother, who is herself incapacitated mentally, physically, or both. The daughter most admires the father because of his status in society and because he pays her positive attention. The father, in turn, takes advantage of the girl's neediness and her sense of importance at being "chosen" by her father for special (sexual) attention.

10. Ammons also describes the lovemaking as the father's display of power (141).

11. Perera's description of the powerful eyes of Ereshkigal, queen of the Netherworld, captures the effect of Ellen's gaze at the Gorgon: "the eyes of death, pitiless, not personally caring. . . . these implacable eyes of death see with an immediate 'isness' that finds pretense, ideals, individuality and relatedness, irrelevant. . . . They bore into the soul to find the naked truth, to see reality beneath all its myriad forms and the illusions and defenses it displays. . . . They also see through collective standards that are false to life itself" (155–56, ellipsis mine). Such seeing "shears us of our defenses and entails a sacrifice of easy collective understandings and the hopes and expectations of looking good and safely belonging. . . . This vision is awful, and yet it bestows a refined perception of reality to those who can bear it. This is the wisdom of the dark feminine that Psyche could not yet sustain" (157, ellipsis mine). This sense that one gains new awareness from facing the Medusa recalls that Medusa represented "female wisdom" as the serpent-goddess of the Libyan Amazons. Medusa's dangerous face was also thought to be that of a menstruating woman, whose "magic blood" could "create and destroy life" (B. Walker 629).

12. Heidegger's theory of the self, *Dasein,* is especially helpful in explaining Ellen's conflict. The self is in "a perpetual tension between an alienated, reified level of existence—existence as an object—and existence as a projective, creative, transcending subject" (Donovan, *Feminist Theory* 118). The self "tries to flee the feeling of 'uncanniness which lies in Dasein' " by "losing itself in the bourgeois familiarity of the everyday world of prefabricated identity" (119). Gimbel discusses Ellen's temptation to regress into childhood and thereby lose her soul (153).

13. Laura Mulvey and E. Ann Kaplan describe the gaze of the male focusing on the female object "in order to possess her, project his fears and desires upon her, and define his identity through her" (quoted in Singley and Sweeney, 186).

14. In her discussion of the Medusa in poems by women, Elias-Button describes a Medusa-like figure of "chthonic female power" in Louise Bogan's poem "The Sleeping Fury," which "remorselessly reveals pretension, hypocrisy, and truths too painful to bear." In facing the Medusa, the "Terrible Mother," within, "we are no longer the protected child but the carriers of the new woman whose birth is our own" (203, 205). Though Gimbel believes as I do that Ellen's journey in the novel is toward mature womanhood, she believes, as I do not, that her facing the Gorgon is a way to confront the "destructive part of herself" that is destroying Newland's and May's marriage (162).

15. Ammons argues that Catherine Mingott is only presumed powerful and that she is really manipulated by the men in the novel (150). Her misreading that Ellen is sent back to Count Olenski's "loathsome marital hold" is perhaps why she overlooks Catherine's role in Ellen's eventual escape to an independent life (128).

16. Lewis (*Biography* 431) and Fryer (127) point out a few ways that Wharton resembles both Newland and Ellen.

17. Elsa Nettels discusses the narrator of "The Young Gentlemen" as one of many blindly arrogant male narrators in Wharton's short fiction (252–53).

18. Barbara White points out that, since Harpledon is supposed to be north of Boston, where the narrator now lives, he should have said "up to Harpledon" rather than "down." The slip, she suggests, emphasizes the "non-ghost-seeing self" of Wharton that refuses to "go down" to see the disturbing experience (*A Study* 90).

19. Northrop Frye discusses dwarfs as "subintelligent and subarticulate" beings that are part of the descent theme in romance, a theme characterized by losing consciousness and descending to a lower world, "which is sometimes a world of cruelty and imprisonment" and always involves a "confusion of identity." As part of this theme also, twins suggest a portrayal of a dreamer and the self he is dreaming about. That Cranch's dwarf twin sons never leave their windowless room emphasizes their timeless, dreamlike existence and Cranch's realization of his stunted masculinity (129, 111).

20. The practical housekeeper who relays important information of which she doesn't understand the spiritual significance is a staple in Gothic fiction (MacAndrew 135–36). Wharton makes her servants wielders of the patriarchal power of suppression. That in "The Young Gentlemen" she names the imperious servant Catherine, the first name of her dedicated housekeeper, Gross, suggests that Wharton was ambivalent about the servant's power.

21. Kahane writes that the grotesque depends on "perceptual distortions" that "assault our sense of a coherent self and world" ("The Maternal Legacy" 244) and Bayer-Berenbaum that "the grotesque insults our need for order, for classification, matching and grouping; it violates a sense of appropriate categories" (29). MacAndrew also points out that "dwarfed and hunchbacked figures, which are traditionally grotesques, appear in Gothic tales and are often also doubles figures symbolizing haunting guilt, paranoia, the split personality, and madness" (161–62).

22. The narrator's perception of the sea recalls Barbara Watson's reference to it as an image of "power and fertility" as well as Wharton's own use of water as a signifier of the feminine (116). Jennice G. Thomas points out that in the story's setting, Wharton draws on a tradition that associates women with nature to demonstrate how "the dread of darkness and death is linked in the masculine imagination with a fear of women" (112).

23. "Bad things come in threes" is an American expression, supposedly derived from Peter's denying Jesus three times "before the cock crows." Actors dislike three candles on a stage or in a dressing room because they indicate a quarrel (Heaps 88).

24. Thomas sees Mary Pask as a figure for the woman artist. Grace, Mary's sister, points to Mary's interest in art as the reason for her solitude. Wharton, in turn, uses Mary to show that "loneliness and contempt were the price patriarchy expected women to pay for their devotion to art or literature" (115).

25. White points out that the Brand family "has been founded on incest or near incest," since Brand had married his cousin (*A Study* 104).

26. The forbidden echoes the "unspeakable," which is associated with the repressed. As Wolstenholme points out in her reference to Freud's "The Uncanny," the unspeakable expresses itself in uncanny recurrence and repetition (121). In this sense Venny's repeated appearances to Saul speak of the uncanny feminine to which Freud alludes.

27. Margaret McDowell calls the stake "undoubtedly a phallic emblem" ("Edith Wharton's Ghost Stories" 84).

28. Sedgwick's observation that the barrier created by the unspeakable (in this

case Venny's femininty) is "breached only at the cost of violence," especially violence at the threshold, is particularly relevant here (16, 32).

29. Wharton mentions Starkfield twice in "Bewitched," as if encouraging us to make the connection with *Ethan Frome.*

30. Jung talks about "Fascination, bewitchment, 'loss of soul,' possession" as "phenomena of the dissociation and suppression of consciousness caused by unconscious contents" (9[1]:281). In this sense Saul's bewitching might be read as a projection of Prudence's intense fear of her own femininity.

31. In the days of ancient Christianity "so many 'grottoes' contained pagan idols that decorative ideas for cathedral sculptures were copied from them: hence the *grotesques* or 'grotto-creatures' swarming in Gothic art" (B. Walker 155). Godfrey makes this connection when he notices that "evil-faced catamawfreys" hanging in the caves are also chiseled in the capital of a column in the church of Saint George.

5. Surviving the Abyss and Revising Gender Roles

1. McDowell discusses the influence of Wharton's preoccupation with death and religion in her late years on the ghost stories she wrote during that period ("Ghost Tales Reconsidered" 291–314).

2. Ammons points out that Bachofen's *Das Mutterrecht* (The Mother Right), published in 1861, was well known among intellectuals and so was probably read by Wharton (192).

3. In "Gender Imprisonment and the Preservation of Houses in 'Mr. Jones,' " a paper presented at the "Edith Wharton at The Mount" conference in Lenox, Massachusetts, June 7–10, 1987, Connie Johnson pointed out that in having all the characters' names begin with "J"—Jones, Juliana, and Jane—Wharton is suggesting that they are, in a sense, all one person. Jones is also, of course, Wharton's father's name.

4. This description bears a strong resemblance to that of Gross, Wharton's "watchfully assiduous, dauntlessly tenacious Alsatian maid, with her wise old puckered face and crumpled smile" (Lubbock, *Portrait* 84). Given Mrs. Clemm's obstructionist role in Jane's experience, the parallel raises questions, as have earlier stories with servants, about Wharton's ambivalent reaction to being cared for by women.

5. Note also Bruno Bettelheim's discussion of apples as symbols in fairy tales (212–13).

6. See Rabuzzi 92ff. See also Wolff, who discusses the threshold as the juncture, for Wharton, of two distinct worlds, one of independent adulthood and sexual maturity and the other of childhood obedience, limitation, and emotional starvation (173).

7. Singley and Sweeney discuss Charlotte as "suspended between two realms of gendered expectation," the role of passive woman and a "potential usurper of texts and the power that they represent" (178). Indeed, they note, all the characters experience "shifting gender roles" (192).

8. Singley and Sweeney point out that Charlotte and Elsie, because of their mutual engagement with reading and writing, become doubles (180, 193).

9. Early Christians opposed the exclusively female Eleusinian rites because of their "overt sexuality" (B. Walker 220).

10. Singley and Sweeney refer to Elsie as androgynous (183–84). Though they discuss the story's "ambiguous allusion" to the Persephone-Demeter myth, their

reading differs from mine in that they assume that it is Kenneth and Charlotte who "each have their turn as Persephone" (191).

11. Sedgwick discusses how faces in Gothic fiction often seem to be "halfway toward becoming a language, a code" (158). In this sense the red faces of both Mrs. Clemm and Mrs. Ashby "speak" of their sexual experience (150, 162–63).

12. Singley and Sweeney refer to Susan Gubar's idea of the subversiveness of the blank page in discussing Elsie's almost blank letters as an assertion of the feminine (197). Elsie's unintelligible letters can also be read as signs of Gothic "unspeakableness" that Sedgwick discusses as creating personal barriers (19).

13. In giving the house this name, Wharton may well have been drawing on earlier occult references. "Willows" is the name of Walter de la Mare's story, collected in *On the Edge,* about a supposedly dead poet whose house of the same name is visited by an American scholar who makes an unsettling discovery there. "The Willows" is also the title of a ghostly story by Algernon Blackwood about a remote island covered with willows that strikes terror and awe in the hearts of the two men who come upon it. De la Mare is the one to whom Wharton dedicates *Ghosts,* which she had considered calling *On the Verge,* an echo of *On the Edge.* Blackwood, a contemporary of Wharton's, could well have been among the many ghost story writers Wharton enjoyed reading.

14. Most critics assume Vance to be the central character in *Hudson River Bracketed* and *The Gods Arrive.* Carol Wershoven was one of the first to take Halo's development in the novels seriously, realizing that she, like Vance, undergoes a journey "back to her own selfhood" (143). Abbey H. P. Werlock goes too far in the opposite direction, arguing that "the real hero" is Halo, the intellectual woman. The unappealing Vance, she explains, is modeled on Morton Fullerton, while Halo mirrors Wharton's own development as writer and woman (182).

15. Mary Suzanne Schriber notes that one reason Wharton may have made the artist in these last two novels male rather than female was to satirize American novelists of the 1920s and "the state of the arts as governed by men" (179).

16. Harold Jantz, in *The Mothers in Faust: The Myth of Time and Creativity,* writes that "the ultimate, deep symbol of motherhood raised to the universal and the cosmic, of the birth, sending forth, death, and return of all things in an eternal cycle, is expressed in the Mothers, the matrices of all forms, at the timeless, placeless originating womb or hearth where chaos is transmuted into cosmos and whence the forms of creation issue forth into the world of place and time" (37).

17. A. J. Downing, who discusses the Hudson River Bracketed style in *The Architecture of Country Houses,* originally published in 1850, comments that the Picturesque depends on the kind of irregularity found in the Hudson River Bracketed style and that the Picturesque manifests Beauty through power. This is the dynamic at work in the Willows and in Halo's personality (29, 113).

18. Sandra Gilbert and Susan Gubar discuss "Kubla Khan" as a representation of Romanticism portrayed as a chasm opening culture to what it had repressed: "the revolutionary and anti-rational forces associated with nature, with imagination, with unconsciousness, and with spontaneity," attributes associated with the "uncanny otherness of 'the feminine.' " The poem, in their view, dramatizes Coleridge's struggle with the concept that artistic creation involves a "quasi-feminine yielding to uncontrollable forces" while at the same time it demonstrates a mastery of form ("The Mirror and the Vamp" 163).

19. Although Ammons reads the Mothers as "figures terrifying but also heal-

ing in their insistence on confronting rather than avoiding pain and suffering," she sees Halo as an unbelievable character whose final act confirms Wharton's sadly romantic conception of women in maternal terms alone (195). In a reading that supports my sense of Halo, Susan Gubar recasts the Virgin Mary's "receptivity to bearing and giving birth to the Incarnate Word" as the female inner space ready "for inspiration and creation, the self conceived and dedicated to its own potential divinity" ("Blank Page" 91). It is also worth noting that Persephone's appearance with a son, the reborn Dionysus, was seen as essential to the Eleusinian mysteries, a strictly female rite (Grace 39). On a less metaphorical (but not necessarily more rational) level, Halo's assumption that this child is a boy might derive from the fact that she lost a son when she was married to Tarrant (*HRB* 195).

20. Julie Olin-Ammentorp observes that reading the ending of *The Gods Arrive* in conjunction with Julia Kristeva's "Stabat Mater" helps us see that Halo "has access to both the semiotic and the symbolic order." Olin-Ammentorp discusses Halo, however, primarily in terms of her embodiment of the semiotic in contrast to Vance as representative of the symbolic. Thus at the end of the novel, "language, the logos, bows before maternality; the symbolic order concedes its dependence upon the semiotic"; in this view, neither character has the power of both orders ("Wharton Through a Kristevan Lens" 305, 306).

21. Erlich notes that in these last two novels, "Wharton moves closer to unifying her feminine self and her artistic self," and she sees elements of Wharton in both Halo and Vance (149). She doesn't pursue the parallels between them, however. Goodman believes as I do that at the end of *The Gods Arrive*, Vance is willing to accept the feminine in himself and that Vance's and Halo's embrace is "a recognition and acceptance of the interdependence of masculinity and femininity." Their union in turn represents Wharton's wish to "wed the male and female in herself" (132). Werlock believes that only Halo is both feminine and masculine by the end of the novel, "both creative and fiercely independent" (196).

22. Wehr notes that Jung sees the drive toward wholeness as consisting of "uniting the 'masculine' and 'feminine' sides of the personality. Following the process through, a new state is achieved" (72).

23. Zilversmit discusses Sara's dependent relationship with her servants as a mother-daughter one ("All Souls' " 320).

24. Zilversmit also refers to the story as reverberating with "almost existential desolation" ("All Souls' " 315).

25. Bayer-Berenbaum writes that "the witches coven is held in the nude, and strange copulations with animals and sexual orgies may be involved" (42). Lewis assumes that Wharton knew about the wild erotic activities of covens (*CSS* 1:xvii). Zilversmit broadens the reading by pointing out that American literature connects witches and covens with "denied or guilty passions" ("Edith Wharton's Last Ghosts" 304). Miriam Robbins Dexter points out that witches possess power not controlled by men and so are *"a projection of men's fears,* fears of energies which they did not control" (182). Allan Gardner Smith refers to Sara as "the crippled intellect" who, "masquerading as male, inherits with her costume the terror of the female that suggests, as in earlier periods, the accusation of witchcraft" (150, 151).

26. White is the only other critic I have found to notice that the narrator's gender isn't indicated. She, like the majority of readers, however, subsequently assumes that the narrator is a woman (*A Study* 105). McDowell disparages the "garrulous

woman" narrator, who she assumes is a gossipy "unattractive maternal figure" ("Ghost Tales Reconsidered" 310, 311). Zilversmit reads the narrator as a young woman who, like Sara, is repressing an "inhibiting deadness" within ("All Souls' " 325).

Bibliography

Correspondence and Manuscripts

Donnée Book 1900. Edith Wharton Archives, Beinecke Library, Yale University, New Haven, Connecticut.

EW to Edward Burlingame. 10 July 1898. Scribner Collection, Firestone Library, Princeton University, Princeton, New Jersey.

EW to Sara Norton. 7 July 1908. Edith Wharton Archives, Beinecke Library, Yale University, New Haven, Connecticut.

"Life and I." Edith Wharton Archives, Beinecke Library, Yale University, New Haven, Connecticut.

"Miss Moynham." Partial manuscript. Edith Wharton Archives, Beinecke Library, Yale University, New Haven, Connecticut.

Notebook, 1924–34. Edith Wharton Archives, Beinecke Library, Yale University, New Haven, Connecticut.

Works by Edith Wharton

The Age of Innocence. New York: D. Appleton, 1920.

A Backward Glance. New York: D. Appleton-Century, 1934.

"Beatrice Palmato." In *Edith Wharton: A Biography*, by R. W. B. Lewis. New York: Harper & Row, 1975.

Certain People. New York: D. Appleton, 1930.

Crucial Instances. New York: Charles Scribner's Sons, 1901.

The Decoration of Houses. New York: Charles Scribner's Sons, 1897.

The Descent of Man and Other Stories. New York: Charles Scribner's Sons, 1904.

Ethan Frome. New York: Charles Scribner's Sons, 1911.

Ethan Frome. New York: Charles Scribner's Sons, 1922.

French Ways and Their Meaning. New York: D. Appleton, 1919.

Ghosts. New York: D. Appleton-Century, 1937.

The Gods Arrive. New York: D. Appleton, 1932.

Here and Beyond. New York: D. Appleton, 1926.

The Hermit and the Wild Woman and Other Stories. New York: Charles Scribner's Sons, 1908.

The House of Mirth. New York: Charles Scribner's Sons, 1905.

Hudson River Bracketed. New York: D. Appleton, 1929.

In Morocco. New York: Charles Scribner's Sons, 1925.

Italian Backgrounds. New York: Charles Scribner's Sons, 1905.

"A Little Girl's New York." *Harper's Magazine*, December 1937–May 1938, pp. 356–64.

A Motor-Flight Through France. New York: Charles Scribner's Sons, 1908.
"Pomegranate Seed." *Scribner's Magazine,* March 1912, pp. 284–91.
Review of Leslie Stephen's *George Eliot. Bookman* 15 (May 1902): 247–51.
Summer. New York: D. Appleton, 1917.
The Writing of Fiction. New York: Charles Scribner's Sons, 1925.
Xingu and Other Stories. New York: Charles Scribner's Sons, 1916.

Secondary Sources

Ammons, Elizabeth. *Edith Wharton's Argument with America.* Athens: University of Georgia Press, 1980.
Baker, Carlos, ed. *Coleridge: Poetry and Prose.* New York: Bantam Books, 1965.
Baker, James Volant. *The Sacred River: Coleridge's Theory of the Imagination.* Baton Rouge: Louisiana State University Press, 1957.
Balzac, Honoré de. "La Grande Bretèche." In *Selected Short Stories,* trans. Sylvia Raphael. New York: Penguin Books, 1977.
Banta, Martha. *Henry James and the Occult: The Great Extension.* Bloomington: Indiana University Press, 1972.
Bayer-Berenbaum, Linda. *The Gothic Imagination: Expansion in Gothic Literature and Art.* East Brunswick: Associated University Presses, 1982.
Bendixen, Alfred, ed. *Haunted Women: The Best Supernatural Tales by American Women Writers.* New York: Frederick Ungar, 1985.
Bendixen, Alfred, and Annette Zilversmit, eds. *Edith Wharton: New Critical Essays.* New York: Garland, 1992.
Berry, Walter Van Rensselaer, to Edith Wharton. November 1898. Edith Wharton Archives, Beinecke Library, Yale University, New Haven, Connecticut.
Bersani, Leo. *A Future for Astyanax: Character and Desire in Literature.* Boston: Little, Brown, 1976.
Bettelheim, Bruno. *The Uses of Enchantment: The Meaning and Importance of Fairy Tales.* New York: Vintage Books, 1977.
Bowman, Barbara. "Victoria Holt's Gothic Romances: A Structuralist Inquiry." In *The Female Gothic,* ed. Juliann E. Fleenor. Montreal: Eden Press, 1983.
Briggs, Julia. *Night Visitors: The Rise and Fall of the English Ghost Story.* London: Faber & Faber, 1977.
Brontë, Charlotte. *Jane Eyre.* 1847. Rpt. New York: Oxford University Press, 1975.
Browning, Robert. "My Last Duchess." In *Poetry of the Victorian Period,* ed. Jerome Hamilton Buckley and George Benjamin Woods. New York: Scott, Foresman, 1965.
Buckley, Jerome Hamilton, and George Benjamin Woods. *Poetry of the Victorian Period.* New York: Scott, Foresman, 1965.
Burnett, Frances Hodgson. *The Secret Garden.* 1911. Rpt. New York: Bantam Books, 1987.
Carpenter, Lynette, and Wendy K. Kolmar. *Haunting the House of Fiction: Feminist Perspectives on Ghost Stories by American Women.* Knoxville: University of Tennessee Press, 1991.
Chandler, Marilyn R. *Dwelling in the Text: Houses in American Fiction.* Berkeley: University of California Press, 1991.
Christ, Carol. *Diving Deep and Surfacing: Women Writers on Spiritual Quest.* Boston: Beacon Press, 1980.

Cixous, Hélène. "Fiction and Its Phantoms: A Reading of *Das Unheimliche* (The "Uncanny"). *New Literary History* 7(Autumn 1975–76): 525–48.
———. "The Laugh of the Medusa." *Signs* 1(Summer 1976): 875–93.
Conger, Syndy McMillan. "The Reconstruction of the Gothic Feminine Ideal in Emily Brontë's *Wuthering Heights*." In *The Female Gothic*, ed. Juliann E. Fleenor. Montreal: Eden Press, 1983.
Daly, Mary. *Beyond God the Father: Toward A Philosophy of Women's Liberation*. Boston: Beacon Press, 1973.
Day, William Patrick. *In The Circles of Fear and Desire: A Study of Gothic Fantasy*. Chicago: University of Chicago Press, 1985.
de Beauvoir, Simone. *The Second Sex*. 1949. Rpt. 1970. Trans. H. M. Parshley. New York: Bantam Books.
Dexter, Miriam Robbins. *Whence the Goddess: A Source Book*. New York: Pergamon Press, 1990.
Dinnerstein, Dorothy. *The Mermaid and the Minotaur: Sexual Arrangement and Human Malaise*. New York: Harper & Row, 1976.
Donovan, Josephine. *Feminist Theory: The Intellectual Traditions of American Feminism*. New York: Frederick Ungar, 1985.
———. *After the Fall: The Demeter-Persephone Myth in Wharton, Cather, and Glasgow*. University Park: Pennsylvania State University Press, 1989.
Downing, A. J. *The Architecture of Country Houses*. 1850. Rpt. New York: Dover, 1969.
Dupree, Ellen. "Wharton, Lewis, and the Nobel Prize Address." *American Literature* 6 (May 1984): 262–270.
Elbert, Monika M. "The Politics of Maternality in *Summer*." *Edith Wharton Review* 7 (Winter 1990): 4–9, 24.
Eliade, Mircea. *The Sacred and the Profane: The Nature of Religion*. New York: Harper & Row, 1961.
Elias-Button, Karen. "The Muse as Medusa." *The Lost Tradition: Mothers and Daughters in Literature*, ed. Cathy N. Davidson and E. M. Broner. New York: Frederick Ungar, 1980.
Ellis, Kate Ferguson. *The Contested Castle: Gothic Novels and the Subversion of Domestic Ideology*, Urbana: University of Illinois Press, 1989.
Erlich, Gloria C. *The Sexual Education of Edith Wharton*. Berkeley: University of California Press, 1992.
Fedorko, Kathy A. "Edith Wharton's Haunted Fiction: 'The Lady's Maid's Bell' and *The House of Mirth*." *Haunting the House of Fiction: Feminist Perspectives on Ghost Stories by American Women*. Ed. Lynette Carpenter and Wendy K. Kolmar. Knoxville: University of Tennessee Press, 1991.
———. " 'Forbidden Things': Gothic Confrontation with the Feminine in 'The Young Gentlemen'.and 'Bewitched.' " *Edith Wharton Review* 11 (Spring 1994): 3–9.
Fiedler, Leslie A. *Love and Death in the American Novel*. New York: Criterion Books, 1960.
Flanner, Janet. "Dearest Edith." *An American in Paris*. New York: Simon & Schuster, 1940.
Fleenor, Juliann E., ed. *The Female Gothic*. Montreal: Eden Press, 1983.
Freire, Pablo. *Pedagogy of the Oppressed*. Trans. Myra Bergman Ramos. New York: Herder & Herder, 1971.
Friedrich, Paul. *The Meaning of Aphrodite*. Chicago: University of Chicago Press, 1978.

Frye, Northrop. *The Secular Scripture.* Cambridge, Mass.: Harvard University Press, 1976.

Fryer, Judith. *Felicitous Space: The Imaginative Structures of Edith Wharton and Willa Cather.* Chapel Hill: University of North Carolina Press, 1986.

Gardiner, Judith Kegan. "On Female Identity and Writing by Women." In *Writing and Sexual Difference,* ed. Elizabeth Abel. Chicago: University of Chicago Press, 1982.

Gilbert, Sandra. "Life's Empty Pack: Notes Toward a Literary Daughteronomy." *Critical Inquiry* 11(March 1985): 355–84.

Gilbert, Sandra M., and Susan Gubar. *The Madwoman in the Attic: The Woman Writer and the Nineteenth Century Literary Imagination.* New Haven: Yale University Press, 1979.

———. "The Mirror and the Vamp: Reflections on Feminist Criticism." In *Future Literary Theory,* ed. Ralph Cohen. New York: Routledge, 1989.

———. *No Man's Land: The Place of the Woman Writer in the Twentieth Century.* Vol. 2. *Sexchanges.* New Haven: Yale University Press, 1989.

Gimbel, Wendy. *Edith Wharton: Orphancy and Survival.* New York: Praeger, 1984.

Gimbutas, Marija. *The Language of the Goddess.* New York: Harper & Row, 1989.

Glaspell, Susan Keating. "A Jury of Her Peers." In *American Voices, American Women,* ed. Lee R. Edwards and Arlyn Diamond. New York: Avon Books, 1973.

Goldenberg, Naomi R. *Returning Words to Flesh: Feminism, Psychoanalysis, and the Resurrection of the Body.* Boston: Beacon Press, 1990.

Goodman, Susan. *Edith Wharton's Women: Friends and Rivals.* Hanover: University Press of New England, 1990.

Grace, Sherrill. "In Search of Demeter." In *Margaret Atwood: Vision and Forms,* ed. Kathryn Van Spanckeren and Jan Garden Castro. Carbondale: Southern Illinois University Press, 1988.

Gribben, Alan. "A Selection from Edith Wharton's Letters to Morton Fullerton, 1907–1915." *Library Chronicle of the University of Texas at Austin,* n.s., no. 31 (1985).

Gubar, Susan. " 'The Blank Page' and the Issues of Female Creativity." In *Writing and Sexual Difference,* ed. Elizabeth Abel. Chicago: University of Chicago Press, 1982.

Harding, M. Esther. *Women's Mysteries Ancient and Modern.* New York: Bantam Books, 1971.

Hart, Francis Russell. "The Experience of Character in the English Gothic Novel." In *Experience in the Novel: Selected Papers from the English Institute,* ed. Roy Harvey Pearce. New York: Columbia University Press, 1968.

Heaps, Willard. *Superstition!* New York: Thomas Nelson, 1972.

Heilman, Robert B. "Charlotte Brontë's 'New Gothic.' " In *From Jane Austen to Joseph Conrad,* ed. Robert Rathburn and Martin Steinmann, Jr. Minneapolis: University of Minnesota Press, 1958.

Herman, Judith, and Lisa Hirschman. "Father-Daughter Incest." In *The Signs Reader: Woman, Gender, and Scholarship,* ed. Elizabeth Abel and Emily K. Abel. Chicago: University of Chicago Press, 1977.

Hillman, James. *The Dream and the Underworld.* New York: Harper & Row, 1979.

Holland, Norman, and Leona Sherman. "Gothic Possibilities." *New Literary History* 8 (1976–77): 279–94.

Homans, Margaret. "Dreaming of Children: Literalization in *Jane Eyre* and *Wuthering Heights.*" In *The Female Gothic,* ed. Juliann E. Fleenor. Montreal: Eden Press, 1983.

Howells, Coral Ann. *Love, Mystery, and Misery*. London: Athlone Press, 1978.

Jacobus, Mary. "The Buried Letter: Feminism and Romanticism in *Villette*." In *Women Writing and Writing About Women*, ed. Mary Jacobus. New York: Barnes & Noble, 1979.

———. "The Difference of View." In *Women Writing and Writing About Women*, ed. Mary Jacobus. New York: Barnes & Noble, 1979.

Jantz, Harold. *The Mothers in Faust: The Myth of Time and Creativity*. Baltimore: Johns Hopkins University Press, 1969.

Johnson, Greg. "Gilman's Gothic Allegory: Rage and Redemption in 'The Yellow Wallpaper.' " *Studies in Short Fiction* 26 (Fall 1989): 521–30.

Joslin, Katherine. *Women Writers: Edith Wharton*. London: Macmillan Education, 1991.

Joslin, Katherine, and Alan Price, eds. *Wretched Exotic: Essays on Edith Wharton in Europe*. New York: Peter Lang, 1993.

Jung, C. G. *Collected Works*. 20 vols. Ed. Gerhard Adler et al. Trans. R. F. C. Hull. Bollingen Series 20. Princeton: Princeton University Press, 1960–85.

Kahane, Claire. "The Maternal Legacy: The Grotesque Tradition in Flannery O'Connor's Female Gothic." In *The Female Gothic*, ed. Juliann E. Fleenor. Montreal: Eden Press, 1983.

———. "The Gothic Mirror." In *The (M)other Tongue, Essays in Feminist Psychoanalytic Interpretation*, ed. Shirley Nelson Garner, Claire Kahane, and Madelon Sprengnether. Ithaca: Cornell University Press, 1985.

Kaplan, Louise J. *Female Perversions: The Temptation of Emma Bovary*. New York: Anchor/Doubleday, 1991.

Kellogg, Grace. *The Two Lives of Edith Wharton: The Woman and Her Work*. New York: Appleton-Century, 1965.

Killoran, Helen. "Pascal, Brontë, and 'Kerfol': The Horrors of a Foolish Quartet." *Edith Wharton Review* 10 (Spring 1993): 12–17.

Knight, G. Wilson. *The Starlit Dome*. London: Methuen, 1941.

Kristeva, Julia. *Powers of Horror: An Essay on Abjection*. Trans. Leon S. Roudiez. New York: Columbia University Press, 1982.

Lacan, Jacques. *Female Sexuality*. Ed. Juliet Mitchell, and Jacqueline Rose. New York: W. W. Norton, 1985.

Lewis, R. W. B. *Edith Wharton: A Biography*. New York: Harper & Row, 1975.

———. "Powers of Darkness." *Times Literary Supplement*, 13 June 1975, 644–46.

———, ed. *The Collected Short Stories of Edith Wharton*. 2 vols. New York: Charles Scribner's Sons, 1968.

Lewis, R. W. B., and Nancy Lewis, eds. *The Letters of Edith Wharton*. New York: Charles Scribner's Sons, 1988.

Lidoff, Joan. "Another Sleeping Beauty: Narcissism in *The House of Mirth*." *American Quarterly* 32 (1980): 519–39.

Lowes, John Livingston. *The Road to Xanadu: A Study in the Ways of the Imagination*. Boston: Houghton Mifflin, 1927.

Lubbock, Percy. "Memoirs." Edith Wharton Archives, Beinecke Library, Yale University, New Haven, Connecticut.

———. *Portrait of Edith Wharton*. New York: D. Appleton-Century Co., 1947.

MacAndrew, Elizabeth. *The Gothic Tradition in Fiction*. New York: Columbia University Press, 1979.

McDowell, Margaret B. "Edith Wharton's Ghost Stories." *Criticism* 12 (Spring 1970): 133–51.

————. *Edith Wharton.* Rev. ed. Boston: Twayne Publishers, 1991.

————. "Edith Wharton's Ghost Tales Reconsidered." In *Edith Wharton: New Critical Essays,* ed. Alfred Bendixen and Annette Zilversmit. New York: Garland, 1992.

McFarland, Thomas. "The Origin and Significance of Coleridge's Theory of Secondary Imagination." In *New Perspectives on Coleridge and Wordsworth,* ed. Geoffrey Hartman. New York: Columbia University Press, 1972.

McMillan, Ann. "The Transforming Eye: *Lady Oracle* and Gothic Tradition." In *Margaret Atwood: Vision and Forms,* ed. Kathryn Van Spanckeren and Jan Garden Castro. Carbondale: Southern Illinois University Press, 1988.

Malcolm, Janet. "The Woman Who Hated Women." *New York Times Book Review,* 16 November 1986, pp. 11–12.

Moers, Ellen. *Literary Women: The Great Writers.* New York: Anchor Books, 1977.

Murray, Margaret P. "The Gothic Arsenal of Edith Wharton." *Journal of Evolutionary Psychology* 10 (August 1989): 315–21.

Nettels, Elsa. "Gender and First-Person Narration in Edith Wharton's Short Stories." In *Edith Wharton: New Critical Essays,* ed. Alfred Bendixen and Annette Zilversmit. New York: Garland, 1992.

Neumann, Erich. *The Great Mother: An Analysis of the Archetype.* Trans. Ralph Manheim. Princeton: Princeton University Press, 1963.

Nichols, Nina daVinci. "Place and Eros in Radcliffe, Lewis, and Brontë." In *The Female Gothic,* ed. Juliann E. Fleenor. Montreal: Eden Press, 1983.

Olin-Ammentorp, Julie. "Wharton's View of Women in *French Ways and Their Meaning.*" *Edith Wharton Review* 9 (Fall 1992): 15–18.

————. "Wharton Through a Kristevan Lens: The Maternality of *The Gods Arrive.*" In *Wretched Exotic: Essays on Edith Wharton in Europe,* ed. Katherine Joslin and Alan Price. New York: Peter Lang, 1993.

Otto, Rudolf. *The Idea of the Holy: An Inquiry into the Non-rational Factor in the Idea of the Divine and Its Relation to the Rational.* Trans. John W. Harvey. New York: Oxford University Press, 1957.

Perera, Sylvia Brinton. "The Descent of Inanna: Myth and Therapy." In *Feminist Archetypal Theory: Interdisciplinary Re-Visions of Jungian Thought,* ed. Estella Lauter and Carol Schreier Rupprecht. Knoxville: University of Tennessee Press, 1985.

Pratt, Annis. *Archetypal Patterns in Women's Fiction.* Bloomington: Indiana University Press, 1981.

————. "Spinning Among Fields: Jung, Frye, Lévi-Strauss, and Feminist Archetypal Theory." In *Feminist Archetypal Theory: Interdisciplinary Re-Visions of Jungian Thought,* ed. Estella Lauter and Carol Schreier Rupprecht. Knoxville: University of Tennessee Press, 1985.

Punter, David. *The Literature of Terror: A History of Gothic Fictions from 1765 to the Present Day.* London: Longman Group, 1980.

Rabuzzi, Kathryn Allen. *Motherself: A Mythic Analysis of Motherhood.* Bloomington: Indiana University Press, 1988.

Radcliffe, Ann. *The Mysteries of Udolpho.* 1794. Rpt. New York: Oxford University Press, 1980.

Radway, Janice. "The Utopian Impulse in Popular Literature: Gothic Romances and 'Feminist' Protest." *American Quarterly* 33 (Summer 1981): 140–62.

Railo, Eino. *The Haunted Castle: A Study of Elements of English Romanticism.* London: George Routledge & Sons, 1927.

Rich, Adrienne. *Of Woman Born: Motherhood as Experience and Institution*. New York: Bantam Books, 1977.

Schneider, Elisabeth. *Coleridge, Opium, and Kubla Khan*. Chicago: University of Chicago Press, 1953.

Schriber, Mary Suzanne. *Gender and the Writer's Imagination: From Cooper to Wharton*. Lexington: University Press of Kentucky, 1987.

Sedgwick, Eve Kosofsky. *The Coherence of Gothic Conventions*. New York: Methuen, 1986.

Showalter, Elaine. *A Literature of Their Own: British Women Novelists from Brontë to Lessing*. Princeton: Princeton University Press, 1977.

———. "The Death of the Lady (Novelist): Wharton's House of Mirth." *Representations* 9 (Winter 1985): 133–49.

———. "American Female Gothic." *Sister's Choice: Tradition and Change in American Women's Writing*. New York: Oxford University Press, 1991.

Singley, Carol J. "Gothic Borrowings and Innovations in Edith Wharton's 'A Bottle of Perrier.'" In *Edith Wharton: New Critical Essays*, ed. Alfred Bendixen and Annette Zilversmit. New York: Garland, 1992.

Singley, Carol J., and Susan Elizabeth Sweeney. "Forbidden Reading and Ghostly Writing: Anxious Power in Wharton's 'Pomegranate Seed.'" *Women's Studies* 20 (1991): 177–203.

Smith, Allan Gardner. "Edith Wharton and the Ghost Story." *Women and Literature* 1 (1980): 149–59.

Stein, Karen F. "Monsters and Madwomen: Changing Female Gothic." In *The Female Gothic*, ed. Juliann E. Fleenor. Montreal: Eden Press, 1983.

Stengel, Ellen Powers. "Edith Wharton Rings 'The Lady's Maid's Bell.'" *Edith Wharton Review* 7 (Spring 1990): 3–9.

Strachey, Barbara, and Jayne Samuels, eds. *Mary Berenson: A Self-Portrait from Her Diaries and Letters*. New York: W. W. Norton, 1983.

Thomas, Jennice G. "Spook or Spinster? Edith Wharton's 'Miss Mary Pask.'" In *Haunting the House of Fiction: Feminist Perspectives on Ghost Stories by American Women*, ed. Lynette Carpenter and Wendy K. Kolmar. Knoxville: University of Tennessee Press, 1991.

Tintner, Adeline. "The Hermit and the Wildwoman: The Fictioning of Henry James." *Journal of Modern Literature* 4 (Fall 1975): 32–42.

Todorov, Tzvetan. *The Fantastic: A Structural Approach to a Literary Genre*. Trans. Richard Howard. Ithaca: Cornell University Press, 1980.

Tyson, Lois. "Beyond Morality: Lily Bart, Lawrence Selden, and the Aesthetic Commodity in *The House of Mirth*." *Edith Wharton Review* 9 (Fall 1992): 3–10.

Van Buren, Jane Silverman. *The Modernist Madonna: Semiotics of the Maternal Metaphor*. Bloomington: Indiana University Press, 1989.

Varnado, S. L. *Haunted Presence: The Numinous in Gothic Fiction*. Tuscaloosa: University of Alabama Press, 1987.

Waggoner, Hyatt H. *Hawthorne: Selected Tales and Sketches*. San Francisco: Rinehart Press, 1970.

Waid, Candace. *Edith Wharton's Letters from the Underworld: Fictions of Women and Writing*. Chapel Hill: University of North Carolina Press, 1991.

Walker, Barbara G. *The Woman's Encyclopedia of Myths and Secrets*. San Francisco: HarperCollins, 1983.

Walker, Nancy A. " 'Seduced and Abandoned': Convention and Reality in Edith Wharton's *Summer.*" *Studies in American Literature* 11 (1983): 107–14.

Walton, Geoffrey. *Edith Wharton: A Critical Interpretation.* Rutherford: Fairleigh Dickinson University Press, 1970.

Watson, Barbara. "On Power and the Literary Text." *Signs* 1 (Autumn 1975): 111–18.

Watson, George. *Coleridge the Poet.* New York: Barnes & Noble, 1966.

Wehr, Demaris S. *Jung and Feminism: Liberating Archetypes.* Boston: Beacon Press, 1987.

Werlock, Abbey H. P. "Edith Wharton's Subtle Revenge? Morton Fullerton and the Female Artist in *Hudson River Bracketed* and *The Gods Arrive.*" In *Edith Wharton: New Critical Essays,* ed. Alfred Bendixen and Annette Zilversmit. New York: Garland, 1992.

Wershoven, Carol. *The Female Intruder in the Novels of Edith Wharton.* Rutherford: Fairleigh Dickinson University Press, 1982.

White, Barbara A. "Edith Wharton's *Summer* and 'Women's Fiction.' " *Essays in Literature* 11 (1984): 223–35.

———. *Edith Wharton: A Study of Her Short Stories.* New York: Twayne, 1991.

Whitmont, Edward C. *The Symbolic Quest: Basic Concepts of Analytical Psychology.* New York: G. P. Putnam's Sons, 1969.

Wiesenfarth, Joseph. *Gothic Manners and the Classic English Novel.* Madison: University of Wisconsin Press, 1988.

Wilt, Judith. *Ghosts of the Gothic: Austen, Eliot, and Lawrence.* Princeton: Princeton University Press, 1980.

Wolff, Cynthia Griffin. *A Feast of Words: The Triumph of Edith Wharton.* New York: Oxford University Press, 1977.

Wolstenholme, Susan. *Gothic (Re)visions: Writing Women as Readers.* Albany: State University of New York Press, 1993.

Woolf, Virginia. *A Room of One's Own.* 1929. Rpt. New York: Harcourt, Brace & World, 1957.

Zilversmit, Annette. "Edith Wharton's Last Ghosts." *College Literature* 14 (Fall 1987): 296–305.

———. "All Souls': Wharton's Last Haunted House and Future Directions for Criticism." In *Edith Wharton: New Critical Essays,* ed. Alfred Bendixen and Annette Zilversmit. New York: Garland, 1992.

Index

ABOUT THE AUTHOR

Kathy A. Fedorko is professor of English at Middlesex County College, Edison, New Jersey, and a past president of the Edith Wharton Society. She serves on the society's executive board and is assistant editor of the *Edith Wharton Review.*